English–Arabic/Arabic–English Translation

Basil Hatim

ENGLISH–ARABIC/ARABIC–ENGLISH TRANSLATION

A Practical Guide

Saqi Books

For Wissam and Lema

British Library Cataloguing-in-Publication Data
A catalogue record for this book is available from the
British Library

ISBN 0 86356 341 4 (hb)
ISBN 0 86356 155 1 (pbk)

© Basil Hatim, 1997
This edition first published 1997
In-house editor: Jana Gough

Saqi Books
26 Westbourne Grove
London W2 5RH

Contents

Preface

This Guide is not envisaged as the last word on grammatical 'well-formedness' (although one of its primary aims is to make a contribution to a more cohesive use of language), nor indeed does it have a mandate to suggest the ultimate in the *mot juste* (although it plays its part in establishing norms of more coherent language use). My aims are rather more global and hopefully more far-reaching than these. I seek to establish and maintain a useful dialogue with colleagues who share my concerns about what text to take to the translation class and how best to go about teaching it in a way that makes learning to translate both enjoyable and durable. I also seek to communicate with those professionals who have left classroom experience well behind them and are now in the thick of things: the success they have achieved so far can lead to further success if the enterprise in which we are engaged is set on a more solid footing. Finally, I seek to reach the greatest asset we have for the future, those thousands of young men and women aspiring to a career in this most valuable of services to the building of a better world. In fact, this Guide would not have seen the light of day had it not been for the some two hundred students I have had the good fortune to teach on the Master Programme at Heriot-Watt University, Scotland, and for the literally thousands who, from Tangier to Irbid, have over the years listened patiently to me arguing about this or that notion of what translation is all about.

Thus the Guide is dedicated to those students who have put up with endless sermons about the virtues of being textually 'competent' and who in the process have got their own back and made me aware the hard way of classroom realities. It is also dedicated to those professionals for whom I have worked and who have often read the riot act when a deadline was not met, in the process bringing me down to earth from the illusions of theoretical ivory towers. And finally, it is dedicated to all my valued colleagues who, whether in agreement or disagreement, have always been gracious enough to show me the warmth and understanding that have kept me going.

As regards acknowledgements, so much is owed to too many to mention by name. Nevertheless, one or two must be singled out for special mention as the expression of my gratitude to them simply cannot be disposed of in terms of the collective. One is my wife, Afaf Bataineh, to whom goes a special, heartfelt thankyou for advising me on the Arabic and, on a more domesticated and thus a much more meaningful level, for allowing home to be turned into a big study in which she granted me an indefinite study leave. Then there are my two colleagues, one from the old days, Gavin Watterson, the other, Ron Buckley, at present with me at Heriot-Watt: to them both I owe a special debt of gratitude for revising the English and advising on general matters of presentation. Mahmood Dhanoon, who was doing his doctorate with me, stepped in at the last minute to save a work in manuscript from oblivion. B. Idrissi-Bouyahyaoui, Director of the King Fahd Advanced School of Translation in Tangier, deserves a special word of thanks for his faith in what I am trying to do. Finally, to Jana Gough my gratitude.

Edinburgh
July 1997

Introduction

Particularly over the last three decades or so, both the theory and the practice of translation have been dominated by a number of dichotomies. We have had 'literal' vs. 'free' translation, the translation of 'form' vs. that of 'function', 'communicative' vs. 'semantic' translation and so on. What is disturbing about such distinctions is not so much the proliferation of unnecessary terminology but the impression that terms give when presented as though they were conscious choices made by the translator according to the school of thought to which he or she belongs. We have also had distinctions such as 'technical' vs. 'non-technical' translation, 'literary' vs. 'non-literary' translation, 'specialized' vs. 'non-specialized' translation, once again often conceived of in doctrinal and almost mutually exclusive terms. These binarisms have proved influential enough not only to inform theories of translation but also to dictate modes of practice enshrined in the kind of training given under headings such as: 'Term I (or Paper A): Specialized Translation'![1]

While in no way wishing to deride the 'literalist' or the 'functionalist', or indeed belittle the value of specialization, particularly at the more advanced stages of translator training, the present Guide adopts a drastically different orientation. Certainly, a literary context is different from a non-literary context, technical language will be handled differently from non-technical use of language and so on. But these are contextual features which will no doubt be evident from the text and will be dealt with appropriately as and when they occur. They will not, however, exclusively predominate in one and the same text from beginning to end,[2] nor will they require an exclusive theory of translation or a translator exclusively trained for this or that purpose.[3] Language varies according to the context and it is this variation,

---

1. Hatim and Mason (1997).
2. O'Donnel and Todd (1980).
3. Hatim and Mason (1990).

incessant and almost seamless, with which the translator has to contend in texts that are essentially multifunctional.

In talking of the essentially open-ended nature of all text production, however, two points must be noted. First, the fact that interaction is intrinsically fuzzy should not justify an 'anything goes' attitude. Being aware of norms is an essential part of appreciating and being able to handle deviations. The second point to be borne in mind is that variation is of many types, and some of these are more crucial to the construction of messages than others. Let us start with the second point first. Language varies according to the geographic, historical or social provenance of texts. Language also varies according to subject matter, level of formality and whether it is spoken or written.[4] But these so-called 'register'* distinctions هوية النص, which are valuable categories with which we as translators work all the time, are surely less vital to overall text development than those which determine whether in handling his or her subject matter, a scientist, for example, intends merely to 'review' a sequence of events fairly impartially or to 'rebut' a stated claim.

It is the latter text-type* أنماط النص view of variation which we endorse in this Guide, a view which takes as a point of departure aspects of the message such as 'intentionality' and the way in which this is linguistically realized. This text-context relationship may be envisaged as a continuum, one end of which caters for the intention to be extremely detached, while the other handles the intention to be extremely involved.[5] Such a view of variation may be represented schematically as follows:

extremely detached   *extremely involved and*
and non-evaluative .... *highly evaluative*

Naturally, extremes are artificial points on any scale and can only have a theoretical value. In reality, texts can never be so neatly categorized and are often found to display characteristics of more than one type. But, as we have pointed out above, accepting polarity, no matter how idealized and unreal this happens to be, is always helpful in determining, as precisely as one needs to, the degree of evaluativeness* possessed by a given text form. This has

---

* Items marked with an asterisk are defined in the Glossary at the end of the Guide.

4. Gregory and Carroll (1978).
5. Beaugrande and Dressler (1980).

important implications for the work of the translator. Being aware of the extent to which a particular text is evaluative determines the translation strategy to be adopted. As made amply clear in this Guide, literal translation works admirably well with legal language لغة النص القانوني, slightly less well with exposition* السرد and not always well with the more involved types of argumentation* الجدل which necessitate a freer approach.[6]

The Guide tries to capture this gradual increase in the degree of evaluativeness across texts and the need to adjust translation strategy accordingly. It starts with legal language which, in English at any rate, displays an extremely high degree of detachment.[7] Responding to a context of non-evaluativeness السياق غير التقويمي with the intention to 'instruct', legal language has developed a finite set of text structure formats* بناء النص that are highly formulaic. In terms of the way language is made to hang together, on the other hand, legal texts display features of a closely knit texture* بنية النص which the translator has to approach in a disciplined and methodical manner. In dealing with this highly conventional use of language, literal translation obviously presents itself as a valid option: the instructional* context is fairly strict, text structure* is generally formulaic, the diction* is highly unemotive and the overall tenor is one of extreme detachment.

Next on the scale of evaluativeness is exposition. While the context of detachment encountered in legal language is also in evidence here, discipline in exposition tends to be a little more relaxed. To reflect this, expository text structure, though fairly well organized, is far less stringently formulaic than that of the legal text. The same goes for texture which, though fairly tight, is far less dense than that of legal language. Bearing in mind that a certain degree of evaluativeness is not uncommon in exposition, we usually find that diction can be fairly emotive, metaphoric expression is not a rarity and a general feel of semi-formality is to be expected. Obviously this varies from one expository text to another, and from one language to another. In terms of translation strategy, a literal approach works well with the more detached end of the spectrum within exposition, but has to be adjusted slightly to handle the freer, more evaluative forms.

Finally, the various forms of argumentation within genres* أجناس كلام such as 'the Editorial', 'the Letter to the Editor' and so on present us with the opportunity to try out our theoretical framework of evaluativeness on

---

6. Werlich (1976).
7. Crystal and Davey (1969).

the more open-ended kinds of texts. The context of argumentation is essentially one in which the need to evaluate in order to persuade is paramount. Text structure responds to this by encouraging creativity within formats that, though not entirely unconstrained, are far less predictable and much more varied than the uniform organization of expository or legal texts. Texture is also fairly innovative, with a predominance of emotive diction, metaphoric expression and highly charged idiom.[*] In dealing with this kind of language variety, both the unit of translation and the strategy of translation have to be adjusted drastically. The word or phrase that works well as a possible unit of translating expository or legal language is not always suitable in dealing with argumentative texts. It follows that a literal approach will not always succeed in handling argumentative style. Of course, the procedures of working with the word or the phrase as a unit of translation, and of adopting the literal approach as a translation strategy, are still valid options and should always be aimed at in dealing with any kind of text. In reality, however, we find that we modify these procedures more often in dealing with argumentative texts than with the less involved kinds of texts. In argumentation, we often find that we must opt for larger stretches of text than, say, the phrase and for freer modes of translation as a general strategy.

The Guide is thus divided into three main parts. Part I deals with the translation of legal texts, Part II with the translation of expository texts and Part III with the translation of argumentative texts. Each part consists of a number of units which present the various text forms identified within a given type in a manner which reflects increasing degrees of evaluativeness. A unit begins with an overview which describes the text form in question in terms of its context[*] (e.g. to inform by summarizing), common structure formats (e.g. scene set, then various aspects of the scene tackled) and typical patterns of texture (e.g. the predominance of the Verbal sentence الجملة الفعلية in Arabic).

The overview is followed by a text (TEXT A) which illustrates the theoretical introduction and is intended for use as a 'sensitizer' only, that is, to be read and considered carefully. The insights gained from this sensitization exercise will hopefully be used in translating TEXT B which follows. The sensitizer TEXT A is then re-presented, this time to be translated. Finally, TEXT C and TEXT D are presented to provide additional practice. All four texts are accompanied by notes and glossaries that are essentially translation-process orientated. Annexed to the Guide are a list of text-linguistic and translation terms used throughout and marked by an asterix (*), and a Select Bibliography which suggests works for further reading.

The Guide is primarily intended for self-study, to be used by professional practising translators who wish to keep abreast of recent developments in both the theory and the practice of translation, and by trainee translators in conjunction with materials prescribed by their courses of study. Colleagues engaged in the training of translators may also find the Guide useful as an additional resource to supplement the course materials. If the Guide is adopted for use in the translation class, however, it is up to the tutor to select his or her own texts to be used in addition to or instead of the text samples presented in the Guide. In whatever mode, it is hoped that the Guide will offer the translation teacher the double advantage of, on the one hand, having his or her students preview or follow up the presentation of a given text form and, on the other hand, having the various text types and the forms and tokens within them presented systematically and in a cognitively valid manner along the text-typological lines suggested.

To conclude, the basic hypothesis entertained in this Guide is that:

DIFFERENT TEXT TYPES PLACE DIFFERENT SETS OF DEMANDS ON THE TRANSLATOR, WITH CERTAIN TYPES BEING OBVIOUSLY MORE DEMANDING THAN OTHERS.

A corollary to this is the further hypothesis that:

IT IS THE DEGREE OF TEXT EVALUATIVENESS THAT SEEMS TO BE THE SINGLE MOST IMPORTANT FEATURE WHICH DISTINGUISHES ONE TYPE FROM ANOTHER

and that:

THE ABILITY TO PERCEIVE AND DEAL WITH THIS CRUCIAL ASPECT OF TEXT CONSTITUTION (DEGREE OF EVALUATIVENESS) IS ONE OF THE MORE VALUABLE TOOLS WITH WHICH TO EQUIP THE TRANSLATOR.

The Guide is envisioned within parameters set by these hypotheses: less evaluative texts are presented first, gradually moving on to tackling higher and higher degrees of involvement.

PART I: *Translating Legal Texts*

UNIT ONE:	The Preamble[*]
UNIT TWO:	The Legal Article[*]
UNIT THREE:	Initial and Concluding Legal Articles

OVERVIEW

The legal document (e.g. the Resolution القرار, the Treaty المعاهدة) may best be viewed as consisting of four major parts: a Preamble الديباجة, an Initial Article[*] فاتحة, a set of articles مواد and a Concluding Article[*] خاتمة.

Each section of the legal document has a 'language' of its own which is essentially of a formulaic nature. The translator must therefore be acquainted with these conventions in both English and Arabic. Involved here are specific formats as well as technical terminology.

Legal discourse is also characterized by close-knit texture.[*] This is primarily intended to keep legal language free from ambiguity. The target text must therefore always reflect this basic quality of legal writing.

Given these basic characteristics of legal language, the approach to translation which seems to present itself most readily is 'literal'[*] translation. Unless there is a good reason to do otherwise, translators must adhere to source text syntax (e.g. word order) and semantics (e.g. the succinct expression of what words denote). The results of failure to observe these rules are all too obvious.

14

UNIT ONE: The Preamble ‫- مقدمة الدستور - مقدمة وشرعة قانونية‬

I. Consider the following text as an example of a Resolution Preamble.

TEXT 1A

قرار
بشأن محكمة العدل الإسلامية الدولية

إن مؤتمر القمة الإسلامي الخامس (دورة التضامن الإسلامي) المنعقد في الكويت في الفترة ٢٦ ـ ٢٩ جمادي الأولى ١٤٠٧هـ الموافق ٢٦ ـ ٢٩ يناير ١٩٨٧م.

اذ يذكر بقرار القمة الإسلامية الثالثة رقم ١١ ـ ٣ ـ س الذي وافق على إنشاء محكمة عدل إسلامية دولية،

وانسجاماً مع أحكام ميثاق منظمة المؤتمر الإسلامي،

ورغبة في إنشاء جهاز قضائي رئيسي يفصل في المنازعات وفقاً لأحكام الشريعة الإسلامية وقواعد القانون الدولي العام سعياً لدعم العلاقات الأخوية وتنقيتها،

وإذ يعرب عن تقديره للجهود التي بذلها خبراء اللجنة المختصة بالتعاون مع الأمانة العامة في إنجاز ما أشارت به القمة الإسلامية الرابعة بشأن اعداد الصيغة النهائية لمشروع النظام الأساسي للمحكمة،

يوافق على مشروع النظام الأساسي لمحكمة العدل الاسلامية الدولية المعتمد على أساس الولاية الاختيارية لأحكامها.

(. . .)

[1]†

---

† Numbers in square brackets refer to the List of Sources provided at the end of the Guide.

II.   Bearing in mind the distinctive features of Arabic preambles, translate the following text into Arabic.

TEXT 1B

Declaration

The World Conference to Combat Racism and Racial Discrimination,

Having met at Geneva from 14 to 25 August 1978 in accordance with General Assembly Resolution 32/129,

Recalling that the Charter of the United Nations is based on the principles of the dignity and equality of all human beings,[1] †

Further recalling the designation by the General Assembly of the period beginning on 10 December 1973 as the Decade for Action to Combat Racism and Racial Discrimination,

Determined to promote the implementation of the Universal Declaration of Human Rights,

Noting the vital need for the mass media to inform public opinion objectively about the liberation struggle in Southern Africa,

Noting further with the gravest concern that racism, racial discrimination and apartheid, which continue to afflict the world,[2] are crimes against the conscience and dignity of mankind,

Solemnly Declares,

1. Any doctrine of racial superiority is scientifically false, morally condemnable, socially unjust and dangerous, and has no justification whatsover.

(. . .)

[2]

NOTES

1.   A literal approach to the translation of legal texts necessitates that we preserve source text word order as far as possible. For example: مبادىء الكرامة والمساواة بين كافة أبناء البشر (*the principles of the dignity and equality of all human beings*) is perhaps more appropriate for this kind of text than مبادىء كرامة كافة أبناء البشر والمساواة بينهم: even though the latter may

---

† Numbers in superscript refer to the notes that follow each text.

be considered 'finer' style or even more grammatical. The same may be said of: *gravest* ابلغ, *based on* مبني على etc.

2. A good example of the 'good reason principle' in deviating from the literal is: *which continue to afflict the world*. The various elements of التي لا يزال العالم يعاني منها hang together (i.e. collocate*) better and are generally less emotive than a more literal rendering such as: التي لا تزال تبتلي العالم.

GLOSSARY

Declaration	إعلان
World Conference	المؤتمر العالمي
Combat Racism	مكافحة العنصرية
Racial Discrimination	التمييز العنصري
Having met	وقد اجتمع
in accordance with . . . Resolution	وفقا لقرار
Recalling that	وإذ يستذكر أن
Charter	ميثاق
Further recalling	وإذ يستذكر أيضاً
designation by the General Assembly	تسمية الجمعية العامة
Determined to	وتصميماً منه على
promote	تعزيز
Noting	وإذ يلاحظ
Southern Africa	افريقيا الجنوبية
Noting further that	وإذ يلاحظ أيضاً
apartheid	سياسة الفصل العنصري
Solemnly Declares	يعلن رسمياً
doctrine of racial superiority	مذهب من مذاهب التفوق العنصري
scientifically false	زائف علمياً
morally condemnable	مدان أخلاقياً
socially unjust	مجحف اجتماعياً
has no justification whatsoever	لا مبرر له على الإطلاق

III. Bearing in mind the distinctive features of Resolution and Declaration preambles in both Arabic and English, translate Text 1A (reproduced here in an unmodified form) into English.

TEXT 1A

قرار
بشأن محكمة العدل الإسلامية الدولية

إن مؤتمر القمة الإسلامي الخامس (دورة التضامن الإسلامي) المنعقد في الكويت في الفترة ٢٦ ـ ٢٩ جمادي الأولى ١٤٠٧هـ الموافق ٢٦ ـ ٢٩ يناير/كانون الثاني ١٩٨٧م.

إذ يذكُر بقرار القمة الإسلامية الثالثة رقم ١١ ـ ٣ ـ س الذي وافق على انشاء محكمة عدل إسلامية دولية،

و¹ انسجاماً مع أحكام ميثاق منظمة المؤتمر الإسلامي،

ورغبة في إنشاء جهاز قضائي رئيسي يفصل في المنازعات وفقاً لأحكام الشريعة الإسلامية وقواعد القانون الدولي العام سعياً لدعم العلاقات الأخوية وتنقيتها،

وإذ يعرب عن تقديره للجهود التي بذلها خبراء اللجنة المختصة بالتعاون مع الأمانة العامة في إنجاز ما أشارت به القمة الإسلامية الرابعة بشأن إعداد الصيغة النهائية لمشروع النظام الأساسي للمحكمة.

يوافق على مشروع النظام الأساسي لمحكمة العدل الإسلامية الدولية المعتمد على أساس الولاية الاختيارية لأحكامها.

(...)

NOTES

1. The additive connector* 'و' which is indispensable for linking the various paragraphs of the Preamble in the Arabic text must be left out in English.

GLOSSARY

resolution	قرار
on the establishment of	بشأن انشاء
International Islamic Court of Justice	محكمة العدل الإسلامية الدولية

The Vth Islamic Summit	مؤتمر القمة الإسلامي الخامس
Islamic Solidarity Session	دورة التضامن الإسلامي
convened in	المنعقد
from AH ... to ...	في الفترة ... هـ
corresponding to ... – ... 1987	الموافق ... – ... م
Recalling	إذ يذكّر بـ
In conformity with	وانسجاماً مع
the provisions of the Charter	أحكام ميثاق
The Organization of the Islamic Conference	منظمة المؤتمر الإسلامي
Desiring to	ورغبة في
a main judicial instrument	جهاز قضائي رئيسي
for the settlement of disputes	يفصل في المنازعات
in accordance with	وفقاً لـ
the Islamic *shari'a*	الشريعة الإسلامية
general international law	القانون الدولي العام
In an endeavour to strengthen	سعياً لدعم
regularize fraternal relations	تنقية العلاقات الأخوية
Expressing its appreciation of	وإذ يعرب عن تقديره
the efforts exerted by	الجهود التي بذلها
the experts on the specialized committee	خبراء اللجنة المختصة
in co-operation with	بالتعاون
the General Secretariat	الأمانة العامة
to implement what the Summit resolved	في إنجاز ما أشارت به القمة
regarding the preparation of	بشأن إعداد
the final version of	الصيغة النهائية
the draft rules of procedure	مشروع النظام الأساسي
Approves	يوافق على

UNIT ONE: Additional Texts

1. The Preamble is arranged in the same way, not only in resolutions and declarations but also in other legal documents such as the Convention, the Agreement and the Decree. Text 1C is an example of a Convention Preamble. Bearing in mind the distinctive features of the Preamble in other text forms studied so far, translate the text into Arabic.

TEXT 1C

Draft Convention on the Law of the Sea

The States Parties to this Convention,

Prompted by the desire to settle, in a spirit of mutual understanding and co-operation,[1] all issues relating to the law of the sea,

Conscious that the problems of ocean space are closely interrelated and need to be considered as a whole,

Recognizing the desirability of establishing, through the Convention, and with due regard for the sovereignty of all States, a legal order for the seas and oceans which would[2] facilitate international communication,

Bearing in mind that the achievement of such goals will contribute to the realization of a just and equitable international economic order which would take into account the interests and needs of mankind as a whole and, in particular, the special interests and needs of developing countries, whether coastal or land-locked,

Affirming that matters not regulated by this Convention[3] continue to be governed by the rules and principles of general international law,

Have agreed as follows:

Part I
Use of Terms

Article 1
Use of Terms

For the purposes of this Convention:

1. 'Area' means the sea-bed and ocean-floor and subsoil thereof beyond the limits of national jurisdiction.

(...)

[3]

NOTES

1. In keeping with the general strategy of literal translation when dealing with legal texts, parenthetical constructions الجمل الاعتراضية are dealt with as and when they occur in the source text, preserving word order as

far as possible: إذ تحدوها الرغبة في أن تسوي وبروح من التفاهم والتعاون المتبادلين. But note that, as punctuation marks are essentially redundant in Arabic, connectors such as 'و' may be necessary here.

2. Pay special attention to the subtle shades of 'modal'* meaning: *would facilitate* = من شأنه أن ييسر.

3. Unless rhetorically motivated,* the agentive passive* (+ by) is turned into active in Arabic: التي لا تحكمها هذه الاتفاقية.

GLOSSARY

Convention	اتفاقية
Prompted by the desire to	وإذ تحدوها الرغبة
Conscious that	وإذ تعي
ocean space	الحيز المحيطي
closely interrelated	وثيقة الترابط
need to be considered	ويلزم النظر فيها
Recognizing the desirability of	وإذ تسلم بأنه من المستحسن
with due regard for	مع إيلاء المراعاة الواجبة
a legal order	نظام قانوني
Bearing in mind	وإذ تضع في اعتبارها
just and equitable	عادل ومنصف
take account	يراعي
interests and needs	مصالح واحتياجات
mankind as a whole	الإنسانية ككل
coastal or land-locked	أساحلية كانت أم غير ساحلية
Affirming that	وإذ تؤكد
continue to be governed by X	سيظل يحكم المسائل
Part	جزء
Terms	مصطلحات
sea-bed	قاع البحار
ocean-floor	قاع المحيطات
subsoil thereof	باطن أرضها
beyond the limits of	خارج نطاق
national jurisdiction	الولاية الوطنية

II. Text 1D is an example of an Agreement Preamble. Bearing in mind the characteristic features of preambles in general, translate the text into English.

TEXT 1D

اتفاقية بشأن الاعتراف بدراسات التعليم العالي وشهاداته ودرجاته العلمية في الدول العربية

إن الدول العربية الأطراف في هذه الاتفاقية،

نظراً للتراث المشترك والروابط القومية والفكرية والثقافية[1] الوثيقة التي تجمع بينها وتأكيداً وتحقيقاً للتعاون الفكري والثقافي الذي نصت عليه المعاهدة الثقافية العربية المؤرخة ١٢ ذي الحجة ١٣٦٤، الموافق ٢٧ نوفمبر ـ تشرين الثاني ١٩٤٥ وإذ تحدوها الرغبة في النهوض بالتربية والبحث العلمي والتدريب واقتناعاً منها بضرورة الاعتراف بدراسات التعليم العالي وشهاداته ودرجاته العلمية لتيسير انتقال الهيئات التعليمية والتدريسية والاختصاصيين والطلبة والباحثين في داخل المنطقة، وإذ تدرك أنه نظراً لتنوع مناهج التعليم وتعقدها، يستحسن أن يؤخذ بعين الاعتبار عند الاعتراف بمراحل التأهيل الدراسات والمعارف والخبرات المكتسبة إلى جانب الشهادات والدرجات الممنوحة، وإذ تعبر عن أملها في أن تشكل هذه الاتفاقية مرحلة في عمل أشمل من شأنه[2] الوصول إلى اتفاقية دولية بين مجموع الدول الأعضاء في منظمة الأمم المتحدة للتربية والعلوم والثقافة :

اتفقت على ما يلي :

أولاً ـ التعاريف
المادة الأولى

١ ـ لأغراض هذه الاتفاقية يقصد بـ «الاعتراف» بإحدى الشهادات أو ألقاب التعليم العالي أو درجاته الممنوحة في إحدى الدول المتعاقدة اعتمادها من جانب السلطات المختصة في دولة متعاقدة أخرى .

< . . . >

[4]

NOTES

1. The order of adjectives in the source text can be significant and must, therefore, be preserved in translation as far as possible: the adjectives ثقافية < فكرية < قومية must appear in this and no other sequence.

2. This is an example of modal/attitudinal meaning to be rendered in English as: 'would'.

GLOSSARY

recognition	الاعتراف
higher education studies	دراسات التعليم العالي
certificates and academic degrees	الشهادات والدرجات العلمية
In view of	نظراً لـ
common heritage	التراث المشترك
close pan-Arab ties	الروابط القومية الوثيقة
intellectual and cultural	فكرية وثقافية
Affirming and verifying	تأكيداً وتحقيقاً
provided for in	الذي نصت عليه
Arab Convention	المعاهدة العربية
Prompted by the desire to	وإذ تحدوها الرغبة في
Convinced of the importance	اقتناعاً منها بضرورة
to facilitate the movement of	تيسير انتقال
teaching staff	الهيئات التعليمية والتدريسية
specialists and researchers	الاختصاصيين والباحثين
Aware that	وإذ تدرك
the diversity of teaching curricula	تنوع مناهج التعليم
it is desirable to	يستحسن
take into consideration	يؤخذ بعين الاعتبار
qualifying stages	مراحل التأهيل
knowledge and acquired skills	المعارف والخبرات المكتسبة
degrees awarded	الدرجات الممنوحة
Expressing their hope	وإذ تعبر عن أملها
constitute	تشكل
within a more comprehensive framework	في عمل أشمل
which would lead to	يكون من شأنه الوصول الى
UNESCO	منظمة الأمم المتحدة للتربية والعلوم والثقافة

academic title or rank	أحد ألقاب التعليم العالي أودرجاته
contracting States	الدول المتعاقدة
adopted	اعتمد
competent authorities	السلطات المختصة

UNIT TWO: The Legal Article

OVERVIEW

The contextual aim of legal article formation is essentially to issue a binding instruction. The most important element in the structure[*] of the article is thus the verbal element الفعل. A finite number of such elements are at the disposal of the law-maker: stating that something is mandatory, allowing exemption, forcing by invoking the law, strongly recommending by invoking reason, logic, etc. In translation, these texture devices of instruction can confront the translator with all kinds of problems. For example, translators sometimes respond to legal 'shall' as though this were a 'futurity' marker. We also sometimes hear 'is permitted to' for legal 'may'.

I. Consider the following text, which contains examples of the various kinds of articles encountered in legal documents.

TEXT 2A

Vienna Convention On Diplomatic Relations
Done at Vienna, on 18 April 1961

The States Parties to the present Convention,
   Recalling that peoples of all nations from ancient times have recognized the status of diplomatic agents,
(. . .)
   Have agreed as follows:

Article 1

For the purpose of the present convention, the following terms shall have the meanings hereunder assigned to them: (a) the 'head of the mission' is the person charged by the sending State with the duty of acting in the capacity; (. . .)

Article 2

The establishment of diplomatic relations between states, and of permanent

25

diplomatic missions, takes place by mutual consent.

Article 3

Nothing in this Convention shall be construed as preventing the performance of consular functions by a diplomatic mission.

Article 4

The sending State must make certain that the agreement of the receiving State has been given for the person it proposes to accredit as head of the mission to that State.

Article 5

The sending State may, after it has given due notification to the receiving States concerned, accredit a head of mission or assign any member of the diplomatic staff to more than one State, unless there is express objection by any of the receiving States.

Article 6

Members of the diplomatic mission should in principle be of the nationality of the sending State.

[5]

II. Bearing in mind the distinctive features of Arabic article formation, translate the following into English as examples of articles in a Decree مرسوم.

TEXT 2B

مرسوم في شأن الوثائق السرية للدولة

بعد الاطلاع على قانون المطبوعات والنشر رقم ٣ لسنة ١٩٦١ والقوانين المعدلة له
< . . . >،

أصدرنا القانون الآتي نصه[1]:

مادة ١

يراد بمصطلح «الوثيقة» في تطبيق أحكام هذا القانون[2] كل ما تتداوله الوزارات[3] والهيئات العامة والمؤسسات العامة والإدارات المستقلة وغيرها من الجهات الحكومية من أوراق ومستندات ومكاتبات ومعلومات وبيانات وخرائط ورسوم وصور وأشرطة تسجيل وأفلام وغيرها من وسائل التسجيل المكتوبة والمسموعة والمرئية .

مادة ٢

مع عدم الإخلال بقواعد السرية المنصوص عليها في أي قانون آخر، تعتبر الوثيقة سرية إذا قرر ذلك كتابةً الوزير المختص لضرورات الأمن الداخلي أو الخارجي أو تتعلق الوثيقة بالسياسة الخارجية أو الشؤون المالية أو الاقتصادية أو بالأسرار المالية أو الاقتصادية للدولة .

مادة ٣

مع عدم الإخلال بأحكام المواد السابقة، يجوز الاطلاع[4] على الوثيقة السرية لمن تتطلب طبيعة عملهم ذلك، بعد الحصول على إذن كتابي خاص من الوزير المختص .

مادة ٨

على الوزراء ــ كل فيما يخصه ــ تنفيذ هذا القانون <. . .> .

رئيس مجلس الوزراء

[6]

NOTES

1. This is an acceptable structure of an Arabic Preamble. But, as made clear in the previous unit, the English format differs slightly: name of signatory > preambular paragraphs parenthetically inserted > the verb of declaring, decreeing, resolving, etc. Thus we must here retrieve the name of the signatory and place it upfront: 'We, the Prime Minister, Having . . ., Have issued . . .'.

2. In legal Arabic, there seem to be two kinds of adverbial elements: one is circumstantial and specific (e.g. في تطبيق أحكام هذا القانون) and is

27

normally short and thus gets embedded; the other is more universal, more or less formulaic and may be fronted thus: (e.g. مع عدم الإخلال بقواعد السرية). However, regardless of whether universal or specific, these adverbial elements are best fronted in English: 'In the application of this law, a "document" means . . . '; 'Without prejudice to the rules of confidentiality, a "document". . .'.

3.   The Arabic construction: كل ما تتداوله الوزارات من س و ص is best tackled in English by having X and Y first and then using a relative clause to bring in the agent and the verb, thus: 'X and Y which the ministries handle', or better still using a truncated relative clause* with the passive, thus: 'X and Y handled by the ministries'.

4.   In legal Arabic, this preposing of the object (تقديم المفعول به) is necessarily unmotivated (i.e. used only for discourse-organizational purposes*). The English text should therefore avoid preserving this word order ('the examination of a secret document may be permitted . . .') and opt instead for the more idiomatic: 'anyone may examine . . . if . . .'.

GLOSSARY

concerning	في شأن
Having examined	بعد الاطلاع
the Law of Printed Matter and Publications	قانون المطبوعات والنشر
the amendments thereto	القوانين المعدلة له
Have issued	أصدرنا
In the application of the provisions of	في تطبيق أحكام
'document' means	يراد بمصطلح «الوثيقة»
records, correspondence	مستندات ومكاتبات
information and data	معلومات وبيانات
drawings and photographs	رسوم وصور
recording tapes	أشرطة تسجيل
written, audio and visual	المكتوبة والمسموعة والمرئية
methods of recording	وسائل التسجيل
Without prejudice to	مع عدم الإخلال بـ
the rules of confidentiality	قواعد السرية
provided for	المنصوص عليها

shall be deemed	تعتبر
decides so in writing	قرر ذلك كتابة
in the interest of	لضرورات
internal security	الأمن الداخلي
concerned with	تعلق بـ
financial secrets	الأسرار المالية
the provisions of the foregoing articles	أحكام المواد السابقة
consult a secret document	يطلع على الوثيقة السرية
the nature of their work demands	تتطلب طبيعة عملهم
after obtaining special written permission	بعد الحصول على إذن كتابي خاص
the Minister concerned	الوزير المختص
Ministers, each in his or her own capacity, must	على الوزراء كل فيما يخصه
implement this law	تنفيذ هذا القانون

III. Bearing in mind the distinctive features of article formation in both English and Arabic, translate Text 2A (reproduced here for easier reference) into Arabic.

TEXT 2A

Vienna Convention On Diplomatic Relations
Done at Vienna, on 18 April 1961

The States Parties to the present Convention,
    Recalling that peoples of all nations from ancient times have recognized the status of diplomatic agents,
(. . .)
    Have agreed as follows:

Article 1

For the purpose of the present convention,[1] the following terms shall have[2] the meanings hereunder assigned to them: (a) the 'head of the mission'[3] is the person charged by the sending State[4] with the duty of acting in the capacity; (. . .)

Article 2

The establishment of diplomatic relations between states, and of permanent diplomatic missions, takes place by mutual consent.

Article 3

Nothing in this Convention shall be construed[5] as preventing the performance of consular functions by a diplomatic mission.

Article 4

The sending State must make[6] certain that the agreement of the receiving State has been given for the person it proposes to accredit as head of the mission to that State.

Article 5

The sending State may, after it has given due notification to the receiving States concerned, accredit a head of mission or assign any member of the diplomatic staff to more than one State, unless there is express objection by any of the receiving States.

Article 6

Members of the diplomatic missions should in principle be of the nationality of the sending State.

NOTES

1. This is an example of what we referred to above as the universal, formulaic kind of adverbial element and could thus be fronted in Arabic: . . . لأغراض هذه الاتفاقية.

2. This is not the future 'shall', but rather an empty, legal 'shall' which forms an inseparable part of the verbal element in which it occurs. Thus we must resist the temptation of going for سوف. Instead we must opt for the Arabic present simple verb which, among its many meanings, relays timelessness and thereby renders the statement legally binding: يراد بـ . . . . This same force accompanies the use in English legal writing of the verb 'to be' (e.g. 'is', ... يراد بـ) or the present simple (e.g. 'takes place', ... يتم) for which the Arabic present simple is once again ideal.

3. It is not the actual head of the mission but the term 'head of the mission' that is being talked about here. Given the redundant nature of punctuation marks in Arabic, this kind of relationship must be made explicit, thus: . . . يراد بمصطلح رئيس البعثة.

4. Unless rhetorically motivated, a by-agent passive is more idiomatically rendered in Arabic as active: الذي تكلفه الدولة المعتمدة. This strategy may also work with nominalized passives such as 'the designation by the UN of X as Y': تسمية الأمم المتحدة لـ س ـ بـ ص, or, in this unit: *as preventing the performance of consular functions by a diplomatic mission:* يمنع البعثة الدبلوماسية من أداء مهامها القنصلية.

5. An agentless passive, on the other hand, would receive a slightly different treatment, though the passive construction is once again avoided: *shall be construed* = يتم تفسير. As we will see in future units, unless there are overriding rhetorical considerations, as in argumentation, the passive construction is normally shunned as 'awkward'.

6. The legal 'shall' is usually misconstrued either as سوف or, perhaps more often, as يجب. This is an understandable response to the force of legal 'shall'. But, as we explained above, this state is attainable through the use of the present simple in Arabic. After all, if we need 'obligatoriness', we can always use 'must' (يجب). This may be compared on the one hand with 'may' (يجوز) and, on the other hand, with 'should' (ينبغي).

GLOSSARY

The States Parties to	إن الدول الأطراف
the present Convention	هذه الاتفاقية
Recalling	إذ تستذكر
from ancient times	منذ القدم
recognized the status of	اعترفت بوضع
diplomatic agents	المبعوثون الدبلوماسيون
hereunder assigned	المحددة أدناه
the sending/receiving State	الدولة المعتمدة ـ المعتمد لديها
duty	مهمة
acting in the capacity	التصرف بهذه الصفة

establishment of diplomatic relations	إقامة علاقات دبلوماسية
establishment of diplomatic missions	إنشاء بعثات دبلوماسية
by mutual consent	بالاتفاق المتبادل
make certain	تضمن
the agreement of	قبول
the person it proposes to accredit	الشخص المزمع اعتماده
give due notification	إعطاء الإشعار اللازم
assign a member of the mission	تعيين أحد الموظفين
express objection by X	اعترض س صراحة
should in principle be of the nationality of	ينبغي من حيث المبدأ أن

UNIT TWO: Additional Texts

I.   Articles are constructed in the same way across a variety of legal text forms. They usually come after the Preamble in Conventions and Decrees, as we have seen, and in Protocols and laws, as we will see shortly. Bearing in mind the distinctive features of legal articles studied so far, translate the following text into English.

TEXT 2C

قانون اتحادي رقم ٨ لسنة ١٩٨٠
في شأن تنظيم علاقات العمل

نحن زايد بن سلطان آل نهيان رئيس دولة الامارات العربية المتحدة،

بعد الاطلاع على أحكام الدستور المؤقت،

وعلى القانون رقم ١ لسنة ١٩٧٢ في شأن اختصاصات الوزارات وصلاحيات الوزراء والقوانين المعدّلة له، وبناءً على ما عرضه وزير العمل والشؤون الاجتماعية،

أصدرنا القانون التالي:

مادة ١: في تطبيق هذا القانون يقصد بالكلمات والعبارات الآتية المعاني المبينة قرين كل منها ما لم يقض السياق بغير ذلك:

صاحب العمل هو[1] كل شخص طبيعي أو اعتباري يستخدم عاملاً أو أكثر لقاء أجر مهما كان نوعه.

32

مادة ٢ : لا تسري أحكام هذا القانون على الفئات التالية :

أ. أفراد أسرة وأقارب وأصهار صاحب العمل من العمال المقيمين معه في مسكنه الذين يعولهم فعلاً بصورة كاملة أياً كانت درجة القرابة أو المصاهرة .

مادة ٣ : يكون حساب المدد والمواعيد المنصوص عليها في هذا القانون بالتقويم الميلادي وتعتبر السنة الميلادية في تطبيق أحكام هذا القانون ٣٦٥ يوماً والشهر ٣٠ يوماً إلا إذا نص عقد العمل على خلاف ذلك .

مادة ٤ : لا يجوز استخدام غير المواطنين بقصد العمل في دولة الامارات الا بعد موافقة دائرة العمل ² .

مادة ٥ : يجوز لوزارة العمل إلغاء بطاقة العمل الممنوحة لغير المواطن إذا ظل العامل متعطلاً عن العمل مدة تتجاوز ثلاثة أشهر متوالية .

مادة ٦ : يجب على صاحب العمل قبل تشغيل أي حدث أن يستحصل منه على موافقة كتابية ممن له الولاية أو الوصاية على الحدث .

مادة ٧ : يحظر تشغيل النساء في الأعمال الخطرة أو الشاقة أو الضارة صحياً .

[7]

NOTES

1. This is an alternative way of presenting definitions in Arabic legal writing. A more idiomatic rendering is perhaps: يراد بمصطلح صاحب العمل الشخص . . . . However, given the long list of terms and the availability of printing conventions such as bold-face type for the terms, the nominal structure may be justified here.

2. The force of 'only' in English cannot be rendered by فقط, but through the use of 'restriction' or قصر in Arabic as this sentence shows.

GLOSSARY

Federal Law	قانون اتحادي
the regulation of labour relations	تنظيم علاقات العمل
Having taken cognizance of	بعد الاطلاع
the provisions of the interim constitution	أحكام الدستور المؤقت
the jurisdiction of ministries	اختصاصات الوزارات
the powers of ministers	صلاحيات الوزراء

PART I: Translating Legal Texts

the submission made by	ما عرضه س
words and expressions	الكلمات والعبارات
shall have the meanings given against each	المعاني المبينة قرين كل منها
natural or corporate	طبيعي أو اعتباري
hires one employee or more	يستخدم عاملاً أو أكثر
in return for a wage of whatsoever nature	لقاء أجر مهما كان نوعه
the provisions shall not apply	لا تسري أحكام
to the following	على الفئات التالية
members of the family of the employer	أفراد أسرة صاحب العمل
relatives by blood or marriage	أقارب وأصهار
shall be calculated on the basis of	يكون حساب ... بـ
the Gregorian calendar	التقويم الميلادي
the Gregorian year	السنة الميلادية
unless provided for otherwise	إلا إذا نص ... على خلاف ذلك
labour contract	عقد العمل
X may be employed only after	لا يجوز استخدام س إلا بعد
non-nationals	غير المواطنين
approval of the Labour Department	موافقة دائرة العمل
X may cancel the work permit	يجوز لـ س إلغاء بطاقة العمل
remains unemployed	ظل متعطلاً عن العمل
for a continuous period in excess of	لفترة تتجاوز
X must obtain	يجب على س أن يستحصل
before employing a minor	قبل تشغيل أي حدث
a written consent	موافقة كتابية
the minor's guardian	من له الولاية أو الوصاية على الحدث
it is prohibited	يحظر
hazardous, arduous or harmful duties	الأعمال الخطرة ـ الشاقة ـ الضارة

II. Text 2D illustrates Preamble and article formation in a Covenant. Bearing in mind the characteristic features of this kind of legal writing studied so far, translate the text into Arabic.

TEXT 2D

International Covenant on Economic, Social and Cultural Rights adopted and opened for signature, ratification and accession by General Assembly Resolution 2200 of 16 December 1966

The States Parties to the present Covenant,

Considering that, in accordance with the principles proclaimed in the Charter of the United Nations, recognition of[1] the inherent dignity and of the equal and inalienable rights of all members of the human family is the foundation of the freedom, justice and peace in the world, . . .

Agreed upon the following articles:

Article . . .

1. All peoples have the right of self-determination. By virtue of that right[2] they freely determine their political status and freely pursue their economic, social and cultural development.
2. All peoples may, for their own ends, freely dispose of their natural wealth and resources without prejudice to any obligations arising out of international cooperation.
3. The States Parties to the present Covenant, including those having responsibilities for the administration of Non-Self-Governing and Trust Territories, shall promote the realization of the right of self-determination, and shall respect that right, in conformity with the provisions of the Charter of the United Nations.

Article . . .

Where relevant information has previously been furnished to the United Nations or to any specialized agency by any State Party to the present Covenant, it will[3] not be necessary to reproduce that information, precise reference to the information so furnished will suffice.

Article . . .

The present Covenant is subject to ratification.

[8]

NOTES

1. A change in word order may be necessary here. This will be done along
    similar lines to the parallel situation we had with: كل ما تتداوله الوزارات من
    أوراق ومستندات the rendering of which involved fronting the items in
    question and following this with a truncated relative clause: 'all the
    papers, documents, etc., handled by ministries'. In Text 2D, *the inherent
    dignity and the equal and inalienable rights of the human family:*

    . . . ما لجميع أعضاء الأسرة البشرية من كرامة أصيلة ومن حقوق متساوية وثابتة.
    The alternative literal rendering would certainly have lost this emphasis,
    thus: الكرامة الأصيلة والحقوق المتساوية والثابتة التي يتمتع بها كافة أعضاء الأسرة
    البشرية . . .

2. This is an example of the transient kind of adverbial which must be
    embedded, thus: . . . وتتمتع بمقتضى هذا الحق . . . تتمتع.

3. Although extremely rare, this use of 'will' is exactly like that of legal
    'shall' and has nothing whatsoever to do with futurity.

GLOSSARY

Considering that	إذ ترى
International Covenant	العهد الدولي
adopted and opened for signature	تم اعتماده وعرضه للتوقيع
ratification and accession	التصديق والانضمام
principles proclaimed in the Charter	المبادىء المعلنة في الميثاق
recognition	الإقرار
is the foundation of	يشكل أساس
have the right	تمتع بحق
freely determine	تتمتع بحرية تقرير
political status	وضعها السياسي
freely pursue economic development	حرية السعي لتحقيق التنمية الاقتصادية
for their own ends	سعياً وراء أهدافها الخاصة
freely dispose of their wealth	التصرف الحر بثرواتها
natural resources	مواردها الطبيعية
without prejudice to any obligations	دون المساس بأية التزامات
arising out of	منبثقة عن
those having responsibilities	تقع على عاتقها مسؤولية

Non-Self-Governing Territories	الأقاليم غير المتمتعة بالحكم الذاتي
Trust Territories	الأقاليم المشمولة بالوصاية
shall promote the realization of	تعمل على تحقيق
relevant information	المعلومات المناسبة
it will not be necessary	ينتفي لزوم
to reproduce information	تكرار ايراد المعلومات
precise reference will suffice	يكون كافياً الإحالة الدقيقة
is subject to	يخضع

UNIT THREE:
Initial and Concluding Legal Articles

OVERVIEW

In dealing with preambles and article formation so far, we have had occasion to touch on the kind of legal language associated with Initial and Concluding Legal Articles. Unit Three specifically addresses the problems encountered in the translation of these text forms.

In terms of context, initializers and concluders serve the dual function of 'instruction' and 'setting the legal framework'. It is the latter purpose, however, which is the more prominent. Hence the conventional nature of the structure formats in use and the formulaic nature of the kind of texture employed. If machine translation is to be at all sustainable as a commercial enterprise, it will be in the area of restricted registers such as 'initializing' and 'concluding' legal documents.

I. As examples of legal writing within this genre,* consider the following texts, which contain the various kinds of linguistic conventions governing the legal register in this area.

TEXT 3A

الفواتح

١. لغرض هذا الاتفاق فإن عبارة «سفينة» تعني أية سفينة ترفع علم أي من الطرفين المتعاقدين.

٢. يقصد بشركات الاستثمار أي شركة تكون أغراضها الأساسية توظيف واستثمار الأموال لحسابها أو لحساب الغير.

٣. في تطبيق أحكام هذا القانون يراد بالكلمات والعبارات الآتية المعاني المبينة قرين كل منها ما لم يقض السياق بغير ذلك:

العامل: هو كل ذكر أو أنثى يعمل لقاء أجر مهما كان نوعه.

الخواتم

١ . يعرض هذا النظام الأساسي للتصديق عليه من قبل الدول الأعضاء وتودع وثائق التصديق لدى حكومة المملكة المغربية .

يودع هذا النظام الأساسي في محفوظات حكومة المملكة المغربية حيث يظل باب التوقيع عليه مفتوحاً . ويتم التوقيع عليه قبل إيداع وثائق التصديق . يصبح هذا النظام الأساسي نافذاً عندما يتم التوقيع عليه من نصف الدول الأعضاء في منظمة المؤتمر الإسلامي .

٢ . يخضع هذا الاتفاق للتصديق عليه وفقاً لتشريعات كلا الطرفين .

٣ . وقع في . . . بتاريخ . . . من نسختين أصليتين باللغات العربية والألمانية والانجليزية وجميع النصوص الثلاثة لها نفس الحجية وفي حالة الاختلاف في تفسير هذا الاتفاق يرجع إلى النص الانجليزي .

٤ . حررت هذه المعاهدة بخمس لغات رسمية متساوية الحجية هي <. . .> تودع في محفوظات الحكومة المغربية التي تناط بها مسؤولية إرسال صور مصدَّقة عنها إلى حكومات الدول الموقعة لها أو المنظمة إليها .

وإثباتاً لما تقدم قام الموقعون أدناه المفوضون حسب الأصول بتوقيع هذه المعاهدة .

[9]

II. Bearing in mind the distinctive features of Arabic Initial and Concluding legal articles, translate the following into Arabic as examples of this kind of legal writing in English.

TEXT 3B

Initializers

1. For the purpose of the present Convention,[1] the following expressions shall have the meanings hereunder assigned to them:
   a) the 'head of the mission' is the person charged by the sending State with the duty of acting in that capacity;
2. For the purpose of the present Protocol, the expression 'members of the mission' shall have the meaning assigned to it in Article I, sub-paragraph (a), of the Convention, namely (. . . .).

3. In this Convention:

(i) The words 'standard clauses' refer to the provisions of Articles II to IX.

Concluders

1. The present Protocol shall be open for signature by all States[2] which may become Parties to the Convention . . .

2. The present Protocol is subject to ratification. The instruments of ratification shall be deposited with the Secretary-General of the United Nations.

3. The present Protocol shall enter into force on the same day as the Convention or on the thirtieth day following the date of deposit of the second instrument of ratification or accession to the Protocol with the Secretary-General, whichever day is the later.[3]

(. . .)

5. The Secretary-General of the United Nations shall inform all States which may become Parties to the Convention of the date on which the present Protocol will enter into force.

6. The original of the present Protocol, of which the Chinese,[4] English, French, Russian and Spanish texts are equally authentic, shall be deposited with the Secretary-General, who shall send certified copies thereof to all States referred to in Article III.

In witness whereof the undersigned Plenipotentiaries,[5] being duly authorized thereto by their respective Governments, have signed the present Protocol.

Done at Vienna, this eighteenth day of April one thousand nine hundred and sixty-one.

7. The Secretary-General shall transmit copies of this Convention to each specialized agency and to the Government of each member (. . .).

[10]

NOTES

1. As pointed out in previous units, not all typically English sentence-initial adverbials remain fronted in legal Arabic, but elements like this one can occupy initial position as they are to some extent universal and formulaic.

2. The likely من قبل for this by-agent passive may be avoided by opting for an *idafa* construction,* thus: لتوقيع جميع الدول.

3. The element *whichever later* is likely to be problematic if left where it is. Thus a neater way of handling the situation may be to introduce the two alternative dates with something like: وفي أحد التاريخين التاليين, to be immediately followed by: أيهما أبعد and then have the two dates.

4. Here, a slight restructuring may also be necessary for: *of which the Chinese, English, . . . texts are equally authentic*: المحرر بخمس لغات متساوية الحجية هي الصينية والانجليزية . . .

5. Once again, this may more usefully be seen as a complete chunk with the need for slight restructuring: وإثباتاً لما تقدم قام الموقعون أدناه والذين فوّضتهم حسب الأصول حكومات كل منهم بالتوقيع على.

GLOSSARY

for the purpose of the present Convention	لأغراض هذه الاتفاقية
the meanings hereunder assigned	المدلولات المحددة أدناه
sub-paragraph	البند
namely	أي
the words 'standard clauses'	عبارة البنود النموذجية
provisions	أحكام
shall be open for signature	يتم عرض . . . لتوقيع
which may become	التي قد تصبح
is subject to ratification	يخضع للتصديق
The instruments of ratification	وثائق التصديق
shall be deposited with	تودع لدى
shall enter into force	يسري
the thirtieth day following	اليوم الثلاثين التالي
The Secretary-General shall inform	يخطر الأمين العام
The original of	أصل
certified copies thereof	صور معتمدة عنه
In witness whereof	وإثباتاً لما تقدم
shall transmit copies of	يبعث بنسخ من

III. Bearing in mind the distinctive features of Initial and Concluding legal articles in both English and Arabic, translate Text 3A (reproduced here for easier reference) into English.

TEXT 3A

الفواتح

١ . لغرض هذا الاتفاق فإن عبارة «سفينة» تعني[1] أية سفينة ترفع علم أي من الطرفين المتعاقدين .

٢ . يقصد بشركات الاستثمار أي شركة تكون أغراضها الأساسية توظيف واستثمار الأموال لحسابها أو لحساب الغير .

٣ . في تطبيق أحكام هذا القانون[2] يراد بالكلمات والعبارات الآتية المعاني المبينة قرين كل منها ما لم يقض السياق بغير ذلك :

العامل : هو كل ذكر أو أنثى يعمل لقاء أجر مهما كان نوعه .

الخواتم

١ . يعرض هذا النظام الأساسي للتصديق عليه من قبل[3] الدول الأعضاء وتودع وثائق التصديق لدى حكومة المملكة المغربية .

يودع هذا النظام الأساسي في محفوظات حكومة المملكة المغربية حيث[4] يظل باب التوقيع عليه مفتوحاً . ويتم التوقيع عليه قبل إيداع وثائق التصديق . يصبح هذا النظام الأساسي نافذاً عندما يتم التوقيع عليه من[5] نصف الدول الأعضاء في منظمة المؤتمر الإسلامي .

٢ . يخضع هذا الاتفاق للتصديق عليه وفقاً لتشريعات كلا الطرفين .

٣ . وقع[6] في . . . بتاريخ . . . من نسختين أصليتين[7] باللغات العربية والألمانية والانجليزية وجميع النصوص الثلاثة لها نفس الحجية وفي حالة الاختلاف في تفسير هذا الاتفاق يرجع إلى النص الانجليزي .

٤ . حررت هذه المعاهدة بخمس لغات رسمية متساوية الحجية هي < . . . > تودع في محفوظات الحكومة المغربية التي تناط بها مسؤولية إرسال صور مصدقة عنها إلى حكومات الدول الموقعة لها أو المنظمة إليها .

وإثباتاً لما تقدم قام الموقعون أدناه المفوضون حسب الأصول بتوقيع هذه المعاهدة .

NOTES

1. In Arabic, while the fronting of لغرض (which, incidentally, is better put in the plural: لأغراض هذا الاتفاق) is perfectly acceptable, this word order is not in any sense rhetorically motivated. Thus the use of the Arabic nominal in the sentence which follows is completely inappropriate. Given the nature of definitions in legal Arabic, only the Verbal structure can be defended here, thus: يعني مصطلح سفينة . . . .

2. As we have already pointed out, the adverbial في تطبيق أحكام هذا القانون is of the transient, specific type and, in Arabic, should not be fronted but embedded, leaving يقصد (which, incidentally, is less idiomatic than يراد) to sentence-initial position.

3. The by-agent من قبل is avoidable here, as elsewhere in Arabic, by opting for something like an إضافة, thus: لتصديق الدول الأعضاء عليه. The non-agentive passive يعرض, on the other hand, is awkward and may be better rephrased as: يتم عرض. However, the way the original text handles both these cases may be accounted for in terms of genre constraints.

4. Here, حيث is redundant and what follows should be treated as an independent instruction both in English and in Arabic.

5. This awkward passive would be more idiomatic in Arabic if put in the active, thus: يوقع عليه نصف الدول الأعضاء.

6. Once again, this agentless passive is better rephrased as: تم التوقيع على هذا. A passive such as حرر could equally be used here and would be perfectly acceptable by virtue of being formulaic and conventional.

7. A chunk-for-chunk translation is necessary here. Study the English Text 3B equivalent of this entire instruction. The same goes for the two items which follow.

GLOSSARY

which flies the flag of	ترفع علم
the two Contracting Parties	الطرفين المتعاقدين
investment companies	شركات الاستثمار
whose main objectives are	تكون أغراضها الأساسية
the management and investment of funds	توظيف واستثمار الأموال

unless the context indicates otherwise	ما لم يقض السياق بغير ذلك
hired for a wage of whatsoever nature	يعمل لقاء أجر مهما كان نوعه
government archives	محفوظات الحكومة
in accordance with the legislation of	وفقاً لتشريعات
Done	تم التوقيع على هذا ـ حُرّر

UNIT THREE: Additional Texts

I. A typical legal document, then, consists of a Preamble (signatory –
    preambular paragraphs – a verb of declaration), a set of initial articles, a
    set of articles (using instructional verbs such as *shall, may, must, should*
    or simply the verb 'to be' *(is/are)* or a verb in the present simple) and,
    finally, a set of concluding articles. Text 3C illustrates the entire format
    of a legal document. Translate the text into English.

TEXT 3C

اتفاقية بشأن الملاحة التجارية البحرية

إن حكومة . . . وحكومة . . . المشار اليهما فيما بعد «الطرفين المتعاقدين»

رغبة منهما في تقوية علاقات الصداقة القائمة بين الدولتين . . .

فقد وافقتا على ما يلي:

مادة ١: لأغراض هذا الاتفاق، تعني عبارة «أفراد طاقم السفينة» الربان وأي شخص مستخدم للقيام بمهام على ظهر السفينة أثناء الرحلة.

مادة ٢: يعمل الطرفان المتعاقدان على مساعدة كل منهما الآخر في تنمية الملاحة التجارية البحرية بين موانئ الطرفين المتعاقدين.

مادة ٣: لا يحق¹ لأي من الطرفين المتعاقدين القيام بأعمال التجارة الساحلية والإنقاذ والإغاثة وغيرها من الأعمال ضمن الموانئ والمياه الإقليمية للطرف الآخر.

مادة ٤: لا تعتبر تجارة ساحلية تلك الحالات التي تبحر فيها سفن أحد الطرفين من ميناء الى ميناء آخر للطرف الآخر من أجل تفريغ أو تحميل البضائع أو إنزال أو صعود الركاب.

مادة ٥: يجوز لأفراد طاقم سفينة أي من الطرفين الذين يحملون مستندات تحديد

هوية صالحة عبور حدود دولة الطرف الآخر .

مادة ٦ : يجب قيد أي تغيير في طاقم بحارة سفينة أي من الطرفين الراسية في ميناء دولة الطرف الآخر في المستندات الخاصة بالسفينة بحيث تبين تاريخ وسبب هذا التغيير .

مادة ٧ : يخضع هذا الاتفاق للتصديق عليه وفقاً لتشريعات كلا الطرفين ويصبح ساري المفعول من تاريخ إشعار الأخير بالموافقة عليه .

حرر في . . . بتاريخ . . . ² من نسختين أصليتين باللغات العربية والألمانية والانجليزية وجميع النصوص الثلاثة لها نفس الحجية ، وفي حالة الاختلاف في تفسير هذا الاتفاق يرجع إلى النص الانجليزي .

[11]

NOTES

1. The meaning of the term حق varies with the context and is thus particularly difficult to render into English. Here, the phrase must be understood as equivalent to لا يجوز = 'may not'.

2. Chunk-for-chunk translation is essential here. See the restructuring involved in the example cited in Text 3A above.

GLOSSARY

mercantile shipping	الملاحة التجارية
hereinunder referred to as	المشار اليهما فيما بعد
the Two Contracting Parties	الطرفين المتعاقدين
Desiring to	رغبة منهما
strengthen the friendly relations	تقوية علاقات الصداقة
existing	القائمة
The expression 'members of the crew'	عبارة «أفراد طاقم السفينة»
captain	الربان
employed to perform particular tasks	مستخدم للقيام بمهام
on board the vessel	على ظهر السفينة
during the passage	أثناء الرحلة
may not	لا يحق
engage in coastal trade	القيام بأعمال التجارة الساحلية
rescue and relief	الإنقاذ والإغاثة

territorial waters	المياه الإقليمية
loading or unloading of goods	تفريغ أو تحميل البضائع
embarkation and disembarkation of passengers	صعود الركاب أو إنزالهم
valid identification papers	مستندات تحديد هوية صالحة
crossing the borders of	عبور حدود
any change must be entered	يجب قيد أي تغيير
berthing	الراسية
This agreement is subject to ratification	يخضع هذا الاتفاق للتصديق عليه
in accordance with the legislation of	وفقاً لتشريعات
shall enter into effect	يصبح ساري المفعول
from the date of the latter's notification of agreement thereto	من تاريخ إشعار الأخير بالموافقة عليه
Done at	حُرِّر في

II. Text 3D illustrates the entire format of a legal document in English. Bearing in mind the distinctive features of the various legal components, translate into Arabic.

TEXT 3D

A Supplementary Convention on the Abolition of Slavery, the Slave Trade, and Institutions and Practices Similar to Slavery

Preamble

The States Parties to the present Convention,

Considering that freedom is the birthright of every human being,

Mindful that the peoples of the United Nations reaffirmed in the Charter their faith in the dignity and worth of the human person,

Having decided, therefore, that the Convention of 1926, which remains operative, should now be augmented by the conclusion of a supplementary convention designed to intensify national as well as international efforts towards the abolition of slavery,

Have agreed as follows:

Article . . .

For the purposes of the present Convention, 'slavery' means the status or condition of a person over whom any or all of the powers attaching to the right of ownership are exercised.

Article . . .

Each of the States Parties to this Convention shall take all practicable and necessary legislative and other measures to bring about progressively and as soon as possible the complete abolition or abandonment of the following institutions and practices: debt bondage, serfdom, and any institution or practice whereby a woman on the death of her husband is liable to be inherited by another person.[1]

Article . . .

With a view to bringing to an end the institutions and practices mentioned in Article I, the States Parties undertake to prescribe, where appropriate, suitable minimum ages of marriage.

Article . . .

This Convention shall be open until 1 July 1957 for signature by any State Member of the UN or of a specialized agency. It shall be subject to ratification by the signatory States, and the instruments of ratification shall be deposited with the Secretary-General of the UN who shall inform each signatory.

Article . . .

This Convention, of which the Chinese, English, French, Russian and Spanish texts are equally authentic, shall be deposited in the archives of the UN Secretariat. The Secretary-General shall send a certified copy thereof to States Parties to the Convention.

In witness whereof the undersigned, being duly authorized thereto by their respective governments, have signed this Convention.

Done at the European Office of the UN at Geneva, this seventh day of September one thousand nine hundred and fifty-six.

[8]

47

NOTES

1. This is a complex structure which may best be rendered as follows: أي من الأعراف أو الممارسات التي تتيح جعل المرأة لدى وفاة زوجها إرثاً ينتقل إلى شخص آخر.

GLOSSARY

Supplementary Convention on	اتفاقية تكميلية بشأن
Abolition of Slavery	إبطال الرق
Slave Trade	تجارة الرقيق
Institutions and Practices	الأعراف والممارسات
Considering	إذ ترى
birthright of every human being	حق يكتسبه كل كائن بشري لدى مولده
Mindful	وإدراكاً منها بأن
reaffirmed their faith	جددت تأكيد إيمانها
the dignity and worth of X	كرامة س وقدره
Having decided, therefore, that	وإذ قررت تبعاً لذلك أن
which remains operative	التي لا تزال سارية المفعول
should now be augmented	أصبح من الواجب أن تضاف إلى
designed to intensify	تهدف إلى تكثيف
'slavery' means	يعني مصطلح «الرق»
the status or condition	حال أو وضع
powers attaching to the right of ownership	السلطات الناجمة عن حق الملكية
over whom any or all of X are exercised	تمارس عليه كافة س أو أي منها
practicable measures	التدابير القابلة للتنفيذ العملي
progressively and as soon as possible	تدريجياً وبالسرعة الممكنة
abandonment	هجر
debt bondage	إسار الدَّين
serfdom	القنانة
With a view to bringing to an end	بغية وضع حد لـ
to prescribe, where appropriate,	تفرض عند الحاجة
suitable minimum ages of marriage	حدوداً دنيا مناسبة لسن الزواج
open for signature	متاحة للتوقيع
instruments of ratification	صكوك التصديق

PART II: *Translating Detached Exposition*

OVERVIEW

Exposition* (السرد) is a text type which has one basic feature in common with the kind of legal discourse with which we have been dealing so far. Both types are essentialy detached and typically unemotive. But unlike legal texts, expository texts are not 'instructional' (i.e. they are not legally binding). Furthermore, exposition can and often does allow a certain measure of evaluativeness. These contextual specifications must always be borne in mind as they are bound to determine the kind of linguistic choices we make in translation.

In terms of structure, exposition, like instructional texts, yields essentially identifiable structure formats. But the kind of structure exhibited by an expository Abstract or Definition, for example, tends to be less rigid or formulaic than that of, say, a Preamble. Generally, expository texts 'set a scene',* then present the various aspects of that scene as comprehensively as deemed appropriate.

Awareness of the typical structure format of an expository text in turn influences the kind of texture that we are likely to encounter in this kind of text. While less closely knit than legal texts, the texture of exposition

49

nevertheless tends to be fairly tight. Expository texts are heavily coordinated (reflected in Arabic by the predominance of the additive 'و') and conspicuously parallelistic (preserved in Arabic by the predominance of the Verb – Subject – Object structure: الجملة الفعلية). Word order, whether in English or in Arabic, is rarely if ever manipulated as rhetorical effect is not what this kind of text is basically about. The idiom is fairly steady and emotive diction is avoided as far as possible.

Finally, in terms of the translation strategy to be adopted in dealing with this kind of exposition, literal translation must be aimed at and is achievable, though to a slightly lesser extent than that possible in legal translation.

A word on what Text 4A (i) below is *not* intended to achieve may perhaps be helpful at the outset. Except for the one sentence in quotation marks to draw your attention to its instructional function, this text is not meant to issue instructions or be in any sense legally binding. Given this kind of context, the structure is not what may at first strike us as much akin to a Preamble. Finally in terms of texture, although the text is predominantly in the Verbal sentence structure, the verbal element is not the same as that found in the instructional text proper where it has the force of law-making.

UNIT FOUR: The Synopsis

I. Consider the following text as an example of the expository Synopsis, which is one form of summarizing.

TEXT 4A (i)

رغبة في إنشاء محكمة العدل الإسلامية الدولية كجهاز من أجهزة المؤتمر الإسلامي صدر القرار ١٣ ـ ٥ <ق.أ> عن المؤتمر الخامس المنعقد في الفترة من ٢٦ إلى ٢٩ يناير ١٩٨٧ وتضمن هذا القرار الموافقة على النظام الأساسي للمحكمة وعلى إضافة فقرة رابعة للمادة الثالثة من ميثاق المؤتمر الإسلامي يكون نصها 'وتؤدي المحكمة مهامها وفقاً لنظامها الأساسي الملحق بهذا الميثاق والذي يعد جزءاً متمماً له' .

وقد تناول النظام الأساسي للمحكمة في مجمله تنظيم تشكيل وبيان الحصانات التي تتمتع بها وواجبات أعضائها وامتيازاتهم ومكافآتهم وأحكام تعيين سائر موظفي المحكمة . وقد حدد النظام اختصاصات المحكمة وولايتها القضائية وتقوم هذه الولاية أساساً على الموافقة الاختيارية على اللجوء إلى المحكمة . كما بين النظام تفصيلاً اجراءات التقاضي وسير الدعوى أمام المحكمة منذ إقامة الدعوى حتى صدور حكم فيها وتعرض لحجية الأحكام التي تصدرها ولأحوال إعادة النظر فيها كما تناول بالتنظيم اختصاص المحكمة في نطاق الوساطة والتوفيق والتحكيم .

[12]

II. To remind you of what legal language is like, Text 4A (ii) is included as an example of an article from the Rules of Procedure of the Islamic Court. This is everything which Text 4A (i) is not and must therefore be translated as a legal text.

TEXT 4A (ii)

إن مؤتمر القمة الإسلامي الخامس .

رغبة في انشاء جهاز قضائي رئيسي يفصل في المنازعات وفقاً لأحكام الشريعة الإسلامية .

يوافق على مشروع النظام الأساسي لمحكمة العدل الإسلامية الدولية .

<. . .>

المادة الثالثة

يتم تشكيل هيئة المحكمة من ستة قضاة بالإضافة إلى الرئيس وتقوم هيئة المحكمة بانتخاب نائب للرئيس من بين أعضائها.

المادة الرابعة

يشترط لانتخاب عضو في المحكمة أن يكون مسلماً عدلاً من ذوي الصفات الخلقية العالية ومن رعايا إحدى الدول الأعضاء على أن لا يقل عمره عن أربعين عاماً وأن يكون من فقهاء الشريعة المشهود لهم أو من الخبراء في القانون الدولي.

[1]

III. Bearing in mind the distinctive features of Arabic expository synopses, translate into Arabic the following example of the Synopsis in English.

TEXT 4B (i)

Organization of the Conference

By resolution 2919 of 15 November 1972,[1] the General Assembly decided to launch the Decade for Action to Combat Racism and Racial Discrimination and to inaugurate the activities of this Decade on 10 December 1973,[2] the twenty-fifth anniversary of the Universal Declaration of Human Rights. The Programme for the Decade provided that *as a major feature during the Decade, a world conference on combating racism should be convened by the General Assembly as soon as possible.*[3] The Programme further[4] provided that the Economic and Social Council would act as the preparatory committee of the Conference.

The Preparatory Committee met from 14 to 25 March 1977 at United Nations Headquarters and submitted its report to the Economic and Social Council. The report included a provisional agenda for the Conference and draft rules of procedure. These were considered and approved[5] by the Council in resolution 2057. That resolution was later endorsed by the General Assembly.

[2]

NOTES

1. A hallmark of expository texture in Arabic is the predominant use of the Verbal sentence structure. Among a number of other features to which we shall have occasion to refer in the coming units, Verbalization entails embedding fronted adverbials, e.g. . . . قررت الجمعية العامة، بالقرار المؤرخ . . .

2. As already mentioned, the 'pragmatic meaning' of punctuation marks must be glossed explicitly in Arabic. Thus the comma here, which means 'coinciding with', is rendered in Arabic as: الموافق للذكرى.

3. A case of an agentive passive = active. Also 'legal' style necessitates the Verbal sentence structure, thus: تدعو الجمعية العامة في أقرب وقت ممكن الى عقد . . . يكون معلماً رئيسياً من معالم العقد.

4. To maintain the consistency of expository texture, resist كما نص and opt for more uniformity through: ونص البرنامج كذلك.

5. It may be more appropriate for the two activities to be separated here, thus: . . . ونظر المجلس في . . . وأقرها بالقرار.

GLOSSARY

launch the Decade for Action	إعلان عقد العمل من أجل
inaugurate the activities	بدأ أنشطة
anniversary	الذكرى
Universal Declaration	الإعلان العالمي
provided	نص
provisional agenda	جدول أعمال مؤقت
draft rules of procedure	مشروع نظام داخلي
was endorsed by X	واعتمدت س . . .

IV. To remind you of what legal language is like, here is an example of an Article from a relevant Declaration. Translate as a legal text.

TEXT 4B (ii)

The General Assembly,

    Alarmed by the manifestations of racial discrimination still in evidence in some areas of the world,

        Proclaims this Declaration:

Article 1

Discrimination between human beings on the grounds of race, colour or ethnic origin is an offence to human dignity and shall be condemned as a denial of the principles of the Charter of the United Nations, as a violation of the human rights and fundamental freedoms proclaimed in the Universal Declaration of Human Rights, as an obstacle to friendly and peaceful relations among nations and as a fact capable of disturbing peace and security among peoples.

[8]

GLOSSARY

Alarmed by the manifestations of	وإذ تثير قلقها مظاهر
still in evidence	لا تزال ظاهرة للعيان
Proclaims this Declaration	تصدر هذا الإعلان
X is an offence	يشكل س إهانة
shall be condemned	ويدان
denial of the principles	انتهاكاً لمبادئ
proclaimed in X	التي نادى بها س
as an obstacle to	بوصفه عقبة في وجه

V. Bearing in mind the distinctive features of the Synopsis in both English and Arabic, translate Texts 4A (i) and 4A (ii) (reproduced here for easier reference) into English.

TEXT 4A (i)

رغبةً¹ في إنشاء محكمة العدل الإسلامية الدولية كجهاز من أجهزة المؤتمر الإسلامي صدر القرار ١٣ ـ ٥ <ق.أ> عن المؤتمر الخامس المنعقد في الفترة من ٢٦ إلى ٢٩ يناير ١٩٨٧ وتضمن هذا القرار الموافقة على النظام الأساسي للمحكمة وعلى إضافة فقرة رابعة للمادة الثالثة من ميثاق المؤتمر الإسلامي يكون نصها 'وتؤدي المحكمة مهامها وفقاً لنظامها الأساسي الملحق بهذا الميثاق والذي يعد جزءاً متمماً له'.

وقد تناول النظام الأساسي للمحكمة في مجمله² تنظيم تشكيل وبيان الحصانات التي تتمتع بها وواجبات أعضائها وامتيازاتهم ومكافآتهم وأحكام تعيين سائر موظفي المحكمة. وقد حدد النظام اختصاصات المحكمة وولايتها القضائية وتقوم هذه الولاية أساساً على الموافقة الاختيارية على اللجوء إلى المحكمة. كما³ بين النظام تفصيلاً اجراءات التقاضي

وسير الدعوى أمام المحكمة منذ إقامة الدعوى حتى صدور حكم فيها وتعرض⁴ لحجية الأحكام التي تصدرها ولأحوال إعادة النظر فيها كما تناول بالتنظيم اختصاص المحكمة في نطاق الوساطة والتوفيق والتحكيم.

NOTES

1. It would certainly have been better exposition in Arabic had this fronted adverbial been embedded as sentence-final here: ... صدر عن س القرار . ...وذلك رغبة في. Considerations of length could have played a part in source text composition. However, the point at issue is to avoid 'instructional' undertones in the English text: 'In the desire to . . ., resolution . . . was issued by . . .'.

2. This is an example of an appropriately embedded adverbial that is normally fronted in English: 'In general, the court . . .'.

3. This كما is an example of the superfluous use of such 'evaluative' additives.

4. Even in Arabic, a more consistent exposition would have benefited from the repetition and not the variation of the Verbal elements: تناول، تناول، تناول. However, Arabic tends to vary. English, on the other hand, goes for strict repetition in this regard: 'dealt with . . . dealt with . . . dealt with . . .'.

GLOSSARY

as an instrument of	جهاز من أجهزة
approval of the rules of procedure	الموافقة على النظام الأساسي
the addition of a paragraph	إضافة فقرة
which provides that	يكون نصها
the court shall perform	تؤدي المحكمة مهامها
annexed to the present Charter	الملحق بهذا الميثاق
form an integral part thereof	الذي يعد جزءاً متمماً له
dealt with	تناول
the organization and composition of	تنظيم وتشكيل
the statement of the immunities	بيان الحصانات
privileges and remuneration	امتيازات ومكافآت

rules of appointing X	أحكام تعيين
define the Court's power	حدد اختصاصات المحكمة
legal jurisdiction	ولايتها القضائية
basically founded on	وتقوم أساساً
discretionary agreement	الموافقة الاختيارية
resort to the Court	اللجوء الى المحكمة
specifically, X made explicit	بين النظام تفصيلاً
the judicial procedures	إجراءات التقاضي
the process of litigation	سير الدعوى
from the time when a case is lodged	منذ إقامة الدعوى
when judgement is issued	حتى صدور الحكم فيها
conditions under which appeal is possible	أحوال إعادة النظر
mediation, reconciliation, arbitration	الوساطة والتوفيق والتحكيم

TEXT 4A (ii)

إن مؤتمر القمة الإسلامي الخامس

رغبة في إنشاء جهاز قضائي رئيسي يفصل في المنازعات وفقاً لأحكام الشريعة الإسلامية،

يوافق على مشروع النظام الأساسي لمحكمة العدل الإسلامية الدولية.

< . . . >

المادة الثالثة

يتم تشكيل هيئة المحكمة من ستة قضاة بالإضافة الى الرئيس وتقوم هيئة المحكمة بانتخاب نائب للرئيس من بين أعضائها.

المادة الرابعة

يشترط لانتخاب عضو في المحكمة أن يكون مسلماً عدلاً من ذوي الصفات الخلقية العالية ومن رعايا إحدى الدول الأعضاء على أن لا يقل عمره عن أربعين عاماً وأن يكون من فقهاء الشريعة المشهود لهم أو من الخبراء في القانون الدولي.

GLOSSARY

Desirous of	رغبة في
adjudicates over disputes	يفصل في المنازعات
the provisions of the Islamic *shari'a*	أحكام الشريعة الإسلامية
the draft rules of procedure	مشروع النظام الأساسي
the board of the court	هيئة المحكمة
X shall consist of	يتم تشكيل س من . . .
a member must be	يشترط أن يكون العضو
a righteous Muslim	مسلماً عدلاً
of high moral standing	من ذوي الصفات الخلقية العالية
a national of . . .	من رعايا
aged not less than	لا يقل عمره عن
an attested jurisprudent	من فقهاء . . . المشهود لهم

UNIT FOUR: Additional Texts

I. Synopses occur in all kinds of documents – legal, journalistic, scientific, etc. The main purpose of the Synopsis is to summarize as objectively as possible the content of a larger text or a body of texts. Bearing in mind the distinctive features of the Synopsis in both English and Arabic, translate the following as examples which illustrate this text form in English and in Arabic.

TEXT 4C (i)

Background to the Conference
on the Least Developed Countries

The General Assembly of the UN, in its resolution 34/203 of 19 December, decided to convene the UN Conference on the Least Developed Countries in 1981 to finalize, adopt and support[1] the Substantial New Programme of Action for the 1980s for the Least Developed Countries outlined in[2] UNCTAD resolution 122. In the same resolution,[3] it designated UNCTAD's Intergovernmental Group on the Least Developed Countries to act as the Preparatory Committee for the Conference and designated the Secretary-General of UNCTAD as Secretary-General of the Conference.

The Preparatory Committee welcomed the offer of the Government of France to host the Conference in Paris and made detailed recommendations on the organization of the UN Conference. These recommendations were subsequently endorsed by the General Assembly which accepted the offer of the Government of France to host the Conference.

The Preparatory Committee decided to make individual least-developed-country reviews the basis for the preparations for the Conference. Accordingly, each least developed country was invited to prepare a presentation of its development programme for the 1980s, for review at individual meetings with its development partners. Each least developed country was left to decide which countries and multilateral agencies or other bodies it wished to invite to its review meeting.

[14]

NOTES

1. Whether to separate between or serially list 'events' like these is a matter for the translator to decide so long as there are no constraining factors. For example, we could here say either.

أ. لوضع الصيغة النهائية وإقرار ودعم

or:

ب. لوضع الصيغة النهاية لـ س وإقرار ودعم هذا البرنامج .

My own preference would be to preserve word order and opt for the first alternative if there are no overriding factors.

2. An example of the agentless passive (positive), which may be rendered as: الذي تمت الإشارة اليه.

3. An adverbial best embedded in exposition: وكلفت الجمعية العامة في نفس القرار . . .

GLOSSARY

the Least Developed Countries	أقل البلدان نمواً
Intergovernmental Group	الفريق الحكومي الدولي
designated X as Secretary-General	وعينت س أميناً عاماً
welcomed the offer	رحبت بعرض
to host the Conference	باستضافة المؤتمر
made detailed recommendations	وضعت توصيات تفصيلية
individual least-developed-country reviews	استعراضات قطرية فردية لأقل البلدان نمواً

to make X the basis	أن تكون س أساساً
the preparations for	الأعمال التحضيرية
prepare a presentation	إعداد عرض
development partners	شركائه في التنمية
X was left to decide	وتم ترك الحرية لكل بلد في اختيار
multilateral agencies	الوكالات متعددة الأطراف

II. Consider and translate into Arabic the following instructional section from the relevant resolution as an example of legal and not expository writing.

TEXT 4C (ii)

The United Nations Conference
on the Least Developed Countries

Recalling resolution 122 of the UN Conference on Trade and Development adopted at Manila on 3 June 1979, in which it was decided as one of its major priorities to launch a Comprehensive New Programme of Action for the Least Developed Countries in two phases, an Immediate Action Programme and a Substantial New Programme, and which was endorsed by the General Assembly in its resolution 34/210 of 19 December 1980. (. . .).

Decides to adopt and recommends the immediate implementation of the following Programme of Action (. . .).

[14]

GLOSSARY

Recalling resolution . . .	إذ يشير إلى
as one of its major priorities	كواحد من أولوياته الرئيسية
to launch X in two phases	الشروع في تنفيذ . . . على مرحلتين
an Immediate Action Programme	برنامج عمل تنفيذي
Substantial New Programme	برنامج عمل جديد مكثف
Decides to adopt	يقرر اعتماد

III. Now consider and translate into English the following extract from an explanatory memorandum as an example of expository writing in Arabic.

TEXT 4D (i)

مذكرة إيضاحية

لما كانت حكومة دولة الكويت تسعى دائماً الى تطوير وتعزيز علاقاتها مع الدول الصديقة ورغبة منها في تعميق الروابط الاقتصادية مع حكومة جمهورية ألمانيا الديموقراطية[1] فقد وقعت الدولتان بتاريخ ١٧ ـ ٦ ـ ١٩٨٧ في بكين اتفاقاً بشأن الملاحة التجارية بهدف التعاون في هذا المجال على أساس من مبادئ السيادة والمساواة.

ويقع الاتفاق في ١٥ مادة اشتملت المادة الأولى منه على بعض التعاريف ونصت المادة الثانية على تعاون الطرفين المتعاقدين من أجل تنمية الملاحة البحرية بين الدولتين وبينت الطرق الكفيلة بذلك.

وأوضحت المادة الثالثة كيفية معاملة كل دولة لسفن الدولة المتعاقدة الأخرى ونصت على أن تكون نفس المعاملة التي يقدمها كل طرف لسفنه المشاركة في الملاحة الدولية وذلك في بعض الأمور التي يمكن مساواة سفن الدولتين فيها مثل الدخول الحر الى مياهها الإقليمية والداخلية.

أما المادة الرابعة فقد نصت على عدم السماح لأي من الطرفين المتعاقدين بممارسة أي من الأعمال الخاصة بالموانئ بما في ذلك أعمال التجارة الساحلية والانقاذ والمساعدة وغيرها. وقد أشارت المادة الخامسة لحالة تعرض سفينة تابعة لأي من الطرفين للجنوح أو التحطم أو إصابتها بأي كارثة أخرى وما يمكن للمسؤولين القيام به تجاهها.

[15]

NOTES

1. This is a good example of a fronted adverbial when the fronting is discourse-organizational and is therefore appropriate. The length of the two items لما كانت س تسعى دائماً ورغبة منها makes embedding them or using them sentence-finally simply too awkward. In English, however, such adverbials would always be fronted: 'As X has always endeavoured to . . . and in the desire to . . .'.

GLOSSARY

Explanatory Memorandum	مذكرة إيضاحية
develop and strengthen	تطوير وتعزيز
consolidate economic links	تعميق الروابط الاقتصادية
an agreement on mercantile shipping	اتفاقية بشأن الملاحة التجارية البحرية
on the basis of the principles of	على أساس من مبادئ
sovereignty and equal rights	السيادة والمساواة
X consists of	ويقع س في
stated the means necessary therefor	بينت الطرق الكفيلة بذلك
reciprocal treatment must be extended	أن تكون نفس المعاملة التي تبديها
when reciprocity is possible	الأمور التي يمكن مساواة سفن الدولتين فيها
X prevented	س قررت عدم السماح
carry out port-related activities	ممارسة أعمال خاصة بالموانئ
coastal trade	أعمال التجارة الساحلية
rescue and relief	الانقاذ والمساعدة
when a ship runs aground	حالة تعرض سفينة للجنوح
wrecked or is stricken by any other disaster	أو التحطم أو اصابتها بأية كارثة

IV. Consider and translate into English the following instructional section from the relevant resolution as an example of legal and not expository writing.

TEXT 4D (ii)

إن حكومة دولة الكويت وحكومة جمهورية المانيا الديموقراطية رغبة منها في تقوية علاقات الصداقة القائمة بين الدولتين فقد وافقتا على ما يلي:

مادة

في حالة جنوح أي سفينة أو تحطمها أو اصابتها بأية كوارث أخرى في المياه الإقليمية أو المياه الداخلية للطرف المتعاقد الآخر يمنح[1] الأشخاص على ظهر السفينة والسفينة والحمولة المساعدة الضرورية.

[15]

NOTES

1. This is an agentless passive and would have been more appropriately
    rendered as: .يتم منح

GLOSSARY

In the event of a ship running aground
necessary assistance shall be extended

في حالة جنوح أية سفينة
يمنح س المساعدة الضرورية

UNIT FIVE: The Summary

OVERVIEW

Synopses, then, are expository forms of text whose function is to summarize as succinctly and as objectively as possible the content of a text or a body of texts. But I feel it is justified to make a distinction between the Synopsis and another expository text form whose function is also essentially to summarize, namely the Summary. I make the distinction on the grounds of a subtle contextual variation between the two forms: summaries tend to allow a certain element of subjectivity which reflects the summarizer's point of view regarding what he or she wants to focus on or whose side is more plausible, etc.

While the structure of both the Synopsis and the Summary is basically the same (scene set and detailed as comprehensively as deemed appropriate), this very notion of appropriateness is left very much to the summarizer in producing a Summary. Hence, one should expect slight variation in the structural configuration characteristic of this particular text form. Put differently, the structure of summaries is inevitably slightly looser than that of the Synopsis, which is bound to influence translation decisions. But in dealing with synopses and summaries, decisions taken by the translator will be markedly different in the area of texture. Here, summaries are often far less stringently written than synopses. Diction is allowed to be more flowery and a certain amount of emotiveness which reflects a bias one way or the other is not ruled out. Translators must therefore aim to preserve this personal touch, which is singularly lacking in synopses.

I. Consider Text 5A (i) as an example of the Synopsis and compare with Text 5A (ii) which illustrates the expository text form of the Summary.

TEXT 5A (i)

UNTANGLING THE WEB: NUTRITION, HEALTH AND EDUCATIONAL ACHIEVEMENT

Over the last several years, five monographs have appeared that, if taken together, shed much light on the web spun by three closely linked variables – nutritional status, health status and educational achievement. Collectively, the monographs also offer a host of approaches for altering the often negative outcomes that stem from the pattern of relationships among these three variables. In other words, the monographs help us to untangle a web that, for many vulnerable children, has indeed been a trap.

UNICEF's 1985 report, *The State of the World's Children,* describes how a minimum of safety net can be provided to protect the growing minds and bodies of the world's most vulnerable children. Through an exploration of case studies, emphasis is given to simple, low-cost techniques that can have a profound influence on the development of every child's physical, social and intellectual potential. (. . .)

Thus far, the foregoing has been a brief synopsis of the major themes touched on in the five monographs. (. . .)

[16]

TEXT 5A (ii)

The five approaches sketched out in the following paragraphs illustrate the diversity of strategies that can be employed to improve the school achievement of children at risk due to poor health and nutritional status. The approaches are not mutually exclusive and, indeed, most effective planners would probably use several of these strategies in combination. (. . .)

The UNICEF report is particularly concerned with the use of mass communication to disseminate four relatively simple and inexpensive methods that enable parents to cut the rate of child mortality in half: growth monitoring, oral rehydration for diarrhoea, breast feeding and immunization against six specific diseases (measles, diphtheria, whooping cough, tetanus, polio and tuberculosis). All four methods save lives by protecting growth. They have a direct impact on school achievement by reducing the prevalence of physical and mental handicap. They also have a unique potential for widespread dissemination through campaigns because of several characteristics. They can be readily distilled. They are based on simple, practical information. They are inexpensive and universal in their relevance. They do not depend on profound changes in values, yet they can lead to dramatic changes.

[16]

II. Text 5B illustrates the expository form of summarizing in Arabic. Consider carefully and translate into English.

TEXT 5B

في هذا اليوم من التاريخ
المؤتمر العربي الأول

في مثل هذا اليوم قبل ٧٩ عاماً، أي في ١٨ حزيران/يونيو سنة ١٩١٣[1]، عقد في باريس «المؤتمر الإسلامي الأول» الذي أحدث صدى كبيراً في مجال الحركة العربية قبيل الحرب العالمية الأولى، وكان أول مؤتمر عربي[2] في الخارج. كان في باريس قبيل الحرب العالمية الأولى[3] نفر من الشباب العرب ومن بينهم[4] من كانوا أعضاء في جمعية «العربية الفتاة» ـ ممن يتتبعون سير الأحداث في بلادهم، وكان الاتحاديون الذين استولوا على الحكم في الدولة العثمانية قد تنكروا للأفكار الإصلاحية التي أقرتها وزارة «حزب الائتلاف» وانبثقت في أوائل عام ١٩١٣ فكرة عقد مؤتمر عربي يعلنون[5] فيه المطالب العربية ويصارحون العالم كله بأن اللامركزية هي قوام حياة العرب وأنهم شركاء في هذه المملكة بل هم الأكثرية المطلقة فيها. وكان أصحاب الفكرة الأصليون خمسة شبان عرب يدرسون في باريس هم عبد الغني العريسي ومحمد المحمصاني وتوفيق فايد (من بيروت) وعوني عبد الهادي (من نابلس) وجميل مردم بك (من دمشق). وقد اتصل هؤلاء الشبان بآخرين من شباب العرب ورجالاتهم[6] في باريس فقوبلت فكرتهم بالترحيب. وبعد مراسلات متعددة مع القاهرة وبيروت ومع رجال الاصلاح العربي تقرر عقد المؤتمر في باريس لأن ذلك[7] سيلفت نظر الرأي العام إلى المطالب العربية. وكانت النية تتجه في البداية إلى أن يعالج المؤتمر القضايا المتعلقة بسورية وحدها، وأن يسمى «المؤتمر السوري» ولكن الطالب العراقي توفيق السويدي (رئيس الوزراء العراقي في ما بعد) أقنع زملاءه بتسميته «المؤتمر العربي».

ودعيت لحضور المؤتمر شخصيات عربية من سورية ولبنان ومصر، فاشترك فيه ممثلون عن حزب اللامركزية في مصر (عبد الحميد الزهراوي وإسكندر عمون) وعن «الجمعية الإصلاحية البيروتية» (برئاسة سليم علي سلام)، وإثنان من أسرة حيدر المعروفة في بعلبك، وعراقيان هما توفيق السويدي وسليمان عنبر، وممثلون عن المهاجرين العرب في الولايات المتحدة والمكسيك، وعن جالية باريس العربية، وممثل عن جالية الآستانة العربية (عبد الكريم الخليل). وانتخب لرئاسة المؤتمر الشيخ عبد الحميد الزهراوي، كما انتخب المحامي اسكندر عمون، من زعماء موارنة لبنان، نائباً للرئيس.

وافتتح المؤتمر في القاعة الكبرى للجمعية الجغرافية بشارع سان جيرمان رقم ١٨٤ في منتصف الساعة الثالثة بعد الظهر يوم الأربعاء ١٨ حزيران (يونيو) ١٩١٣، وألقى

كلمة الافتتاح «ندرة مطران» وعقد المؤتمر أربع جلسات (من ١٨ حزيران الى ٢٣ منه) ألقيت خلالها خطب ودارت مناقشات حول الموضوعات الثلاثة التالية :

(١) الحياة الوطنية ومناهضة الاحتلال (٢) حقوق العرب في المملكة العثمانية (٣) المهاجرون من سورية وإلى سورية .

واتخذ المؤتمر قرارات مهمة منها مطالبة الحكومة العثمانية بضمان تمتع العرب بحقوقهم السياسية والاشتراك في الإدارة المركزية للمملكة اشتراكاً فعلياً ، وبأن تكون في كل ولاية عربية إدارة لامركزية ، وأن تعتبر اللغة العربية لغة رسمية في الولايات العربية ، وأن تكون الخدمة العسكرية محلية في تلك الولايات إلا في الحالات الاستثنائية[8] .

وقد أحدث «المؤتمر العربي الأول» ضجة قوية في داخل الدولة العثمانية وخارجها وأثر في حكومة الاتحاديين تأثيراً غير يسير ، وجعلها تسعى إلى رجاله وتعرض الوفاق بين العرب والترك على أساس الاستجابة للمطالب العربية أو بعضها . ولكنها كانت مناورة مرحلية حاول بها الاتحاديون مسايرة الضجة ، وما لبثوا أن[9] اتخذوا المؤتمر حجة على زعمائه فلاحقوهم وأعدموا من بأيديهم ومنهم (عبد الحميد الزهراوي وعبد الغني العريسي ومحمد المحمصاني) . ومع كل ذلك فقد كان للمؤتمر العربي أثره التاريخي المهم ، وهو[10] الذي أخرج المسألة العربية من الصعيد المحلي إلى الصعيد الدولي .

[17]

NOTES

1. I suggest that 'On this day 79 years ago' be used as a title, and only 'On 18 June 1913' be retained in the actual body of the text.

2. The addition of 'to be held outside . . .' is necessary.

3. The adverbial 'prior to the First World War' may best be fronted.

4. Resist the temping 'including' and start a new sentence: 'This group included'.

5. The reference to 'the Arab youths' must be made explicit in English: 'in which the Arab youths would declare the Arab demands . . . .'.

6. This is a tricky element which may best be rendered: 'other Arabs both from among the young and the leading figures'.

7. The reference must also be retrieved here and modality must be adjusted: 'as this venue would draw the attention of public opinion . . .'.

8. The 'exception' may best be fronted: 'and that, except in a state of

emergency, conscription in a *vilayet* be restricted to members of that *vilayet* only'.

9. This is particularly difficult to render and a more idiomatic, though rather wordy, way of going about this may be something like: 'No sooner had this come to pass than the Unionists went back to the old ways and used the conference as a pretext to clamp down on the men who had taken part in organizing it, executing some of those who were caught.'

10. The emphasis relayed by the use of the 'pronoun of separation' (هو) may be preserved thus: 'and was in itself the event which took the Arab cause from its parochial setting to the wider international arena . . .'.

GLOSSARY

had a considerable impact on	أحدث صدى كبيراً في
on the Arab movement	في مجال الحركة العربية
just before	قبيل
convene	يعقد (مؤتمراً)
a group of young Arabs	نفر من الشباب العربي
the 'Young Arab Society'	جمعية «العربية الفتاة»
who were particularly aware of	ممن يتتبعون
the course of events	سير الأحداث
the Unionists	الاتحاديون
who had seized power	الذين استولوا على الحكم
the Ottoman empire	الدولة العثمانية
turn against	يتنكر لـ . . .
reformist ideas	الأفكار الاصلاحية
the Coalition Party	حزب الائتلاف
give rise	انبثق
tell the whole world	يصارح العالم كله
decentralism	اللامركزية
the cornerstone of Arab existence	قوام حياة العرب
in fact they are the majority	بل هم الأكثرية المطلقة
the original proponents of the idea	أصحاب الفكرة الأصليون
five young Arabs	خمسة شبان عرب
make contact	اتصل بـ . . .
and their proposal was greeted warmly	فقوبلت فكرتهم بالترحيب

after much correspondence	بعد مراسلات متعددة
leaders of Arab reform	رجال الإصلاح العرب
issues relating to	القضايا المتعلقة
later to become prime minister	رئيس الوزراء فيما بعد
persuaded his colleagues	أقنع زملاءه
leading figures	شخصيات
the Decentralist Party	حزب اللامركزية
the Beirut Reform Society	الجمعية الإصلاحية البيروتية
Arab emigrés	المهاجرين العرب
Istanbul	الآستانة
the Great Hall of the Geographical Society	القاعة الكبرى للجمعية الجغرافية
at 184 Boulevard St Germain	بشارع سان جيرمان رقم ١٨٤
at precisely 3.30 in the afternoon of . . .	في منتصف الساعة الثالثة بعد ظهر يوم . . .
the opening speech	كلمة الافتتاح
had four sessions	عقد المؤتمر (أربع) جلسات
speeches were made	ألقيت (خلالها) الخطب
discussions took place on	ودارت مناقشات
life in the homeland	الحياة الوطنية
resisting occupation	مناهضة الاحتلال
immigrants from and into Syria	المهاجرون من سورية والى سورية
safeguard Arab political rights	ضمان تمتع العرب بحقوقهم السياسية
their effective participation	الاشتراك في . . . اشتراكاً فعلياً
vilayet	ولاية
created a tremendous stir	أحدث ضجة قوية
had a significant effect on	أثر في . . . تأثيراً غير يسير
seek to make contact with the organizers	يسعى الى رجال (المؤتمر)
reconciliation between	الوفاق بين . . .
based on responding to	على أساس الاستجابة لـ . . .
all or some of	(المطالب العربية) أو لبعضها
only a subterfuge	كانت مناورة مرحلية
absorb the clamour	يساير الضجة
had an important historic impact	كان له أثره التاريخي المهم

III. Bearing in mind the distinctive features identified so far of both the expository Synopsis and the Summary, translate Texts 5A (i) (Synopsis) and 5A (ii) (Summary) (reproduced here for easier reference) into English.

TEXT 5A (i)

UNTANGLING THE WEB: NUTRITION, HEALTH AND EDUCATIONAL ACHIEVEMENT

Over the last several years, five monographs have appeared that, if taken together, shed much light[1] on the web spun[2] by three closely linked variables – nutritional status, health status and educational achievement. Collectively, the monographs also offer[3] a host of approaches for altering the often negative outcomes that stem from the pattern of relationships among these three variables. In other words, the monographs help us to untangle a web that, for many vulnerable children, has indeed been a trap.

UNICEF's 1985 report, *The State of the World's Children,* describes how a minimum safety net can be provided to protect the growing minds and bodies of the world's most vulnerable children. Through an exploration of case studies,[4] emphasis is given to simple, low-cost techniques that can have a profound influence on the development of every child's physical, social and intellectual potential. (. . .)

Thus far, the foregoing has been[5] a brief synopsis of the major themes touched on in the five monographs. (. . .)

NOTES

1. To preserve the expository tone, this pseudo-conditional may be 'verbalized' as follows: في السنوات الأخيرة، ظهرت خمس دراسات تعلمنا، مجتمعة، الكثير بشأن . . .

2. The title *Untangling the Web* may be rendered by the catchy, dramatic phrase: الخروج من الحلقة المفرغة.

   However, in keeping with expository academic writing conventions, *the web spun* in the body of the text must be rendered more neutrally by something like: بشأن العلاقات المتشابكة التي تربط ما بين ثلاثة متغيرات وثيقة الترابط.

   The other occurrence later on in the paragraph of more or less the same

phrase – *help us to untangle a web* – may also be fairly neutrally rendered
simply as: . . . تسهم في إزالة تشابك الخطوط في وضع هو.

3. To preserve and maintain the expository tone, this initial adverbial may
    be embedded, and a Verbal sentence structure used: وتقترح هذه الدراسات
    أيضاً، بالإجمال، طرائق عدة . . .

4. Once again, the initial adverbial elements must be embedded to
    maintain the flow of Verbal sentences: ويلفت التقرير الانتباه، استناداً الى
    دراسات لحالات مفردة، إلى تقنيات . . .

5. Resist a likely Nominal here and opt for a Verbal: كانت هذه إذن باختصار
    المباحث الرئيسية التي تم . . .

GLOSSARY

Over the last several years	في السنوات الأخيرة
monographs	دراسات
closely linked variables	متغيرات وثيقة الترابط
nutritional status	الحالة التغذوية
health status	الحالة الصحية
educational achievement	النتائج المدرسية
a host of approaches	طرائق عدة
the often negative outcomes	السلبية في كثير من الأحيان
stem from	التي تنتج عن
the pattern of relationships	التفاعل ما بين هذه المتغيرات
In other words	أي
vulnerable children	الأولاد الأقل حظاً
has indeed been a trap	هو بالنسبة لـ . . . فخ حقيقي
a minimum safety net	شبكة أمان لا غنى عنها إطلاقاً
the growing minds and bodies	النمو البدني والفكري
simple, low-cost techniques	تقنيات بسيطة وقليلة التكلفة
have a profound influence	بإمكانها الإسهام إلى حد بعيد في تحقيق
the development of X's potential	تحقيق الطاقة الكافية عند س
physical and intellectual potential	الطاقة البدنية والفكرية الكافية
major themes	المباحث الرئيسية
touched on	التي تم التطرق إليها

TEXT 5A (ii)

The five approaches sketched out in the following paragraphs illustrate the diversity of strategies that can be employed to improve the school achievement of children at risk due to poor health and nutritional status. The approaches are[1] not mutually exclusive and, indeed, most effective planners would probably use several of the strategies in combination. (. . .)

The UNICEF report is particularly concerned with the use of mass communication to disseminate four relatively simple and inexpensive methods that enable parents to cut the rate of child mortality in half: growth monitoring, oral rehydration for diarrhoea, breast feeding and immunization against six specific diseases (measles, diphtheria, whooping cough, tetanus, polio and tuberculosis). All four methods save lives by protecting growth. They have a direct impact on school achievement by reducing the prevalence of physical and mental handicap. They also[2] have a unique potential for widespread dissemination through campaigns because of several characteristics. They can be readily distilled.[3] They are based on simple, practical information. They are inexpensive and universal in their relevance. They do not depend on profound changes in values, yet they can lead to dramatic changes.

NOTES

1. In rendering this sentence, the previous sentence and the sentence which follows, the Verbal sentence structure must be adhered to: تمثل الطرائق الخمس التي يرد وصفها في الفقرات التالية . . . ولا تستبعد هذه الطرائق بعضها البعض الآخر.

    Only for discourse-organizational purposes, however, the sentence which follows is nominalized: بل إنها ربما أعطت وفي غالبية البرامج الأكثر فاعلية نتائج أفضل عند تآزرها.

2. As the last item in the list, and in an attempt to preserve 'also', this sentence may be presented thus: ومن جهة أخرى يتوافق بعض خصائص هذه الطرائق مع طبيعة الحملات الواسعة.

3. What may be called pseudo-substantiation starts here. This is a discourse-organizational device to signal the 'subset' status of the elements which follow: . . . إذ تتميز بسهولة التعميم وتستند إلى معلومات بسيطة . . . ولا تكلف إلا القليل وتتسم بالقابلية على التطبيق في كل مكان.

GLOSSARY

sketched out in the following . . . illustrate	تمثل . . . التي يرد وصفها
the diversity of strategies	مختلف الاستراتيجيات
at risk due to	الأكثر عرضة بفعل
in combination	عند تآزرها
is particularly concerned with	وتركز اليونيسف في تقريرها
mass communication	وسائل الإعلام
disseminate	التعريف بـ . . .
enable parents	بوسعها السماح للآباء والأمهات
cut in half	يخفض الى النصف
the rate of child mortality	معدل وفيات الأطفال
growth monitoring	مراقبة النمو
oral rehydration for diarrhoea	إعادة التمييه عن طريق الفم عند حصول إسهال
breast feeding	الرضاعة الطبيعية
immunization against	التلقيح ضد
measles	الحصبة
diphtheria	الخناق الغشائي
whooping cough	الشهاق/ السعال الديكي
tetanus	الكزاز
polio	الشلل
tuberculosis	السل
the prevalence of	كثرة حالات
physical and mental handicap	الإعاقة البدنية والتخلف العقلي
universal in their relevance	وتتسم بقابلية التطبيق في كل مكان
They do not depend on	غير مرهونة بـ
profound changes in values	اللجوء إلى تغيير جذري في طرق التفكير
yet they can lead	وقادرة ومع ذلك على
dramatic changes	إحداث تغييرات ملفتة

UNIT FIVE: Additional Texts

I. Summaries occur in a variety of documents. For example, Text 5C illustrates the kind of summarizing normally found in conclusions to books and articles. Such summaries are bound to be selective as they reflect the summarizer's view of what is to be retained or left out, and on what to focus and how. Bearing in mind the distinctive features of summarizing studied so far, translate the text into English.

TEXT 5C

الخلاصة

استهدفت هذه الدراسة التعرف على العلاقة بين[1] بعض المتغيرات المتعلقة بالوالدين كالجنس والعمر والمستوى التعليمي وعدد الأبناء وبين اتجاهات التسلط والحماية الزائدة والإهمال والتدليل والقسوة والألم النفسي والتذبذب والتفرقة والسواء كما يكشف عنها مقياس الاتجاهات الوالدية المستخدم في البحث.

وشملت عينة البحث ٥٠٠ من الكويتيين نصفهم من الآباء ونصفهم من الأمهات وتتراوح أعمارهم بين ١٨ و٦٤ سنة. وقد تم اختيار العينة بطريقة الحصص بحيث[2] تغطي معظم مناطق الكويت وتوفر أعداداً ملائمة من المتغيرات الديموغرافية موضوع البحث.

وقد اعتمد التحليل الإحصائي للبيانات على تحليل التباين الثلاثي لمعرفة الفروق بين الفئات المختلفة لكل متغير من المتغيرات المستقلة وللكشف عن أي تأثير للتفاعل فيما بينها، كما استخدم اختبار «ت» لبيان موقع هذه الفروق بدقة ـ إن وجدت ـ[3] وتحديد اتجاهها.

ويمكن إيجاز أهم نتائج البحث فيما يلي:

أولاً: فيما يتعلق بالصورة العامة للاتجاهات الوالدية، لوحظ أن الوالدين من أفراد العينة لا يميلون عموماً في اتجاهاتهم في تنشئة الأبناء إلى القسوة أو الإهمال أو التدليل حيث كانت درجاتهم على هذه المقاييس منخفضة نسبياً بالمقارنة ببقية الاتجاهات الأخرى ويعتبر هذا المؤشر إيجابياً.

[19]

NOTES

1. As we will have two sets of concepts, the use of 'on the one hand' to introduce the first set, and 'on the other hand' to introduce the second, would be a helpful organizational device.

2. An important linker which functionally means 'so as to ensure that'.

3. The position of the parenthesis is variable and language-specific. In

English, the parenthesis in question will be disposed of as follows: 'precisely to locate where differences, if any, lie'.

GLOSSARY

the aim of this study is to identify	استهدفت هذه الدراسة التعرف على
variables concerning	المتغيرات المتعلقة بـ
level of education	المستوى التعليمي
domination	التسلط
over-protectiveness	الحماية الزائدة
negligence	الإهمال
cosseting	التدليل
cruelty	القسوة
psychological maltreatment	الألم النفسي
unpredictability	التذبذب
discrimination	التفرقة
equality	السواء
The Parental Trends Measure	مقياس الاتجاهات الوالدية
population sample consisted of	شملت عينة البحث
aged between – and –	تتراوح أعمالهم بين – و –
the quota method	طريقة الحصص
relevant demographic variables	متغيرات ديموغرافية موضوع البحث
statistical analysis of the data	التحليل الاحصائي للبيانات
three-way analysis of variance	تحليل التباين الثلاثي
the various categories	الفئات المختلفة
independent variables	المتغيرات المستقلة
interaction	التفاعل
T-test	اختيار «ت»
precisely to locate the differences	لبيان موقع الفروق بدقة
the general picture of parental trends	الصورة العامة للاتجاهات الوالدية
it is noted	لوحظ
generally tend towards	يميلون عموماً
raising children	تنشئة الأبناء
relatively low	منخفضة نسبياً

II. Text 5D is another example which illustrates the kind of summarizing often encountered in the concluding sections of articles, books or Background Notes as is the case in the present sample. Translate into Arabic.

TEXT 5D

OBSERVATIONS

The preceding paragraphs have examined some of the difficulties which have been encountered[1] in adapting the tariff-based GATT system, which was left[2] as the only contractual framework for multilateral trade relations after the failure of the Havana Charter to come into force, due to the increasing complexity and dynamism of international trade. This paper has attempted to highlight some of the key characteristics and developments which illustrate certain weaknesses or contradictions that have given rise to a generally perceived impasse in international trade relations and which, if not corrected, could well have[3] serious consequences for the future growth of world trade. The analysis has been illustrative, not[4] exhaustive, and has been intended to substantiate and elaborate upon ideas expressed at earlier sessions of the Trade and Development Board.

[20]

NOTES

1. Strictly speaking, this is an 'agentless تم passive'. However, the 'تم structure' does not seem to work with 'negative' concepts such as 'encountering difficulties'. The actual passive, which is permissible in cases like this but *only* if rhetorically motivated, cannot be entertained either, so a way out of this seems to be 'a passivized active' – a set of verbs which are active in form but passive in meaning: بعض الصعوبات الناجمة عن محاولة تكييف.

2. The same 'negative' agentless passive as that dealt with in note 1 above: الذي بقي الإطار التعاقدي الوحيد.

3. There are two basic problems here: one is the position of the parenthesis, which has to wait until the end of the sentence in Arabic. The second problem is that of the peculiar modal meaning of 'could', highlighted by

75

'well', producing the cliché-like modality of 'minimal tentativeness'. Note, finally, the fact that مأزق is indefinite, so the relative pronoun 'which' cannot be retained: كمأزق . . . من شأنه أن تكون له نتائج . . . ما لم يتم تصحيحه.

4. In keeping with the conventions of detached exposition, resist كان إلا أنه لم يكن شاملاً توضيحياً must. This is not an argument and the contrast be subdued. Resist also a قصر in handling *intended to substantiate*, that is avoid ولم يكن يستهدف سوى which is very tempting here. However, we have to keep within total detachment, even without a كما, by simply: وكان يرمي إلى إثبات صحة الأفكار التي تم طرحها.

GLOSSARY

X have examined	لقد بحثت س في
the tariff-based GATT system	نظام آلغات القائم على التعريفات
multilateral trade relations	العلاقات التجارية متعددة الأطراف
the failure of X to come into force	بعد الإخفاق في وضع س موضع التنفيذ
due to	وذلك نتيجة
the increasing complexity and dynamism of X	تزايد تعقيد س وحركتها
This paper has attempted	وقد حاول هذا البحث
highlight some of the key characteristics	إلقاء الضوء على بعض الخصائص الرئيسية
certain weaknesses or characteristics	نقاط ضعف وتناقضات معينة
that have given rise to	كانت السبب في
a generally perceived impasse	ما يمكن وصفه بشكل عام كمأزق
substantiate	التوسع في
Trade and Development Board	مجلس التجارة والتنمية

UNIT SIX: The Abstract

OVERVIEW

Along similar lines to the distinction between legal writing and exposition with which we have been dealing so far and which marks a shift from ultra-formality to a slightly lower degree of formality, and along similar lines to a further distinction we have established between the almost frozen style of the Synopsis and the more casual Summary, two variants of a particular text form may be identified within what is essentially an expository text-type. This distinction is, on the one hand, between the more 'serious' Abstract and the more 'relaxed' variety in both English and Arabic and, on the other hand, between English abstracts and Arabic abstracts in general, with the latter tending to be slightly less formal.

Although proper, text-linguistic descriptions of Arabic abstracts are very few and far between, we can nevertheless suggest how abstracting could ideally be envisaged in Arabic. Our proposals would derive their validity from, on the one hand, available descriptions of abstracting in general and, on the other, from our knowledge of text in context. These pointers, together with common sense and a disciplined form of intuition about texts, would seem to point us in the direction of the need in abstracting to maintain the highest standards of objectivity and succinctness.

In translating from English, there are always sufficient clues to guide us towards this aim of preserving objectivity. In translating from Arabic, however, the problem seems to be more acute: the translator must make sure that evaluativeness, loose structure and emotive diction, which are features likely to be predominant in the Arabic text, are neutralized and kept within limits acceptable to the English target reader.

I.   Consider the following text as an example of the fairly formal Abstract.

TEXT 6A

ملخص

تتناول هذه الدراسة خلفية تاريخية عن «ملكة سبأ» التي أشار اليها بعض الدارسين إشارات عابرة في كتاباتهم عن تاريخ اليمن القديم بل اعتبرها بعض المؤرخين الأجانب

أسطورة شرقية . ولذا رأيت أن أستعين بأهم المصادر التي تناولت موضوع هذه الملكة
وفي مقدمتها الكتب المقدسة : التوراة والانجيل والقرآن الكريم، ثم المصادر العربية
ورأي بعض الرواة والمفسرين، ولاستكمال الموضوع أضفت ما جاء في الأساطير
الحبشية التي نسبت هذه الملكة الى الحبشة، معلقاً على النقاط التي تستدعي المناقشة في
كل فصل من فصول الدراسة والتي يظهر منها أن هذه «الملكة» عاشت في حوالي
منتصف القرن العاشر قبل الميلاد وهي الفترة الموازية لحكم سليمان في فلسطين، خاصة
وأنها قامت بزيارته وهي الزيارة التي أشارت اليها الكتب المقدسة واختتمها القرآن
الكريم مؤكداً أحداثها .

وتناولت الدراسة بعد ذلك دور دولة سبأ المؤثر في تاريخ اليمن القديم ومناقشة
الآراء المختلفة عن الزمن الذي استقر فيه السبئيون في جنوب الجزيرة العربية .

وتناولت الدراسة أيضاً اسم الملكة «بلقيس» واحتمالات اشتقاقه مع الإشارة إلى أن
هذا الاسم أو غيره لم يظهر حتى الآن على أية آثار يمنية قديمة، وهذا ينطبق أيضاً على
اللقب «ملكة» الذي اقترح أن نستبدله بلقب «حاكمة» إلى أن يتضح غير ذلك من الآثار
التي ما زالت مطمورة تحت الرمال وتنتظر الكشف والدراسة العلمية التي ستظل بلا
شك الكثير من النقاط التي ما زالت غامضة في تاريخ اليمن القديم خاصة وفي تاريخ
الجزيرة العربية عامة .

[21]

II. Bearing in mind the distinctive features of the fairly formal expository abstracts in Arabic, translate Text 6B into Arabic.

TEXT 6B

Introductory Note

Volume I of the Official Records contains[1] the Final Act, the resolutions adopted by the Diplomatic Conference, and the draft Additional Protocols prepared by the International Committee of the Red Cross. Volume II contains the rules of procedure,[2] the list of participants, the reports of the Drafting Committee and the reports of the Credentials Committee for the four sessions of the Conference. Volumes III and IV contain the table of amendments. Volume V to VII contain the summary records of the plenary meetings of the Conference. Volumes VIII to X contain the summary records of Committee I. Volumes XI to XIII contain the summary records and reports of Committee II. Volumes XIV and XV contain the summary records and reports of the ad hoc Committee on Conventional Weapons. Volume XVII contains the table of contents of the sixteen volumes.

The Official Records of the Conference are published in all of the official and working languages of the Conference. In the Russian edition, as Russian was an official and working language of the Conference only from the beginning of the second session, the documents of which no official translation was made in Russian are reproduced in English. The Arabic edition of the Official Records[3] contains only the documents originally issued in Arabic and those translated officially into Arabic after Arabic became an official and working language at the end of the third session. The Final Act only has been translated into Chinese.

[22]

NOTES

1. In this text, not only will the Verbal sentence structure dominate: يتضمن
    المجلد الأول من السجلات الرسمية . . . but repetition and not variation will
    also be maintained throughout: ويتضمن المجلد الثاني. Resist a كما along the
    line and use the additive 'و' only: . . . ويتضمن.

2. As usual with 'listing' in Arabic, and unless ambiguity is likely to occur, the various items linked by the use of commas in English must be connected by the Arabic additive 'و'.

3. This adverbial may be fronted and إما used, but neither the fronting nor إما are in any way 'functional' in this highly non-evaluative context. The non-functionality extends to the use of 'restriction' (قصر) in the following elements (e.g. *only from* . . .).

GLOSSARY

the Final Act	الوثيقة الختامية
the draft Additional Protocols	مشاريع الملحق (البروتوكول) الإضافية
the rules of procedure	النظام الداخلي
Drafting Committee	لجنة الصياغة
Credentials Committee	لجنة تدقيق أوراق الاعتماد
table of amendments	جدول التعديلات
the summary records	المحاضر التحليلية

the plenary meetings	الجلسات العامة
the ad hoc Committee	اللجنة الخاصة
on Conventional Weapons	بشأن الأسلحة التقليدية
table of contents	فهرس المحتويات
are published in all of . . .	طبعت بجميع (اللغات)
the official and working languages	اللغات الرسمية ولغات العمل
as Russian was . . . only from	ولما لم تصبح اللغة الروسية . . . إلا في . . .
reproduced in English	وردت باللغة الانجليزية
originally issued in Arabic	صدرت في الأصل باللغة العربية

III. Bearing in mind the distinctive features identified so far of the Abstract in both English and Arabic, translate text 6A (reproduced here for easier reference) into English.

TEXT 6A

ملخص

تتناول هذه الدراسة خلفية تاريخية عن «ملكة سبأ» التي أشار اليها بعض الدارسين إشارات عابرة في كتاباتهم عن تاريخ اليمن القديم بل اعتبرها بعض المؤرخين الأجانب أسطورة شرقية[1]. ولذا رأيت أن أستعين بأهم المصادر التي تناولت موضوع هذه الملكة وفي مقدمتها الكتب المقدسة: التوراة والانجيل والقرآن الكريم، ثم المصادر العربية ورأي بعض الرواة والمفسرين، ولاستكمال الموضوع أضفت ما جاء في الأساطير الحبشية التي نسبت هذه الملكة الى الحبشة، معلقاً على النقاط التي تستدعي المناقشة في كل فصل من فصول الدراسة والتي يظهر منها أن هذه «الملكة» عاشت في حوالي منتصف القرن العاشر قبل الميلاد وهي الفترة الموازية لحكم سليمان في فلسطين، خاصة وأنها قامت بزيارته وهي الزيارة التي أشارت اليها الكتب المقدسة واختتمها القرآن الكريم مؤكداً أحداثها.

وتناولت الدراسة بعد ذلك دور دولة سبأ المؤثر في تاريخ اليمن القديم ومناقشة الآراء المختلفة عن الزمن الذي استقر فيه السبئيون في جنوب الجزيرة العربية.

وتناولت الدراسة أيضاً اسم الملكة «بلقيس» واحتمالات اشتقاقه مع الإشارة إلى أن هذا الاسم أو غيره لم يظهر حتى الآن على أية آثار يمنية قديمة، وهذا ينطبق أيضاً على اللقب «ملكة» الذي اقترح أن نستبدله بلقب «حاكمة» إلى أن يتضح غير ذلك من الآثار

التي ما زالت مطمورة تحت الرمال وتنتظر الكشف والدراسة العلمية التي ستظئ بلا
شك الكثير من النقاط التي ما زالت غامضة في تاريخ اليمن القديم خاصة وفي تاريخ
الجزيرة العربية عامة .

NOTES

1. In translating this highly detached form of text into English, one should
    endeavour to 'neutralize' the unnecessarily high degree of evaluativeness
    encountered in the Arabic. I have preserved بل ('even'), and لذا ('for this
    reason'), but I am not entirely sure that these could legitimately be
    retained. I have a feeling that the English text would be the better for it
    if these were left out. Certainly رأيت must go, leaving us with: 'I have
    consulted'.

GLOSSARY

the historical backgound of	خلفية تاريخية عن
the queen of Sheba	ملكة سبأ
to whom X have made passing references	التي أشار اليها س اشارة عابرة
researchers . . . in their works on	الدارسين . . . في كتاباتهم عن
the ancient history of	تاريخ ــ القديم
have even considered her	بل اعتبرها
as eastern legend	أسطورة شرقية
for this reason	ولذا
deal with this queen	التي تناولت موضوع هذه الملكة
the most important of which	وفي مقدمتها
the Torah, the New Testament and the Qur'an	الكتب المقدسة : التوراة والانجيل والقرآن
and referred to the opinion of some	ورأي بعض
narrators and commentators	الرواة والمفسرين
in order to be more comprehensive	ولاستكمال الموضوع
what was said in	ما جاء في
the Ethiopian legends	الأساطير الحبشية
which trace X back to	التي نسبت س إلى
which point to the fact that	التي يظهر منها
the mid-tenth century BC approximately	في حوالي منتصف القرن العاشر ق.م
would coincide with	موازية

81

the rule of Solomon	لحكم سليمان
and would thus fit in with reports of	خاصة
the visit which X is said to have made	أنها قامت بزيارته
a story which the holy books cite	الزيارة التي أشارت إليها الكتب المقدسة
and which the Qur'an was finally to confirm	واختتمها القرآن الكريم مؤكداً أحداثها
the various views regarding	الآراء المختلفة عن
and its probable etymologies	واحتمالات اشتقاقه
ancient Yemeni relics	آثار يمنية قديمة
this is similarly true of	وهذا ينطبق أيضاً على
are still buried under the sands	ما زالت مطمورة تحت الرمال
awaiting discovery	تنتظر الاكتشاف

UNIT SIX: Additional Texts

I.   Texts 6A and 6B are examples of what one might label as the more 'serious Abstract'. However, and much more so in Arabic, abstracts are not always as stringently written. While still catering for the context of objective information, and retaining an expository structure format (scene set then detailed), abstracts can have a slightly looser texture than that which we have seen so far. Vocabulary items tend to be varied and not slavishly repeated and at times diction borders on the evaluative. In terms of translation strategy, we should always aim at a rendering which is as literal as possible and, in working from Arabic, excessively ornate language in non-fiction must be neutralized in the English version. With this in mind, translate the following text into English.

TEXT 6C

ملخص

تهدف هذه الدراسة بلوغ أهداف أكبر بكثير من حجمها الكمي المتمثل في عدد صفحاتها[1] فهي تهدف أساساً إلى إجراء تقييم عام وشامل[2] لمجمل الدراسات التي تمت حتى الآن في ميدان الحضارة الإسلامية وإظهار الطابع العفوي التلقائي الذي يمثل ـ حين يكتب[3] لهذه الدراسات درجة من درجات الإيجابية ـ مستوى خفيضاً من مستويات الوعي بقيمة هذه الحضارة ودورها في حياتنا الراهنة والمستقبلية. والدراسات التي تم إنجازها حتى الآن داخل ميدان الحضارة الإسلامية تنقسم الى قسمين أساسيين: دراسات

المستشرقين أصحاب «العقل المستفيد» ـ القسم الأول ـ من دراسة الحضارة الإسلامية
وهي دراسات أصيبت بعيب لا خلاص منه وهو كونها جزء من المشروع الثقافي الغربي
<الاستشراق> أداة الاستعمار الغربي ووسيلته الثقافية في التعامل مع الشرق. وانتهينا
الى تأكيد الطابع المغرض المزيف لهذه الدراسات من خلال تقسيمنا لتاريخ الاستشراق
الى مراحله الأساسية واستخلاص الخصائص المميزة لكل مرحلة مع الاستشهاد بنصوص
من أعمال المستشرقين أنفسهم.

والقسم الثاني من هذه الدراسات هو أعمال الباحثين المسلمين وتنقسم هذه
الدراسات بدورها الى قسمين: أبحاث المدرسة التقليدية الدينية <الأزهر مثلا> وهي
دراسات تنصب على الأبعاد الهامشية من الحضارة الإسلامية بالإضافة إلى كونها دراسات
عقيمة وغير مؤثرة. هذه هي أعمال «المدرسة الركامية» أو «العقل المستقيل» من دراسة
الحضارة الإسلامية. والقسم الأخير من هذا القسم الثاني هو دراسات الباحثين العرب
تلاميذ المستشرقين المباشرين أو أولئك الذين تأهلوا في الجامعات الغربية الحديثة. هؤلاء
هم أصحاب «العقل العربي المستجيب» في دراسة الحضارة الإسلامية والذي لاحظناه
على أبحاث هذا الفريق من الباحثين العرب هو الاستلاب شبه الكامل في المركزية
الأوروبية أو الحاضر الثقافي الغربي بشكل عام.

وانتهينا الى التأكيد على أن الدراسات في العلوم الحضارية الإسلامية ما زالت تمر ـ
سواء في أيدي المستشرقين أو الباحثين العرب ـ بما أطلقنا عليه اسم «مرحلة الممارسة
العفوية» وذلك لعدم ارتباط هذه الدراسات بهدف أو بمشروع عربي شامل يمتزج فيه
ماضي العقل العربي بحاضره من أجل الإعداد للمستقبل. هذه هي خلاصة الجانب
النقدي أو السلبي ـ بلغة فرنسيس بيكون ـ من هذا البحث.

[18]

NOTES

1. In this text, we have an even more serious problem of evaluativeness
   than in the previous text. Literal translation would not be a
   recommended procedure here: تهدف هذه الدراسة إلى بلوغ أهداف أكبر بكثير
   is simply: 'This study is intended من حجمها الكمي المتمثل في عدد صفحاتها
   to achieve a number of ambitious objectives.'

2. An interesting area in which evaluativeness in Arabic may be effectively
   neutralized is the proliferation of synonyms when such a device is not
   functional: الطابع is simply: 'a comprehensive assessment'; تقييم عام وشامل
   العفوي التلقائي is: 'ad hoc nature.'

3. Some pragmatic* glossing to bring out the irony in ‫حين يكتب‬ ‫لـ‬ may be necessary: 'in the rare cases where . . .'; ‫درجة من درجات الإيجابية‬: 'are at all constructive' and ‫يمثل مستوى خفيفاً من مستويات الوعي‬: 'can only reflect a low level of awareness'.

GLOSSARY

aims to embark on	‫تهدف إلى إجراء‬
contemporary and future existence	‫حياتنا الراهنة والمستقبلية‬
fall into two basic categories	‫تنقسم الى قسمين أساسيين‬
utilitarian-minded orientalists	‫المستشرقين أصحاب «العقل المستفيد»‬
western cultural programme	‫المشروع الثقافي الغربي‬
orientalism	‫الاستشراق‬
imperialistic tool	‫أداة الاستعمار‬
suffer from a fatal flaw	‫أصيبت بعيب لا خلاص منه‬
a deviously distortive nature	‫طابع مغرض مزيف‬
illustrated by citations drawn from	‫مع الاستشهاد بنصوص من أعمال‬
Muslim scholars	‫الباحثين المسلمين‬
focus on marginal issues	‫تنصب على الأبعاد الهامشية‬
the 'Collapsed School'	‫المدرسة الركامية‬
the resigned mind	‫العقل المستقيل‬
schooled directly at the hands of orientalists	‫تلاميذ المستشرقين المباشرين‬
the responsive mind	‫العقل المستجيب‬
we have taken X to task	‫الذي لاحظناه على أبحاث س‬
almost wholesale abandon to	‫الاستلاب شبه الكامل‬
Eurocentricity	‫المركزية الأوروبية‬
the present western cultural scene has to offer	‫الحاضر الثقافي الغربي‬
passing through the phase of ad hoc practice	‫تمر بمرحلة الممارسة العفوية‬
the absence of any link	‫لعدم ارتباط هذه الدراسة بـ‬
merges with	‫يمتزج‬
the past of Arab thought	‫ماضي العقل العربي‬
the critical or negative conclusion	‫خلاصة الجانب النقدي أو السلبي‬
after Francis Bacon	‫بلغة فرانسيس بيكون‬

TEXT 6D

Non-Government Resources for Education[†]

ABSTRACT

The challenge posed by resource gaps in education confronts all countries[1] and not just the less-developed ones. Every nation has unfinished agendas of expansion[2] of education and improvement of education quality which could be met with additional resources:[3] or else could propose many programmes in other sectors of socio-economic activity on which it could with advantage spend resources released by more effective management of education. From an analytical point of view, the options for closing the resource gap represent as valid a taxonomy of possibilities for the United States as for the least developed countries.

In this article, I shall successively[4] review briefly the options for closing the resource gap in education; then concentrate more specifically on private funding for education; and thirdly, examine in particular the potential of community financing. In doing so, I shall be drawing in particular on work undertaken and published by the World Bank in the financing of education. [13]

[†] *The ideas expressed in this article are those of the author and in no way reflect official positions of the Commonwealth Secretariat.*

NOTES

1. By way of setting the scene for the Abstract-proper, the writer wishes to set the tone of the debate that is to follow in the body of the article. This tone-setting function may be preserved by: (a) nominalizing the thesis (with 'resource gaps' made salient); and (b) providing a subsequent substantiation: إن نقص الموارد في المجال التربوي تحد يواجه جميع بلدان العالم دون استثناء ولا يقتصر على تلك البلدان الأقل نمواً فـ . . .

2. An effective way of substantiating the claim made is by turning the two sentences used for this purpose into 'rhetorical questions':

وهل من بلد لا يستطيع أن يستخدم بشكل مفيد . . .؟ فأية دولة ليس لديها مشروع غير مستكمل . . .؟

This will enhance the attention-attracting function of the Abstract in addition to what it is normally intended to achieve.

3. There is an implicit restriction (قصر) here: لا يمكن إدخاله حيز الواقع إلا باستخدام موارد إضافية.

4. The element 'successively' is a listing device. In Arabic this may be done by opting for a slightly more serial structure: سأبدأ أولاً بإلقاء نظرة سريعة . . . ثم أتوقف . . . وأتطرق أخيراً لـ . . .

GLOSSARY

unfinished agendas of expansion	مشاريع غير مستكملة
sectors of socio-economic activity	القطاعات الاجتماعية الاقتصادية
with advantage	بشكل مفيد
released by more effective . . .	يتيسر توفيرها عن طريق تحسين
From an analytical point of view	أما على صعيد التحليل
closing the resource gap	سد العجز في الموارد
taxonomy of possibilities	قائمة التدابير
for X . . . as for Y	بالنسبة إلى س . . . كما بالنسبة إلى ص
review briefly	إلقاء نظرة سريعة
then concentrate on	أتوقف عند
private funding	تمويل القطاع الخاص لـ . . .
examine in particular	أتطرق بصورة خاصة لـ . . .
the potential of	الإمكانات التي يتيحها
community financing	التمويل الصادر عن المجتمع المحلي
In doing so	وفي هذا السبيل
draw on	استند إلى
work undertaken and published	أجراها وقام بنشرها س
The ideas expressed	الآراء المعبر عنها
in no way reflect	لا تمثل بأي حال من الأحوال
official positions	المواقف الرسمية لـ . . .

UNIT SEVEN:

The Report (Person-oriented/Entity-oriented)

OVERVIEW

Within exposition, we have so far dealt with the Synopsis, the Summary and the Abstract. This unit introduces another expository text form – the Report. Reports may be classified initially into person-oriented and entity-oriented. Person-oriented reports focus on what a particular person has said or done. Entity-oriented reports, on the other hand, are more like definitions and present a descriptive account of an entity such as an institution, an agency, etc.

Like all expository forms covered so far, the Report writer responds to a context which essentially demands succinctness and impartiality in relaying a set of facts. This orientation determines the kind of structure that reporting texts ideally take: a scene set, then the various aspects of the scene detailed. Finally, the texture of the report reflects the relative absence of evaluativeness: diction is by and large unemotive (factual vocabulary which basically means what it says and neutral sentence structure in which word order is essentially basic). In Arabic, one predominant feature of exposition is once again much in evidence in reports. This is the use of the Verbal sentence structure and the maintenance of heavy parallelistic arrangement in sequencing the various sentences of the text.

It may be wise to voice a note of caution here. The above account of reporting necessarily takes the ideal situation, the unmarked* case, as it were. But for a variety of rhetorical effects (e.g. in propaganda or advertising) reporters depart from their primary function, which is to report, and cater for other functions such as persuading, selling, etc. In cases like these, a certain element of evaluativeness is allowed to creep in and texture is bound to respond to this contextual requirement. Vocabulary will be heavily charged, and sentence structure drastically manipulated. The Nominal sentence structure will have to be used in Arabic, as will be demonstrated in later units.

I.   Consider the following text samples and compare them with each other. Text 7A (i) illustrates the person-oriented report, while Text 7A (ii) is an entity-oriented report. Pay special attention to both the structure and the texture of the texts which, despite the difference in focus, are both characterized by features typical of exposition in general.

TEXT 7A (i)

تقرير عن المؤتمر التربوي الثامن عشر

تحت شعار «التربية في الوطن العربي ومقومات الإنسان الصالح» افتتح وزير التربية وزير التعليم العالي بالوكالة المؤتمر التربوي الثامن عشر الذي أقامته جمعية المعلمين الكويتية في الفترة من ٢٦ ـ ٣١ مارس/آذار.

واستهل الحفل بتلاوة آيات عطرة من الذكر الحكيم، ثم ألقى بعد ذلك وزير التربية كلمة رحب فيها بضيوف المؤتمر وشكر فيها جمعية المعلمين نهجها هذا في عقد المؤتمرات التربوية.

ونوه السيد الوزير إلى أهمية المؤتمر حيث أنه يتناول أهداف التربية ويردها إلى استشقاقها في شمول وتكامل وأشار الى أن مقومات الإنسان الصالح تتحد في خمسة منطلقات هي طبيعة المجتمع العربي المسلم ومواجهة تحديات العصر وجعل الإنسان محور العملية التربوية وأهمية دراسة الفكر التربوي المعاصر وحاجة المجتمع العربي إلى نهوض أبنائه به وتفاعلهم معه. وأضاف أن هذا المؤتمر يعتبر دعوة للتمسك بوحدة الأمة وفيه مواضيع متعددة تؤدي إلى توحيد الجهود والتعاون على سبيل الخير. وقال إن الأمم لا تنهض إلا إذا غرست قيمة العمل في نفوس أبنائها وربت الإنسان على الاعتماد على نفسه في كسب الرزق.

[25]

TEXT 7A (ii)

الأمة العربية

تشمل عبارة «الأمة العربية» مجموعة من الشعوب العربية الممتدة من الخليج العربي إلى المحيط الأطلسي وتربط بينها قومية مشتركة قائمة على أساس من الجوار ووحدة اللغة والتاريخ والأماني والأهداف والمصير المشترك.

وقد وردت العبارة المذكورة في دساتير بعض الدول العربية بعد استقلالها إذ نصت مختلف دساتير سوريا التي صدرت بعد عام ١٩٥٠ على أن «الشعب السوري جزء من

الأمة العربية»، وورد أيضاً في الدساتير المصرية منذ عام ١٩٥٦ على أن «الشعب المصري جزء من الأمة العربية». أي أن مصير أي دولة عربية مرتبط بمصير كامل الأمة العربية .

وعلى هذا الأساس أضافت بعض الدول العربية كلمة «عربية» إلى اسم الدولة ومنها المملكة العربية السعودية وجمهورية اليمن العربية .

وتضم الأمة العربية حالياً ١٨ دولة منتسبة جميعها الى جامعة الدول العربية وإلى منظمة الأمم المتحدة وتشكل نسبة تقدر بـ ١٣ بالمئة من عدد أعضائها .

[26]

II. Bearing in mind the characteristic features of person-oriented and entity-oriented reports in Arabic, translate Texts 7B (i) and 7B (ii) as examples of this type of reporting in English.

TEXT 7B (i)

Report on the General Debate

The United Nations Conference on Technical Co-operation among Developing Countries was held[1] at Buenos Aires from 30 August to 12 September 1978. The Conference was opened by the Secretary-General of the United Nations. Representatives of States – many of them of ministerial rank, observers for a number of intergovernmental bodies and representatives of specialized agencies, regional commissions and other UN bodies, programmes and offices attended by special invitation and took part in the work of the Conference.

Opening the general debate[2] at the afternoon meeting on 30 August 1978, the Secretary-General of the Conference said he was convinced that the Conference would lay the foundations for enhancing all forms of co-operation among developing countries and for transforming relationships for the benefit of the entire world community.[3] The success of the Conference would depend on the extent of the commitment of governments to the concept and promotion of technical co-operation among developing countries; evidence of their commitment was the fact that national reports had been received from more than 100 governments. Further evidence of the importance attached by governments to the Conference was the fact[4] that their delegations included outstanding personalities and experts in the subject. The Secretary-General of the special Conference expressed his appreciation of the special contributions made by the governments of Iraq, Kuwait and Qatar towards the costs of participation of specially financially disadvantaged countries.

[27]

NOTES

1. A steady flow of parallel Verbal sentences (active constructions) must be maintained throughout: . . . وشارك . . . وافتتح . . . انعقد.

2. Particularly when cataphoric, and unless considerations of length and the need for clarity intervene, English source text adverbials are embedded in this kind of exposition: قال أمين عام المؤتمر أثناء فتحه باب النقاش العام في جلسة بعد الظهر المنعقدة في ٣ أغسطس ١٩٧٨.

3. We may here revert back to conventions of reporting in Arabic: a verb of saying normally introduces each of the various segments of the statement reported. Here, for example, something like: وأضاف. The segment which follows may be introduced by something like: واستطرد, etc.

4. A rare example of redundancy in English: *the fact* is normally left out in Arabic as the following verbal noun states 'the fact' itself: واستطرد الأمين العام قائلاً إن الدليل على هذا الالتزام كان واضحاً عندما قام ما يزيد على ١٠٠ حكومة بإرسال تقارير تتعلق ببلدانها.

GLOSSARY

General Debate	النقاش العام
Conference on Technical Co-operation	مؤتمر . . . المعني بالتعاون التقني
of ministerial rank	برتبة وزير
X attended by special invitation	وتم توجيه دعوات خاصة إلى . . .
took part in the work of the Conference	وحضر هؤلاء وشاركوا في أعمال المؤتمر
observers for a number of bodies	مراقبين من مختلف الهيئات
intergovernmental bodies	الهيئات الحكومية الدولية
specialized agencies	الوكالات الخاصة
regional commissions	اللجان الإقليمية
UN bodies, programmes and offices	هيئات الأمم المتحدة وبرامجها ومكاتبها

he was convinced that	وعبر عن ثقته من أن . . .
lay the foundations for	سيضع أسس
enhancing all forms of co-operation	تعزيز كافة أشكال التعاون
transforming relationships	تطوير العلاقات
for the benefit of	لصالح
the entire world community	الأسرة الدولية برمتها
would depend on the extent of	يعتمد على مدى
the commitment of governments to	التزام الحكومات بـ
the concept and promotion of	فحوى مفهوم . . . والعمل على تعزيزه
evidence of their commitment was	وكان الدليل على هذا الالتزام واضحاً
national reports	تقارير عن بلادهم
Further evidence of	ويكمن الدليل الآخر على . . . في أن . . .
the importance attached by X to Y	الأهمية التي يوليها س لـ ص
included outstanding personalities	ضمت شخصيات رفيعة المستوى
experts in the subject	خبراء في الموضوع قيد البحث
expressed his appreciation	عبر عن تقديره العميق
the special contributions	المساهمات الخاصة
costs of participation of	تغطية تكلفتها لاشتراك
specially financially disadvantaged countries	البلدان التي تعاني بشكل خاص من عجز مالي

TEXT 7B (ii)

Scottish Development Agency

The Agency was set up in 1975 as[1] the government's principal instrument of industrial and economic development in Scotland. As well as its own wide-ranging powers to invest directly in new enterprise,[2] it provides factory space and industrial management advice. The Agency also acts as a central Scottish information bureau for international business and guides other organizations, particularly about industrial plant location and development. Head office:[3] 120 Bothwell Street, Glasgow.

[28]

NOTES

1. Here, 'as' is equivalent to the agentive 'by' in the passive, and the

structure may thus be rendered as active: أنشأت الحكومة وكالة التنمية
الاسكتلندية لكي تكون الجهة الرئيسية التي عن طريقها يتم الإشراف على . . .

2. This fronted cataphoric element may either be postponed or dealt with initially but with the cataphora 'decoded'. I recommend the second solution as the cataphora in this kind of text is merely discourse-organizational and not rhetorically functional: وبالإضافة إلى السلطات
الواسعة التي تتمتع بها وكالة التنمية في الاستثمار مباشرة بمشاريع جديدة . . .

   This can be continued with فإنها تقوم بـ; but in keeping with the overall expository tone, the Verbal structure is more appropriate: تقوم
الوكالة.

3. A PR element is present here and the address may be introduced in Arabic by something like: وللحصول على مزيد من المعلومات يمكن الاتصال
بالوكالة على عنوانها التالي: . . .

GLOSSARY

principal instrument of	الجهة الرئيسية
provides factory space	توفير الأراضي لإقامة المصانع
industrial management advice	المشورة في مجال الإدارة الصناعية
acts as a central Scottish	يعد بمثابة مركز اسكتلندي
information bureau	لتوفير المعلومات
for international business	لرجال الأعمال من مختلف أنحاء العالم
industrial plant locations	مواقع الوحدات الصناعية
plant development	تطوير المصانع

III. With the features of English person-oriented and entity-oriented reporting in mind, translate Texts 7A (i) and 7A (ii) (reproduced here for easier reference) into English.

TEXT 7A (i)

تقرير عن المؤتمر التربوي الثامن عشر

تحت شعار «التربية في الوطن العربي ومقومات الإنسان الصالح» افتتح وزير التربية وزير التعليم العالي بالوكالة المؤتمر التربوي الثامن عشر الذي أقامته جمعية المعلمين الكويتية في

الفترة من ٢٦ ـ ٣١ مارس/آذار .

واستهل الحفل بتلاوة آيات عطرة من الذكر الحكيم، ثم ألقى بعد ذلك وزير التربية كلمة رحب فيها بضيوف المؤتمر وشكر فيها جمعية المعلمين نهجها هذا في عقد المؤتمرات التربوية .

ونوه[1] السيد الوزير إلى أهمية المؤتمر حيث أنه يتناول أهداف التربية ويردها إلى استشقاقها في شمول وتكامل وأشار الى أن مقومات الإنسان الصالح تتحدد في خمسة منطلقات هي طبيعة المجتمع العربي المسلم ومواجهة تحديات العصر وجعل الإنسان محور العملية التربوية وأهمية دراسة الفكر التربوي المعاصر وحاجة المجتمع العربية إلى نهوض أبنائه به وتفاعلهم معه . وأضاف أن هذا المؤتمر يعتبر دعوة للتمسك بوحدة الأمة وفيه مواضيع متعددة تؤدي إلى توحيد الجهود والتعاون على سبيل الخير . وقال إن الأمم لا تنهض إلا إذا غرست قيمة العمل في نفوس أبنائها وربت الإنسان على الاعتماد على نفسه في كسب الرزق .

NOTES

1. As we have seen in the English parallel text, English reporting conventions dictate that the various elements of, say, a speech are presented as unsignalled independent chunks. That is, while the Arabic text introduces each element with a verb of saying, in English this does not seem necessary: a verb of saying (e.g. commonly 'said') is used with the first and last elements only. The intervening elements are simply listed. Therefore, forget about: وأشار، وأضاف.

GLOSSARY

on the theme	تحت شعار
constituents of upright citizenship	مقومات الإنسان الصالح
acting Minister, [name follows]	وزير . . . بالوكالة
Association of Teachers	جمعية المعلمين
The ceremony began with a recitation from the Holy Qur'an	واستهل الحفل بتلاوة عطرة من الذكر الحكيم
thanked X for its plans to hold	شكر فيها س نهجها هذا في عقد
stressed the significance of	نوّه الى أهمية
it comprehensively deals with	يتناول . . . في شمول وتكامل
and the way X have developed	ويردها الى استشقاقها
are definable in terms of five basic concepts	تتحدد في خمسة منطلقات

confronting the challenges of the modern age	مواجهة تحديات العصر
the focus of the educational process	محور العملية التربوية
contemporary educational thought	الفكر التربوي المعاصر
the need of society for its members to contribute	حاجة المجتمع الى نهوض أبنائه به
The conference is thus tantamount to a call	هذا المؤتمر يعتبر دعوة
adherence to the unity	التمسك بوحدة
for the common good	على سبيل الخير
rise up only when they	لا تنهض إلا إذا . . .
plant in the souls . . . the value of	غرست في نفوس . . . قيمة العمل
nurture man on the need for	ربت الإنسان على
self-reliance	الاعتماد على النفس
earning one's livelihood	كسب الرزق

TEXT 7A (ii)

الأمة العربية

تشمل عبارة «الأمة العربية» مجموعة من الشعوب العربية الممتدة من الخليج العربي إلى المحيط الأطلسي وتربط بينها قومية مشتركة قائمة على أساس من الجوار ووحدة اللغة والتاريخ والأماني والأهداف والمصير المشترك .

وقد وردت العبارة المذكورة في دساتير بعض الدول العربية بعد استقلالها إذ نصت مختلف دساتير سوريا التي صدرت بعد عام ١٩٥٠ على أن «الشعب السوري¹ جزء من الأمة العربية»، وورد أيضاً في الدساتير المصرية منذ عام ١٩٥٦ على أن «الشعب المصري جزء من الأمة العربية» . أي أن مصير أي دولة عربية مرتبط بمصير كامل الأمة العربية .

وعلى هذا الأساس أضافت بعض الدول العربية كلمة «عربية» إلى اسم الدولة ومنها المملكة العربية السعودية وجمهورية اليمن العربية .

وتضم الأمة العربية حالياً ١٨ دولة منتسبة جميعها الى جامعة الدول العربية وإلى منظمة الأمم المتحدة وتشكل نسبة تقدر بـ ١٣ بالمئة من عدد أعضائها .

NOTES

1. Legal formulation is required here: 'X shall be . . .'. To reflect the

universality of the principle, 'X is . . .' is adequate here.

GLOSSARY

The expression subsumes	تشمل عبارة
stretching from . . . and linked by	المتدة . . . وتربط بينها
a shared national identity	قومية مشتركة
based on neighbourliness	قائمة على أساس من الجوار
one language, one history, one set of aspirations	وحدة اللغة والتاريخ والأماني
a common destiny	المصير المشترك
occur	ورد
post-independence constitutions	دساتير بعض الدول بعد استقلالها
drawn up after	التي صدرت بعد . . .
state that (provide)	نصت
The people of Syria are a part	الشعب السوري جزء
X now includes	ويضم . . . حالياً
which are all members of the Arab League	منتسبة جميعها إلى جامعة الدول العربية
represent . . . of the organization's total membership	تشكل نسبة س من عدد أعضائها

UNIT SEVEN: Additional Texts

I. Bearing in mind the features of reports in both English and Arabic studied so far, translate the following texts into Arabic. Texts 7C (i) and 7C (ii) present person-orientation and entity-orientation separately, while Text 7D combines both modes.

TEXT 7C (i)

Statements made upon the adoption of the Substantial New Programme of Action

The representative of the United States said that his Government was pleased to join in the consensus on the Substantial New Programme of Action which provided a solid basis for action by all governments.[1] The programme was especially strong for its full recognition of the complex interrelationships in the development process. The complementarity among domestic and international measures was well reflected[2] and had been a hallmark of the discussions. This reflection of reality strengthened the international community's resolution to achieve accelerated growth for the least developed of its members in the decade ahead.

With respect to possible new mechanisms,[3] he noted that IMF had already considered and, as appropriate, would continue to review most of these proposals.

The United States continued to oppose a link between Special Drawing Rights and aid and remained concerned that any such link could damage efforts to make Special Drawing Rights the principal reserve asset in the international monetary system.

The United States considered that IMF was the appropriate and best qualified forum for dealing with financial difficulties caused by export earnings shortfalls. In fact, the IMF Compensatory Financing Facility had been a very useful mechanism for providing assistance of this type.
[20]

NOTES

1. This is the reverse of what was recommended in dealing with Text 7A (i) (into English). Here, Arabic conventions must be invoked and the various elements of the statement (listed unsignalled by a verb of saying in English) must now be properly signalled. Arabic would probably also opt for variation of these verbs of saying. However, given the genre of the Report and the detached discourse of summarizing, it may perhaps be helpful to suggest that repetition and not variation will be more appropriate here: ‏قال . . . وقال . . . وقال‎.

2. Two points need to be made here. One is that, while we endorse the Arabic convention of signalling the various elements of the statement, we have also recommended that this be constrained by repeating and not varying these verbs. As a further constraint, we suggest that these signals should not be overused. That is, not every single sentence should be considered an element of the statement and as such has to be signalled. For example, ‏وقال إن البرنامج الجديد يتصف‎ . . . in ‏قال‎ would be a sufficient signal for the following two sentences before another signal is required.

    The other point to be made relates to the implicitness of the agentive

passive construction here: 'X was well reflected' (by the programme) وقد
جاء مرآة صادقة لـ . . .

3. Resist أما + 'fronting' (أما فيما يتعلق بـ، فقد لاحظ) and instead, and in
keeping with expository style, opt for: ولاحظ المندوب فيما يتعلق بإمكانية
إنشاء آليات جديدة أن صندوق النقد الدولي . . .

GLOSSARY

was pleased to join in the consensus on	مغتبطة للانضمام الى توافق الآراء على
the Substantial New Programme	برنامج العمل الجديد المكثف
provided a solid basis	يوفر قاعدة متينة
X was especially strong for its	س يتصف بمزية خاصة لأن فيه
full recognition of	ادراكاً كاملاً لـ
complex interrelationships	تعقيد العلاقات
development process	عملية التنمية
The complementarity among . . . measures	التكامل بين التدابير
X had been a hallmark of	كان من السمات البارزة لـ
reflection of reality	التعبير عن الواقع
strengthened the international community's resolution	شد من عزم المجتمع الدولي
accelerated growth	نمواً سريعاً
achieve X for Y	العزم أن يحقق س ص
in the decade ahead	في العقد المقبل
X had already considered Y	قد نظر بالفعل في هذا الأمر
as appropriate	، وكما يرى مناسباً،
would continue to review most of	وسوف يواصل ، ـ، استعراض غالبية
continued to oppose a link	لا تزال تعارض الربط
Special Drawing Rights and aid	حقوق السحب الخاصة والمعونة
and remained concerned that	وتظل معربة عن قلقها
damage	يلحق الضرر
efforts to make	الجهود الرامية
the principal reserve asset	الأصول الاحتياطية الرئيسية
the appropriate and best qualified forum	المحفل الملائم والمؤهل أكثر من غيره
export earnings shortfalls	العجز في عائدات الصادرات

Compensatory Financing Facility　　　　　تسهيلات التمويل التعويضي

a useful mechanism　　　　　　　　　　　　آلية مفيدة

TEXT 7C (ii)

International Monetary Fund

The Articles of Agreement of the International Monetary Fund (IMF) were drawn up,[1] along with those of IBRO, at the 1944 Bretton Woods conference, and IMF came into being on 27 December 1945, when representatives of countries whose quotas amounted to 80 per cent of the Fund's resources had deposited their ratifications of the agreement. The Articles have been twice amended, in 1969 and in 1978.

The Fund seeks to promote international monetary co-operation and to facilitate the expansion of trade, and thus to contribute to increased employment and improved economic conditions in all member countries.

To achieve its purposes,[2] IMF makes financing available to members in balance-of-payment difficulties and provides them with technical assistance to improve their economic management. The fund maintains a pool of financial resources that it makes available to member countries to enable them to carry out economic reform programmes to remedy their payment deficits.

The Fund's Special Drawing Rights (SDR's) are[3] an international currency, created by IMF in 1969. They can be used by its members for making international payments – for example, to obtain currency in a spot transaction, for the settlement of a financial obligation, as a loan or as security for a loan.

[29]

NOTES

1. The 'تم passive structure' would be most appropriate for the predominantly agentless passive in this kind of text.

2. Resist fronting this cataphoric expression and embed instead: ويسعى
   الصندوق ولكي يتمكن من تحقيق أهدافه الى . . .

3. Resist an equational/Nominal sentence structure and activate the verbal
   elements: . . . وتعتبر حقوق السحب الخاصة بمثابة.

GLOSSARY

X were drawn up	تم وضع
along with those of	في نفس الوقت الذي تم فيه وضع
IBRO	المجلس الدولي للبحوث والتنمية
IMF came into being	وقد بدأ الصندوق أعماله فعلاً
whose quotas amounted to . . .	بلغت حصصها
deposit ratifications	أودعت وثائق إبرام الاتفاقية
seeks to promote	يسعى الى تعزيز
facilitate the expansion of trade	تسهيل النمو التجاري
and thus to contribute	وبالتالي الإسهام
increased employment	زيادة فرص العمل
improved economic conditions	تحسين الأوضاع الاقتصادية
in balance-of-payment difficulties	تواجه صعوبات في موازين مدفوعاتها
X maintains a pool of financial resources	يدير مركزاً للخدمات المالية
it makes available to	تكون (الخدمات) في متناول س
making international payments	القيام بالمدفوعات الدولية
obtain currency in spot transactions	الحصول على سيولة نقدية في التحويلات الفورية
settlement of a financial obligation	الإيفاء بالتزام مالي

II. Text 7D serves both a person-oriented reporting mode and a more entity-oriented mode. Translate into English, paying special attention to features of the two modes of reporting which are in evidence in the text.

TEXT 7D

رئيس صندوق النقد العربي يتحدث الى الغرفة

ألقى الدكتور جواد هاشم رئيس صندوق النقد العربي كلمة في الحفل الذي أقامته غرفة[1] التجارة العربية البريطانية في ٢٣ أيلول/سبتمبر[2] ودعت إليه أكثر من ٦٠ من كبار الشخصيات يمثلون العديد من المصارف العالمية والعربية والبريطانية. كما ضم الحفل أيضاً ممثلين عن الصحف اليومية البريطانية والعربية الصادرة في لندن[3] وممثلين عن وكالات الأنباء والصحف المالية والاقتصادية. وقد استعرض الدكتور هاشم،[4] الذي شغل سابقاً منصب وزير التخطيط في العراق، أنشطة صندوق النقد العربي خلال

99

السنوات الأربع الماضية . كما استعرض خطط الصندوق للسنوات العشر القادمة وخاصة
المتعلقة بالزيادة المقترحة في رأسمال الصندوق ليصل الى حوالي ١٠٠٠٠ مليون دولار
أمريكي . وأعلن⁵ الدكتور هاشم أن تلك الزيادة ضرورية لتمكين الصندوق من مواجهة
الارتفاع المتوقع في معدل الاقراض خلال السنوات القليلة المقبلة .

وقم تم إنشاء صندوق النقد العربي بواسطة جامعة الدول العربية وتم وضع قواعده
على غرار صندوق النقد الدولي إلى حد ما . ومن أبرز أهداف الصندوق تقديم تسهيلات
إئتمانية ميسرة للدول الأعضاء التي تتعرض موازين مدفوعاتها لعجز خطير ، والمساعدة
في تنسيق السياسات الاقتصادية والمالية والنقدية الطويلة الأجل في الدول العربية .⁶ ولا
يقوم الصندوق بتمويل مشاريع التنمية مباشرة إذ⁷ يستخدم في الإقراض الدينار العربي
الحسابي الذي يمثل الوحدة النقدية للصندوق . ويماثل الدينار العربي الحسابي ثلاثة من
حقوق السحب الخاصة التي يصدرها صندوق النقد الدولي . وقد بلغ مجموع القروض
التي منحها الصندوق حتى الآن لسبع من الدول الأعضاء حوالي ٤٠٠ مليون دولار
أمريكي .

[28]

NOTES

1. To have 'the chamber' as 'agent' is unidiomatic in English. This 'agency', however, must be somehow preserved. One way of achieving this is through using the possessive 'the Chamber's reception' and through using the passive 'to which were invited some 60 . . .'.

2. Fronting the date helps the subsequent text to flow better and is more in keeping with reporting conventions in English: 'On 23 September, X gave a speech at the Chamber . . .'.

3. To lighten the 'additive' load, this final item in the series may be introduced with: 'as well as those from news agencies . . .'.

4. A truncated relative clause used parenthetically is most appropriate here: '. . . , a former minister of planning in Iraq, . . . '.

5. The conventions of reporting in English require that 'verbs of saying' should literally mean what they actually say. That is, 'reviewed' is retained in English not because the Arabic text has it but because the verb denotes an activity (reviewing) that is true to what the speaker did and is thus important to preserve. The activity 'declaring', however, is not what actually happened and the verb 'declared' is mere padding, an extravagance Arabic reports seem to allow. In this respect, English is more strict and a mere 'said' should suffice: 'Dr Hashim said that this

increase was necessary . . . '.

6. A signal such as 'but' or 'however' may be useful here, not as a functional 'adversative', but merely as a discourse-organization device.

7. As the preceding element has not been a genuine adversative, إذ here would not be a functional substantiator but, once again, a discourse-organizational device. As such, إذ is best neutralized as 'and' in English: 'and uses . . . '.

GLOSSARY

Arab Monetary Fund	صندوق النقد العربي
AMF President Speaks at the Chamber	رئيس صندوق النقد العربي يتحدث في حفل الغرفة
at the Chamber's reception	في الحفل الذي أقامته الغرفة
high-ranking representatives	(من) كبار الشخصيات يمثلون
Also present at the reception	كما ضم الحفل
London-based Arab press	الصحف العربية الصادرة في لندن
X reviewed	استعرض
during the last four years	خلال السنوات الأربع الماضية
the Fund's plans for the next decade	خطط الصندوق للسنوات العشر القادمة
particularly those relating to	وخاصة المتعلقة
the proposed increase in	الزيادة المقترحة لـ . . .
to X million . . .	ليصل س مليون . . .
to enable the Fund to meet	لتمكين الصندوق من مواجهة
increase in lending	الارتفاع في معدل الإقراض
during the next few years	خلال السنوات القليلة القادمة
was established by	أنشأت
the Arab League	جامعة الدول العربية
is partly modelled on	ووضعت قواعده على غرار . . . الى حد ما
The Fund's main aims include	ومن أبرز أهداف الصندوق
the provision of soft credit	تقديم تسهيلات إئتمانية ميسرة
members with serious deficits	للدول الأعضاء التي تتعرض لعجز خطير
balance-of-payments deficits	تتعرض موازين مدفوعاتها لعجز خطير
the assistance with coordinating	المساعدة في تنسيق . . .
long-term financial policies	السياسات المالية طويلة الأجل
finance development projects directly	تمويل مشاريع التنمية مباشرة

its own currency, the Arab Accounting Dinar,	عملته الخاصة الدينار العربي الحسابي
it uses X for lending	يستخدم في عمليات الإقراض س
X is equal to	يماثل
Special Drawing Rights	حقوق السحب الخاصة
loans which X has so far made to	مجموع القروض التي منحها الصندوق حتى الآن
amount to	بلغ

UNIT EIGHT:
The News Report (Non-evaluative/Evaluative)

OVERVIEW

A domain which makes heavy use of reporting is that of journalism. A basic variety of journalistic reporting is one which we will refer to as the 'non-evaluative news report'. Here, an overriding requirement of context would be to 'monitor'* a situation, and to report a series of events as objectively as one can.

In response to such a context, the structure of the text would be highly unmarked. That is, the format 'scene-set' 'details of the scene' would be strictly adhered to.

Finally, the kind of texture which is compatible with this organization of text would be both semantically and syntactically basic. Vocabulary would be unemotive, sentence structure would display highly unmarked word order and connectivity would be established on the basis of a parallelism which threads its way through the text. In terms of translation strategy, this fairly sombre tone justifies little deviation from linguistic norms, and literal translation seems to work in the majority of cases.

Non-evaluative reporting may usefully be compared with another less detached kind of reporting. In this more involved form of the news report, the context responded to would be one in which the journalist's aim is to 'manage'* and not simply monitor a situation. The 'news' is not only reported but evaluated as well.

Text structure in this evaluative kind of context is bound to be more marked. The report could start off with the details and build up to reach some form of a summing-up which could easily have been an initial scene-setter. It could also employ structures borrowed from other text types such as counter-argumentation.

By the same token, texture would be slightly more turbulent than that of the non-evaluative news report. Here, vocabulary would normally carry significant connotations* and not mere denotation*. Furthermore, syntax would be highly manipulated to relay all sorts of rhetorical effect. As far as translation strategy is concerned, evaluative discourse necessitates a freer translation style, and, to relay a variety of rhetorical purposes, translators need to depart from a strictly literal rendering.

But one slight departure from recognized norms is present in news reports whatever the degree of evaluativeness. This relates to the specific kind of diction that is employed by the news report as a genre within the register of journalism. Certain features will be used as signals that we are in the mode of reporting news and not dealing with, say, a particular inauguration ceremony (person-oriented) or the structure and aims of a particular organization (entity-oriented). An example of such discourse signals is وجدير بالذكر whose function is the introduction of background information.

I.   Texts 8A (i) and 8A (ii) are examples of the non-evaluative and the evaluative news reports respectively.

TEXT 8A (i)

مجموعة من عشرة اغتالت في باريس
مسؤول الأمن الخارجي الفلسطيني

اغتيل في باريس ليل الأحد ـ الاثنين السيد عاطف بسيسو < ٤٤ عاماً> المسؤول عن العلاقات الخارجية في جهاز الأمن التابع لمنظمة التحرير الفلسطينية وضابط الاتصال بين المنظمة وأجهزة الأمن الأوروبية. واتهم الرئيس الفلسطيني ياسر عرفات جهاز الاستخبارات الاسرائيلي <موساد> باغتياله.

وتولى تنفيذ العملية التي اتسمت بالدقة الشديدة شخصان اقتربا من بسيسو اثر نزوله من سيارته التي كان يقودها بنفسه وتوجهه لدخول فندق «ميرديان» في حي مونبارناس. وأصيب المسؤول الأمني الفلسطيني بثماني رصاصات وقتل على الفور، في حين فر المنفذان في سيارة كانت في انتظارهما ويقودها شخص ثالث.

وكان شخصان صديقان لبسيسو يرافقانه لدى اغتياله، وقد حاولا اللحاق بالقاتلين إلا أنهما تراجعا بعدما هددهما الجانيان وقالت مصادر على اتصال بأحد هذين الشخصين إن مجموعتين تضم كل منهما خمسة شاركتا في العملية التي شملت مراقبة بسيسو الذي كان في مرحلة إعادة تنظيم الأجهزة الأمنية للمنظمة بعد اغتيال «أبو أياد» و«أبو الهول» في ١٤ كانون الثاني/يناير ١٩٩١ في تونس. وأوضحت إن احدى المجموعتين تولت مراقبته منذ دخوله الأراضي الفرنسية آتياً من برلين بعد ظهر الأحد في سيارته، فيما تولت المجموعة الثانية التنفيذ. وكانت هذه تضم إضافة الى مطلقي النار سائق السيارة التي استخدمت في الفرار وشخصين آخرين توليا توفير الحماية لمطلقي النار.

ويذكر أن المغدور الذي درس الحقوق في بيروت كان قد شارك في سلسلة من

العمليات الخارجية واعتقل في العام ١٩٧٣ في إيطاليا بعدما حاول مع مجموعة إسقاط طائرة اسرائيلية بواسطة صواريخ أرض ـ جو من طراز سام ٧ لكنه تحول في الثمانينات مسؤولاً أمنياً يتعاون مع الأجهزة الأوروبية في كبح الإرهاب.

[30]

TEXT 8A (ii)

صعايدة مصر يخرجون الفرعون امنحتب الثالث
من تحت رمال الأقصر

أهم ما في هذا الاكتشاف الآثاري العظيم، الأضخم والأخطر من نوعه في هذا القرن منذ اكتشاف كنوز توت عنخ آمون الأسطورية انه لن يرتبط باسم أي منقب أجنبي كما جرت العادة في غالبية اكتشافات آثار الفراعنة حتى الآن ذلك أنه حدث بمحض الصدفة وعلى يد صعايدة مصر السمر البسطاء وكأن الفرعون امنحتب الثالث لم يشأ أن يظهر وحاشيته إلا على يد أحفاده.

وفي التفاصيل، كما رواها الدكتور سيد توفيق رئيس منظمة الآثار المصرية القديمة بالقاهرة، أن مجموعة من العمال كانت تحفر الأرض بالمعاول والرفوش عند قاعدة أعمدة ميدان امنحتب الثالث في هيكل الأقصر ذلك أن الأعمدة بدأت في الآونة الأخيرة تميل بشكل خطير مما دفع بالمسؤولين المصريين الى اتخاذ القرار باستحداث دعائم تحت الأرضية لحمايتها من الانهيار.

أعمال الحفر كانت قد بدأت منذ مطلع كانون الثاني/يناير من العام الجاري وكانت تجري ببطء وحذر شديدين نظراً لأهمية الأعمدة والمنطقة الآثارية التي تقع فيها وكان المشرف على العمال قد قرر ألا يتجاوز الحفر المتر الواحد عمقاً.

فجأة في الثاني والعشرين من كانون الثاني سمع الريس فرج صوت ارتطام معول أحد العمال بجسم صلب فصرخ بأعلى صوته أن يتوقف الجميع عن الحفر وأسرع بنفسه الى الحفرة وراح يزيل الرمال بكلتا يديه عن ذلك الجسم الصلب ويا للهول ما اكتشف: قطعة من الصخر البركاني البلوري أرسلت بريقاً ساطعاً عند انكشافها على أشعة الشمس. انه تمثال الفرعون امنحتب الثالث ورأسه مكللاً بالتاجين اللذين يرمزان الى مصر العليا والسفلى.

[31]

105

II. Bearing in mind the distinctive features of non-evaluative and evaluative news reporting in Arabic, and the basic differences between the two modes, consider Texts 8B (i) and 8B (ii) as examples of the two text forms in English, then translate them into Arabic.

TEXT 8B (i)

DOUBLE BLAST BRINGS LONDON BOMBING TOTAL TO 10

Two bombs exploded in London early yesterday,[1] bringing to 10 the number of explosions in the capital in the past two weeks.

No one was injured,[2] although extensive damage was caused. The devices bore the hallmarks of the IRA's recent mainland campaign. The first bomb exploded outside the Novotel hotel in Hammersmith, West London, at 12.40. It had apparently been placed at the back of a coach which was damaged by the blast.

The second device was placed either in or under a car outside the Comedy Pub in Oxendon Street, near Leicester Square in the West End. It exploded around 1.30 a.m., shattering windows and setting alight two vehicles and damaging others nearby.

The area was closed[3] as police searched the area for other devices. Staff in the pub were treated at the scene for shock. Scotland Yard said a 'vague'[4] warning had been given in a telephone message to Capital Radio 10 minutes before the first explosion. It had not given sufficient details to locate the device immediately.

A man reported to have been arrested running away from the scene in the West End turned out to be a passer-by.

In Hammersmith, police decided against evacuating the 600 people in the hotel. Guests reported hearing a loud explosion and seeing smoke engulfing the area.

[5]The explosions come a week after the bomb at the Sussex Pub in Covent Garden in which a nurse, David Heffer, was fatally injured.

[32]

NOTES

1. In Arabic, to capture the saliency of *Two bombs exploded* and thus reflect the secondary importance of the circumstantials *in London early yesterday,* the latter are disposed of first, leaving the most salient to end-

The same may انفجرت في لندن في وقت مبكر من يوم أمس قنبلتان :position
be done with the following sentence in which *to 10* is a salient element:
.وبذلك يصل عدد الانفجارات في العاصمة خلال الأسبوعين الماضيين الى عشرة

2. This is an example of a rhetorically motivated passive construction: for
    all kinds of reasons (anonymity, etc.), the agency is deliberately
    suppressed. Furthermore, this passive verbalizes negative agency and
    thus rules out 'تم'. Arabic must therefore preserve it as passive: ولم يصب
    أحد بجروح. Still, one ought to try to avoid passivizing as in the following
    element: *although extensive damage was caused:* على الرغم من حصول أضرار
    جسيمة. But if all else fails, the passive would be an appropriate last
    resort.

3. Compare this agentless passive with the preceding examples. Though
    formally suppressed, the agency is conceptually present (the police); also
    the agency is positive. Thus, تم اغلاق would work.

4. Punctuation must be glossed: وذكرت سكوتلانديارد أن س كان قد تلقى عبر
    الهاتف تحذيراً وصفته بأنه كان مبهماً.

5. A background signal (e.g. وجدير بالذكر) may be useful here.

GLOSSARY

The devices	المتفجرات
bore the hallmarks of	تشير بشكل قاطع إلى أن الانفجارين هما جزء من
recent mainland campaign	الحملة التي شنها س أخيراً داخل الجزر البريطانية
at 12.40	في الساعة الثانية عشر وأربعين دقيقة من بعد منتصف الليل
It had apparently been placed at the back of a coach	ويبدو أن القنبلة كانت قد وضعت في مؤخرة حافلة
shattering windows	محطمة بذلك الواجهات الزجاجية
setting alight two vehicles	ومشعلة النار في سيارتين أخريين
nearby	كانت موجودة بالقرب من مكان الحادث
turned out to be a passer-by	لم يكن سوى أحد المارة
decided against evacuating the 600 people	أرتأوا عدم إخلاء نزلائه الـ ٦٠٠
was fatally injured	أصيب بجروح أودت بحياته

TEXT 8B (ii)

From Snow to Shining Snow

It was a moment of pure, bewitching political theatre.[1] The cheering crowd of 5,000 gathered inside a vast hangar at Denver airport fell silent and then screamed in disbelief as a 60ft high door slid majestically open to reveal the nose of his[2] plane and then Clinton's waving figure, and behind him the dawn rising in grandeur over the Rocky Mountains.

The Clinton campaign ended in snow in Denver yesterday morning, as it had begun in the snows of New Hampshire last January. From breakfast diners to airport hangars to tarmac rallies on what seemed like half the runways in America, Bill Clinton campaigned from dawn to dusk and on to dawn again in a relentless, sleepless trek across this vast nation which is finally comprehending the implacable nature of his pursuit of the presidency. He started from Philadelphia, the 18th-century birthplace of the nation, sipping Mountainberry apple tea in a classic 1950s aluminium diner that looked like a train carriage, just as it did when John Kennedy campaigned there 32 years ago.

He raced across the midwest to Cleveland, where Hillary clapped her hands in delight at the stray shafts of sun bouncing from Lake Erie. On to the cold, hard rain of Detroit, just across the river from Canada. Then he flew south for a thousand miles for more rallies down to the mariachi bands and sombreros of the Rio Grande valley in Texas, where he was introduced in Spanish in the warm softness of a tropical midnight.

But the sun was glinting everywhere.

[33]

NOTES

1. To convey the evaluativeness involved, the Verbal sentence structure begins to give in to the pressure of the need to nominalize: فالجمع الهاتف
   الذي ضم ٥٠٠ شخص ران عليه الصمت لحظة، ثم صرخ . . .

2. To keep the mystery of the cataphoric* 'his plane', and in order not to give the game away in Arabic, we opt for the equally mysterious: كاشفاً
   عن مقدمة طائرة الضيف المنتظر.

GLOSSARY

It was a moment of   لم تكن سوى لحظة من لحظات

pure, bewitching political theatre	العرض السياسي الساحر
gathered inside a vast hangar	احتشد داخل عنبر طائرات ضخم
screamed in disbelief	صرخ في حالة من الذهول
slid majestically	انفتح وبشكل يوحي بجلال العظمة
then Clinton's waving figure appeared	ثم ظهر كلنتون وهو
the dawn rising in grandeur	الفجر المنشق بأبهى
from breakfast diners to . . . to . . .	من مطعم شعبي إلى . . . وإلى . . .
on what seemed like	ما بدا وكأنه
from dawn to dusk and on to dawn	من الفجر حتى الغروب وحتى فجر اليوم التالي
relentless, sleepless trek	مشوار شاق لم تغمض فيه عيناه
implacable nature of his pursuit of	التصميم الذي لا يتزعزع والذي يميز سعيه للفوز
birthplace of the nation	مسقط رأس هذه الأمة
sipping	وهو يرشف
a classic 1950s aluminium diner	في مطعم شعبي تقليدي من القصدير يذكرنا بأيام الخمسينات
just as it did	تماماً كما كان يبدو
raced across	وهرع مسرعاً
clapped her hands in delight	صفقت بابتهاج
at the stray shafts of sun bouncing	وهي تستقبل أشعة الشمس المتناثرة
cold, hard rain of Detroit	ديترويت بطقسها البارد ومطرها الغزير
just across the river from	لا يفصلها عن . . . سوى نهر صغير
the mariachi bands	فرقة المرياتشيد الشعبية
sombreros	وقبعات الصمبريرة التقليدية
warm softness of a tropical midnight	في دفء منتصف ليل إستوائي ناعم
glinting everywhere	تلألأ في كل مكان وكأنها اسم على مسمى

III. Bearing in mind the features of evaluative and non-evaluative reporting styles studied so far, translate Texts 8A (i) and 8A (ii) (reproduced here for easier reference) into English.

TEXT 8A (i)

مجموعة من عشرة اغتالت في باريس
مسؤول الأمن الخارجي الفلسطيني

اغتيل في باريس ليل الأحد ـ الاثنين السيد عاطف بسيسو < ٤٤ عاماً >[1] المسؤول عن العلاقات الخارجية في جهاز الأمن التابع لمنظمة التحرير الفلسطينية وضابط الاتصال بين المنظمة وأجهزة الأمن الأوروبية. واتهم الرئيس الفلسطيني ياسر عرفات جهاز الاستخبارات الاسرائيلي < موساد > باغتياله.

وتولى تنفيذ العملية التي اتسمت بالدقة الشديدة شخصان اقتربا من بسيسو إثر نزوله من سيارته التي كان يقودها بنفسه وتوجهه لدخول فندق «ميرديان» في حي مونبارناس. وأصيب المسؤول الأمني الفلسطيني بثماني رصاصات وقتل على الفور، في حين فر المنفذان في سيارة كانت في انتظارهما ويقودها شخص ثالث.

وكان شخصان صديقان لبسيسو يرافقانه لدى اغتياله[2]، وقد حاولا اللحاق بالقاتلين إلا أنهما تراجعا بعدما هددهما الجانيان وقالت مصادر على اتصال بأحد هذين الشخصين إن مجموعتين تضم كل منهما خمسة شاركتا في العملية التي شملت مراقبة بسيسو الذي كان في مرحلة إعادة تنظيم الأجهزة الأمنية للمنظمة بعد اغتيال «أبو أياد» و«أبو الهول» في ١٤ كانون الثاني/ يناير ١٩٩١ في تونس. وأوضحت أن احدى المجموعتين تولت مراقبته منذ دخوله الأراضي الفرنسية آتياً من برلين بعد ظهر الأحد في سيارته، فيما تولت المجموعة الثانية التنفيذ. وكانت هذه تضم إضافة الى مطلقي النار[3] سائق السيارة التي استخدمت في الفرار وشخصين آخرين توليا توفير الحماية لمطلقي النار.

ويذكر أن[4] المغدور الذي درس الحقوق في بيروت كان قد شارك في سلسلة من العمليات الخارجية واعتقل في العام ١٩٧٣ في ايطاليا بعدما حاول مع مجموعة إسقاط طائرة اسرائيلية بواسطة صواريخ أرض ـ جو من طراز سام ٧ لكنه تحول في الثمانينات[5] مسؤولاً أمنياً يتعاون مع الأجهزة الأوروبية في كبح الإرهاب.

NOTES

1. First, observe the effective agentless passive اغتيل, etc., here and elsewhere in this text. Second, the defining sentence المسؤول is best presented separately as a new sentence: 'He was the official in charge of external relations'. The defined entity بسيسو is already overloaded.

2. The adverb لدى اغتياله may be fronted cataphorically, as the sentence could usefully be extended with the details of what the companions did: 'At the time of the assassination, X was accompanied by two friends who tried . . . '.

3. Another example of an adverbial element that is best disposed of cataphorically: 'In addition to the two assassins . . . '.

4. A background signal best omitted in English.

5. This point is of immense ideological significance and the 'opposition' involved must be presented forcefully as: 'In the eighties, however, . . . '.

GLOSSARY

A group of ten assassinate . . .	مجموعة من عشرة اغتالت
security apparatus of the PLO	جهاز الأمن التابع لمنظمة التحرير الفلسطينية
the liaison officer	ضابط الاتصالات بين
European security organizations	أجهزة الأمن الأوروبية
accused X of carrying out the assassination	اتهم س باغتيال
executed with extreme precision	اتسمت بالدقة الشديدة
approach	اقترب من
after he got out of the car	إثر نزوله من سيارته
the car he was driving	سيارته التي كان يقودها بنفسه
was heading towards the entrance of	وتوجهه لدخول . . .
was hit by eight bullets	أصيب بثماني رصاصات
died immediately	وقتل على الفور
while the two attackers fled	في حين فر المنفذان
but had to retreat	إلا أنهما تراجعا
when the assassins threatened them	بعدما هددهما الجانيان
sources in contact with . . . revealed	وقالت مصادر على اتصال بـ
watching X who had embarked on	مراقبة س الذي كان في مرحلة
a reorganization of the PLO's security organs	اعادة تنظيم الأجهزة الأمنية لـ
in the wake of the assassination of	بعد اغتيال س
the sources added that	وأوضحت
had had him under surveillance since	تولت مراقبته منذ
while X carried it out	فيما تولت س التنفيذ
shoot down X with	إسقاط س بواسطة

ground-to-air SAM 7 missiles	صواريخ أرض جو من طراز سام
he became . . . and was cooperating with	تحول مسؤولاً أمنياً يتعاون مع
in curbing terrorism	في كبح الإرهاب

TEXT 8A (ii)

صعايدة مصر يخرجون الفرعون امنحتب الثالث
من تحت رمال الأقصر

أهم ما في هذا الاكتشاف الآثاري العظيم، الأضخم والأخطر من نوعه في هذا[1] القرن منذ اكتشاف كنوز توت عنخ آمون الأسطورية أنه لن يرتبط باسم أي منقب أجنبي كما جرت العادة في غالبية اكتشافات آثار الفراعنة حتى الآن ذلك أنه[2] حدث بمحض الصدفة وعلى يد صعايدة مصر السمر البسطاء وكأن الفرعون امنحتب الثالث لم يشأ أن يظهر وحاشيته إلا على يد أحفاده .

وفي التفاصيل كما رواها الدكتور سيد توفيق رئيس منظمة الآثار المصرية القديمة بالقاهرة أن مجموعة من العمال كانت تحفر الأرض بالمعاول والرفوش عند قاعدة أعمدة ميدان امنحتب الثالث في هيكل الأقصر ذلك أن الأعمدة بدأت في الآونة الأخيرة تميل بشكل خطير مما دفع بالمسؤولين المصريين الى اتخاذ القرار باستحداث دعائم تحت الأرضية لحمايتها من الانهيار .

أعمال الحفر كانت قد بدأت منذ مطلع كانون الثاني/يناير من العام الجاري[3] وكانت تجري ببطء وحذر شديدين نظراً لأهمية الأعمدة والمنطقة الآثارية التي تقع فيها وكان المشرف على العمال قد قرر ألا يتجاوز الحفر المتر الواحد عمقاً .

فجأة في الثاني والعشرين من كانون الثاني سمع الريس فرج صوت ارتطام معول أحد العمال بجسم صلب فصرخ بأعلى صوته أن يتوقف الجميع عن الحفر وأسرع بنفسه الى الحفرة وراح يزيل الرمال بكلتا يديه عن ذلك الجسم الصلب ويا للهول ما اكتشف : قطعة من الصخر البركاني البلوري أرسلت بريقاً ساطعاً عند انكشافها على أشعة الشمس . إنه تمثال الفرعون امنحتب الثالث ورأسه مكللاً بالتاجين اللذين يرمزان الى مصر العليا والسفلى .

NOTES

1. To respond to the highly marked use of the nominal structure in this kind of reporting, a form of emphasis may be necessary in English, a

cleft sentence* perhaps: 'What is most significant in this gigantic, huge and most crucial of archaeological discoveries this century is . . . '.

2. This is an implicit connector in English, with the following element beginning a new sentence, thus: 'It happened by sheer coincidence . . . '.

3. As in note 2 above, this extraordinarily marked nominal structure cannot simply be rendered literally. Perhaps a 'restriction'* of some kind may be necessary, as in: 'The digging operation did not begin until January of this year . . . ', which reflects the critical nature of the situation.

GLOSSARY

The Saeedis of Upper Egypt	صعايدة مصر
uncover X from beneath the sands of Luxor	يخرجون س من تحت رمال الأقصر
The Pharaoh Amenhotep III	الفرعون امنحتب الثالث
ever since the discovery of	منذ اكتشاف . . . الأسطورية
the legendary treasures of Tutankhamun	كنوز توت عنخ آمون
foreign excavator	منقب أجنبي
as has been customary	كما جرت العادة
pharaonic antiquities	الآثار الفرعونية
at the hands of the brown and simple X	على يد صعايدة مصر السمر البسطاء
it was as though X wished only to appear to . . .	وكأن س لم يشأ أن يظهر إلا على يد
descendants	أحفاده
Narrating the details of the story, X said	وفي التفاصيل كما رواها س أن
the Department of Ancient Egyptian Antiquities	منظمة الآثار المصرية القديمة
digging with their picks and shovels	تحفر بالمعاول والرفوش
at the base of the columns in X square	عند قاعدة أعمدة ميدان س
Temple of Luxor	في هيكل الأقصر
This had become necessary as . . .	ذلك أن
lean dangerously	تميل بشكل خطير
To deal with the problem, X decided	مما دفع بالمسؤولين الى اتخاذ القرار
to put in underground supports	باستحداث دعائم تحت الأرضية
to prevent collapse	لحمايتها من الانهيار
given the importance	لأهمية

archaeological site	المنطقة الآثارية
digging must be no deeper than one metre	ألا يتجاوز الحفر المتر الواحد عمقاً
heard the labourer's pick hit a solid object	سمع ارتطام معول بجسم صلب
at the top of his voice, he shouted ordering	فصرخ بأعلى صوته أن توقف
and 'Good Heavens!'	يا للهول!
crystalline volcanic rock	الصخر البركاني البلوري
sparkled	أرسلت بريقاً ساطعاً
in the sun	عند انكشافها على أشعة الشمس
with his head adorned by two crowns	ورأسه مكلل بالتاجين

UNIT EIGHT: Additional Texts

I.   Texts 8C (i)/8D (i) and Texts 8C (ii)/8D (ii) are examples of semi-evaluative and evaluative news reporting respectively. However, the texts are different from those presented above, but only in the occasion of their occurrence. The following additional texts are drawn from the type of journalism found in the 'weeklies', such as *The Economist* and *Time*, which accounts for the slightly higher degree of evaluativeness throughout. The element of commentary involved basically ensures news durability.

TEXT 8C (i)

A Thin Ray of Hope in Sarajevo

The wall that Serbian forces had formed around the Bosnian capital of Sarajevo was pierced just enough[1] to let in a ray of hope. More[2] than 1,000 Canadian peacekeepers under the United Nations flag rolled in through the mountains from Croatia to buttress a small UN force already in place. The contingent quickly cleared and reopened the airport that had been closed by Serbian shelling and sniper fire for 87 days.

With that, a full-scale international relief effort got underway. Almost 100 tons of emergency supplies from the US arrived in the first two days. Giant cargo planes also flew from Britain and France. The food and medicine were then trucked – under Canadian guard – into the desperate city of 400,000 people. In Washington, Defense Secretary Dick Cheney said American air and naval forces would be available if they were needed to protect the relief flights or future truck convoys. But relief shipments, welcome as they are, can only be a palliative. They do not end the siege of

Sarajevo or the Serbian occupation.

(. . .)

[34]

NOTES

1. The use of 'قصر' may be justified to relay the element of evaluativeness
    involved: لم يتم اختراق الجدار الذي أقامته القوات الصربية إلا بقدر يكشف عن بارقة
    ضئيلة من الأمل.

2. It is clear that this is to an extent evaluative, with the element in question
    substantiating and not merely adding – as would be the case in non-
    evaluative news reports: إذ وصل. The same happens with the second
    sentence of the second paragraph: فقد وصل.

GLOSSARY

1,000 Canadian peacekeepers	ألف كندي من قوات حفظ السلام
rolled in through	وصلوا بكامل معداتهم
to buttress	لدعم
a UN force	قوة تابعة للأمم المتحدة
already in place	كانت متمركزة هناك
contingent cleared and reopened the airport	قامت السرية بتنظيف المطار وإعادة فتحه
the airport that had been closed	بعد أن ظل مغلقاً (٨٧ يوماً)
closed by Serbian shelling and sniper fire	مغلقاً بنيران القصف الصربي ورصاص القناصة
With that X got underway	وبذلك بدأت بالفعل . . .
a full-scale relief effort	حملة إغاثة شاملة
emergency supplies	امدادات ضرورية
Giant cargo planes	طائرات شحن ضخمة
X were then trucked – under Canadian guard –	وتم بعد ذلك براً وتحت حراسة كندية
the desperate city	المدينة اليائسة
would be available	ستكون على أهبة الاستعداد
if they were needed	إذا دعت الحاجة
future truck convoys	القوافل البرية مستقبلاً

But X, welcome as they are,	لكن س، بالرغم من أنها جاءت في وقتها،
can only be a palliative	لا تمثل سوى اجراءً مرحلياً فهي

TEXT 8C (ii)

Culture Shocks End in Tragedy

Tokyo. Yoshihiro Hattori, a 16-year-old Japanese exchange student from Nagoya, and his friend Web Haymaker, also 16, were out[1] to have a good time last week, little suspecting that their evening would end in tragedy. The two boys had been invited to a Hallowe'en party in Baton Rouge, Louisiana, and Yoshihiro had dressed up in a white jacket, mimicking John Travolta in the old disco film, *Saturday Night Fever*. It was Saturday night.

Yoshihiro had not been in the US for long, and his command of English was not very good, but he had become good friends with Web, with whose family he was staying.

At about 7.30, the boys knocked on the front door of the house where they thought the party was being held. There was no answer, so they went around to the garage door and knocked again. A woman appeared and looked startled. The boys stood there. Then the woman's husband came out with a .44 magnum revolver and told the boys to 'freeze'. Web did so, but Yoshihiro, not understanding and apparently thinking it was part of a joke, stepped forward and asked, 'Where's the party?' The husband shot him in the chest, killing him almost instantly. The party[2] was several doors down the street.

The tragedy was cruelly ironic, as one of Yoshihiro's relatives said later: Yoshihiro 'came to learn cultural differences, and it seems these cultural differences[3] killed him'.

[34]

NOTES

1. The use of the Nominal is most appropriate here to relay a necessary element of evaluativeness: س وص كانا قد خرجا لقضاء وقت ممتع في الأسبوع الماضي.

2. A good example of the use of أما الحفل to bring out the contrast and hence the irony.

3. There is a cleft meaning here: ويبدو أن هذه الفوارق هي ذاتها التي أودت بحياته.

GLOSSARY

little suspecting that	غير مدركين على الإطلاق
16-year-old Japanese exchange student	الطالب الياباني الزائر والبالغ من العمر
evening	سهرة
Hallowe'en party	حفلة تنكرية
dressed up in a white jacket	قد ارتدى سترة بيضاء أنيقة
mimicking X in the old disco film	مقلداً الممثل الراقص س في الفلم الغنائي الشهير
It was Saturday night	وشاء القدر أن تكون الليلة ليلة سبت بالفعل
had not been in the US for long	كان قد وصل الى الولايات المتحدة منذ فترة قصيرة
his command of English was not very good	كما لم يكن ذا إلمام جيد باللغة الانجليزية
become good friends	كوّن صداقة وطيدة مع
At about 7.30	وفي حوالي الساعة السابعة والنصف مساءً
knocked on the front door	طرق على باب منزل
went around to the garage door	(مما اضطرهما) أن يقصدا باب الكراج الخلفي
looked startled	وعلى وجهها علامات الذعر
told the boys to 'freeze'	وطلب من الولدَين باللهجة العامية الأمريكية أن يجمدا في مكانيهما
Web did so	فأطاعه وب
not understanding	ولعدم فهمه قصد الرجل
apparently thinking	واعتقد على ما يبدو أن
part of a joke	من قبيل المزاح
shot him in the chest	أطلق الرصاص وأصابه في صدره
killing him almost instantly	مودياً بحياته في الحال
was several doors down the street	كان في منزل آخر لا يبعد سوى عدة أمتار وفي الشارع نفسه
cruelly ironic	قاسية ساخرة

TEXT 8D (i)

اتهام عشرة نواب مصريين بالإتجار بالمخدرات

دخلت قضية نواب البرلمان المصري المتهمين بالإتجار بالمخدرات مرحلتها الأخيرة بعد وصول رسالة من اللواء محمد موسى وزير الداخلية الى رئيس البرلمان متضمنة كشفاً بأسماء هؤلاء النواب والاتهامات الموجهة اليهم وعددهم عشرة.

ورغم العطلة البرلمانية فقد قطع نواب البرلمان من أعضاء اللجنة التشريعية اجازتهم لحضور الاجتماع السري الذي دعت إليه اللجنة لمناقشة رسالة وزير الداخلية وبحث الموقف القانوني للنواب العشرة في أول سابقة من نوعها في تاريخ الحياة البرلمانية المصرية.

وخلت رسالة وزير الداخلية[1] من صدور أحكام قضائية نهائية باتهام أي من النواب العشرة في عمليات تجارة وتهريب المخدرات إلا أن تحريات أجهزة مكافحة المخدرات في مصر تؤكد وجود دلائل على مشاركة النواب في عمليات جلب وتهريب مخدرات غير أن حرصهم الشديد يجعلهم في مأمن باعتبارهم كمسؤولين عن عمليات التمويل والتخطيط ولا يقومون بالتنفيذ.

ويترقب الرأي العام في مصر قرار البرلمان بشأن النواب العشرة والمتوقع صدوره خلال الدورة الجديدة للبرلمان ويعتبر هذا الموضوع الاختبار الثاني للبرلمان بعد حسم قضية تزوير انتخابات دائرة النزهة وبطلان عضوية نائبها في إطار حرص البرلمان على مصداقيته وسمعته.

[35]

NOTES

1. The reporting becomes slightly more involved here as it merges with commentary: 'The minister's letter did not make a mention of . . .'. But the investigations carried out . . .'. Following from this, there is another adversative: غير أن حرصهم الشديد. This may be introduced with a background/commentary signal such as: 'It is worth noting, however, that the MPs' extreme caution in . . . which makes them feel safe . . .'. Also the explanation of the 'caution' may have to be made more explicit as in: 'caution in planning for, financing and directing the operations but not actually carrying them out . . .'.

GLOSSARY

drug trafficking	الإتجار بالمخدرات
after Y received from X a letter containing	بعد وصول رسالة من ص الى س متضمنة
The Speaker of the House	رئيس البرلمان
Rear-Admiral	اللواء
a list of the names	كشفاً بأسماء
the accusations levelled against them	الاتهامات الموجهة اليهم
parliamentary recess	العطلة البرلمانية
the legislative committee	اللجنة التشريعية
interrupted their holidays	قطعوا إجازتهم
to attend a meeting held *in camera*	لحضور الاجتماع السري
this meeting was called by	الاجتماع الذي دعت اليه . . .
the legal position	الموقف القانوني
in the first case of its kind	في أول سابقة من نوعها
in the history of the Egyptian parliament	في تاريخ الحياة البرلمانية المصرية
did not make a mention of	خلت
any final judicial rulings	من صدور أحكام قضائية نهائية
investigations carried out by drug combating agencies	تحريات أجهزة مكافحة المخدرات
confirmed that there is evidence	تؤكد وجود دلائل على
procurement and smuggling of	جلب وتهريب
public opinion awaits	ويترقب الرأي العام
parliamentary session	دورة البرلمان
test case for	الاختبار لـ
rigging the elections	تزوير الانتخابات
and the consequent invalidity of the	وبطلان عضوية
in its concern that	في إطار حرص
its credibility and reputation remain untarnished	حرص البرلمان على مصداقيته وسمعته

TEXT 8D (ii)

السود يحرقون العلم الاسرائيلي في نيويورك

التوتر الدموي بين السود واليهود في مدينة نيويورك أوضح الحساسية[1] بين جماعتين تدعي كل منهما أنها مضطهدة وأن الجماعة الأخرى تهددها، وأوضح كذلك أن انغلاق اليهود المتطرفين لن يسبب إلا مزيداً من المشاكل لهم ولبقية اليهود.

وذكر عدد من يهود نيويورك أنهم أصيبوا بالذعر والخوف وهم يشاهدون المتظاهرين السود يحرقون العلم الاسرائيلي أمام معبد اليهود «الأرثودكس» في حي كراون هايتز، الذي يمتلئ بالمهاجرين من كثير من بلاد العالم الثالث. ويرى المراقبون أن حرق العلم الاسرائيلي في نيويورك، حيث أكبر جالية يهودية في الولايات المتحدة، ستكون له دلالات كثيرة.

والتوتر بدأ بحادثة مرور[2] عندما تجاهل سائق سيارة يهودي أرثودكسي الضوء الأحمر وعبر الشارع وصعد على رصيف المشاة، وصدم طفلاً وطفلة من السود. وعندما سرت إشاعة في الحي الذي يسكنه عدد كبير من السود أن الشرطة لم تعتقل اليهودي وأن سيارة إسعاف تابعة للطائفة اليهودية رفضت نقل المصابين الى المستشفى، تظاهر السود احتجاجاً. وزادت المظاهرات والتوتر عندما أعلن أن الطفل توفي وأن الطفلة في حالة خطيرة واتجه السود نحو حي اليهود الأرثودكس يقذفونهم بالحجارة ويشعلون النار في سياراتهم. وهجم السود على يهودي أرثودكسي من استراليا كان يزور المنطقة وضربوه حتى مات رغم أنه لم يشترك في حادث المرور.

عمدة نيويورك الأسود ديفيد ديكنز هرع الى المنطقة وحاول تهدئة المشاعر ولأكثر من أسبوع كان يزور المنطقة كل يوم لكنه قال: «اعلم أن هذه ليست نهاية المشكلة».

[35]

NOTES

1. This is another example of the need to respond to the highly evaluative use of the Nominal sentence structure in reporting by perhaps opting for a cleft sentence: 'It was the tension between X and Y which ended in bloodshed that glaringly exposed how precarious the relations are between the two groups, each of which claims . . . '.

2. Once again, to exploit the force of the Nominal structure, a restrictive

adverb may be necessary: 'The tension simply began . . .'; or 'The tension began with a mere traffic incident . . .'.

GLOSSARY

being persecuted and threatened by cliquishness	مضطهدة وأن الجماعة الأخرى تهددها انغلاق
will only cause more problems	لن يسبب إلا مزيداً من المشاكل
were seized with fear and were terrified	أصيبوا بالذعر والخوف
synagogue	معبد
the largest Jewish community	أكبر جالية يهودية
will have numerous repercussions	ستكون له دلالات كثيرة
crossed the street and mounted the pavement	عبر الشارع وصعد على رصيف المشاة
hitting two small black children, a boy and a girl	وصدم طفلاً وطفلة من السود
when rumour spread in the district	وعندما سرت إشاعة في الحي
transport the casualties	نقل المصابين
demonstrated in protest	تظاهر السود احتجاجاً
was in a critical condition	في حالة خطرة
headed towards . . . , hurling stones at them	واتجه . . . نحو . . . يقذفونهم بالحجارة
and setting their cars on fire	ويشعلون النار في سياراتهم
beat him to death	وضربوه حتى مات
rushed to	هرع
trying to calm feelings	حاول تهدئة المشاعر

UNIT NINE:
The Report (Formulaic/Executive/Personalized)

OVERVIEW

Within this form of reporting, we shall distinguish between the Formulaic, the Executive and the more involved Personalized Report. The first type follows strict conventional formats and may be illustrated by the Auditor's Report. The second type covers the highly formal, albeit still personalized, reports such as the UN Secretary-General's annual report to the General Assembly. The third type is the most open-ended form of personalized reporting, with actual texts ranging from the student reference to reporting on a personal mission.

In terms of contextual specification, the three types of personalized reporting all perform the same kind of function. Formally, however, the various types follow different textual procedures. As already pointed out, the Formulaic Report leaves little room for innovativeness: there is a cliché-like format to be followed. The producers of the Executive and the more involved variety, on the other hand, enjoy a greater degree of freedom in developing their texts. In fact, these forms could use any or all of the text forms covered so far, legal or expository, as well as forms to be covered later under argumentation.

The texture of Formulaic reports would thus be far more constrained than that of the other two forms. In the latter, and particularly in the more involved variety, a certain degree of evaluativeness is inevitable. Vocabulary is bound to be slightly more emotive than deemed appropriate in other forms of exposition. Syntax would be somehow manipulated to persuade as well as inform:

The translation strategy to be adopted in dealing with the Personalized kind of reporting will vary as the reporting focus varies: a literal rendering would be appropriate for the Formulaic, a less literal approach is ideal for translating the Executive variety and, finally, a least literal method of translating would be required when dealing with the more involved variety.

It is perhaps worth reiterating here that, across the board, Arabic tends to opt for a slightly higher degree of evaluativeness than English. That is, there will be some evaluativeness, albeit minimal, even in Formulaic reports, and the more involved reports will obviously be more evaluative.

I. Consider the following text samples as examples of the Formulaic, the
    Executive and the more involved forms of Personalized reporting. Pay
    special attention to the cliché-like nature of linguistic expression typical
    of this form of reporting in English.

TEXT 9A (i)

Report of the Auditors to the Proprietor
Edinburgh, 28th April 1992

We have audited the accounts of the Bank of Scotland presented on pages 50
to 70 in accordance with Auditing Standards. In our opinion the accounts
give a true and fair view of the state of affairs of the Bank and of the Group
at 29th February 1992 and of the profit and cash flows of the Group for the
year then ended and have been properly prepared in accordance with the
Companies Act 1985.

[36]

TEXT 9A (ii)

UN Secretary-General's Annual Report
to the General Assembly

At the beginning of this year, I undertook a special effort to pursue the
convening of an international peace conference on the Middle East. With the
widespread support of the international community, I held numerous
consultations with the parties and the members of the Security Council.
These consultations focused on both the principle of a conference and
questions of procedure. The views expressed to me differed in nuance and
detail, but it was generally hoped that they could be sufficiently narrowed to
make possible the convening of a conference at which the more difficult
substantive issues could be tackled in a constructive spirit. Unfortunately, it
has not yet proved possible to obtain the agreement of all the parties to the
principle of an international conference and this has hindered my efforts to
make progress on the procedural issues. Bilateral efforts to promote the
peace process have also apparently run into difficulties. In spite of these set-
backs the search must by all means be sustained for a comprehensive

settlement through a negotiating process, under United Nations auspices, in which all parties would participate.

[24]

TEXT 9A (iii)

Norman Schwartzkopf's Memoirs
The Gulf War Ceasefire

I looked at the map. 'OK. Let's go with Safwan airfield' [as a possible site for the ceasefire talks with the Iraqis]. Safwan was the Iraqi military landing strip just north of the Kuwaiti border and only two miles from the road junction I'd ordered the US VII Corps to take the morning before.

Minutes later [General John] Yeosock called back. 'We don't have any forces there.'

I stared hard at the situation map. The entire sector around the airfield was clearly marked as being held by us. I'd also been given confirmation reports to that effect when I'd arrived in the war room that morning. 'If we're not on the airfield itself, we must have units nearby, right? Just move some troops into that area'. Yeosock said he would.

I was becoming uneasy. Safwan was in a sector crucial to our ability to block the escape of Iraqi heavy equipment from Kuwait and root out any remaining Scud storage bunkers. I'd assumed our forces had spent the time since the shooting stopped doing just that. Now I wasn't so sure.

Then Yeosock called back and confirmed my worst fears: we had nobody at Safwan – not at the airfield and not at the nearby mountain where the Scuds were reportedly hidden, let alone at the road junction I had explicitly ordered the army to take. Helicopters had flown combat patrols along the highway and had reported no enemy forces, he said, but troops had never set foot in the sector. I felt as though I'd been punched in the gut.

[38]

II. Bearing in mind the basic features characteristic of the three modes of reporting (the Formulaic, the Executive and the Personalized), consider the following text samples which illustrate the three forms in Arabic. Translate into English.

TEXT 9B (i)

تقرير فاحصي الحسابات

الدوحة ـ قطر

حضرات السادة مساهمي بنك قطر الوطني ش.م.ق

لقد فحصنا ميزانية بنك قطر الوطني ش.م.ق ـ الدوحة ـ قطر كما في ٣١ كانون الأول/ديسمبر ١٩٧٦، وبياني توزيع الأرباح والأرباح والخسائر للسنة المنتهية بذلك التاريخ وفقاً لقواعد المراقبة المتعارف عليها وقد شمل[1] فحصنا إجراء الامتحان اللازم للقيود والسجلات الحسابية، كما شمل إجراءات المراقبة الأخرى التي وجدناها مناسبة وقد حصلنا على المعلومات التي رأيناها ضرورية لأداء مهمتنا على وجه مرضٍ.

برأينا أن الميزانية المذكورة تعبّر بأمانة ووضوح عن المركز المالي الحقيقي للبنك بتاريخ ٣١ كانون الأول/ديسمبر ١٩٧٦ وأن بياني الأرباح والخسائر وتوزيع الأرباح يظهران بصورة عادلة نتيجة أعمال البنك للسنة المنتهية بذلك التاريخ، وأن البيانات المذكورة متفقة مع الواقع وتتضمن كل ما نص القانون ونظام البنك وأن البنك يمسك حسابات منتظمة وأن الجرد السنوي أجري وفقاً للأصول المرعية وأن البيانات الواردة في تقرير مجلس الإدارة فيما يتعلق بالحسابات متفقة مع ما هو وارد في دفاتر البنك وأنه في حدود المعلومات التي توفرت لدينا لم تقع خلال السنة المالية مخالفات لأحكام القانون على وجه يؤثر في نشاط البنك أو في مركزه المالي. وباعتقادنا أن البيانات المذكورة جهزت على أساس مماثل للأصول المتبعة سابقاً ووفقاً للأصول المحاسبية المتعارف عليها.

[39]

NOTES

1. Here, it may be helpful to start a new sentence in English: 'Our examination was made in accordance with generally accepted auditing standards . . .'.

GLOSSARY

The shareholders, Qatar National Bank S.A.Q.	حضرات السادة مساهمي بنك قطر الوطني ش.م.ق.
we have examined	لقد فحصنا
balance sheet	ميزانية

as at 31 December	كما في ٣١ كانون الأول/ ديسمبر
statement of profit and loss	بيان الأرباح والخسائر
statement of appropriation	بيان توزيع الأرباح
for the year then ended	للسنة المنتهية بذلك التاريخ
and (accordingly included)	وقد شمل فحصنا
such tests . . . as we considered necessary	إجراء الامتحان اللازم
accounting records	القيود والسجلات الحسابية
other auditing procedures	إجراءات المراقبة (الأخرى)
we have obtained all the information and explanations	وقد حصلنا على كافة المعلومات
which were necessary for the purpose of our examination	التي رأيناها ضرورية لأداء مهمتنا
in our opinion	برأينا فإن
the above-mentioned balance sheet	الميزانية المذكورة
gives a true and fair view	يعبر بأمانة ووضوح
the financial position	المركز المالي (الحقيقي)
the result of its operations	نتيجة أعمال البنك
are consistent	متفقة مع الواقع
and give all the information required by law and the bank's statutes	وتتضمن كل ما نص القانون ونظام البنك
proper books of account were kept by the bank	وأن البنك يمسك حسابات منتظمة
stocktaking was carried out in accordance with recognized principles	وأن الجرد السنوي أجري وفقاً للأصول المرعية
to the best of our knowledge and belief and according to the information given to us	وفي حدود المعلومات التي توافرت لدينا
no contraventions of the law were committed	لم تقع مخالفات لأحكام القانون
in such a way as to affect materially the bank's activities	على وجه يؤثر في نشاط البنك

TEXT 9B (ii)

عرض عام للحالة الاقتصادية

بحلول العام المالي ١٤٠٢ ـ ١٤٠٣ (١٩٨٢ ـ ١٩٨٣) دخل الاقتصاد السعودي مرحلة جديدة من مراحل[1] تطوره الحديث. فقد مر الاقتصاد[2] عبر ثلاث مراحل ساهمت جيعها بوضع الأسس الراسخة للنمو المستقر والمتوازن لاقتصاد البلاد على المدى البعيد.

بدأت أولى هذه المراحل بتوحيد البلاد في عام ١٣٥١ (١٩٣٢) وانتهت بالتطبيق الناجح لبرنامج التوازن والاستقرار في عام ١٣٧٩ ـ ١٣٨٠ (١٩٦٠). واستغرقت فترة زمنية تزيد عن الربع قرن، وأدى اكتشاف الزيت الى توفير الموارد التي حركت عجلة التنمية الاقتصادية، وتميزت[3] هذه الفترة بأنها أطول المراحل وأكثرها مشقة وتحدياً لأن البلاد قد بدأت بموارد محدودة جداً. وبالرغم من أن المملكة باتت موحدة وكانت غنية بقيمها وتطلعاتها، فإنها في الحقيقة كانت تفتقر لتجهيزات البنية الأساسية. وكانت امكانيات التنمية كبيرة إلا أن إيرادات الزيت في ذلك الوقت لم تكن كافية لسد الاحتياجات ولذلك كانت المملكة أمام مهمة طويلة وشاقة.

ومع ذلك[4] تحقق العديد من المنجزات خلال تلك الفترة وأنشئ جهاز حكومي متكامل كبداية لعملية التغيير الاجتماعي والاقتصادي للبلاد وانقطعت صلة الاقتصاد السعودي بحالة الكفاف التي سادت في الماضي وبدأت ترسية دعائم التنمية لإقامة اقتصاد حديث.

[40]

NOTES

1. In Arabic, the structure مرحلة جديدة من مراحل is a highly idiomatic way of rendering the English indefinite: 'a new phase . . . '.

2. In English, focusing on the 'the three phases' in subject position, together with the present perfect, may help in preserving the full force of this pseudo-substantiation + قد + the past tense: 'the three phases through which the economy has already passed have together laid . . . '.

3. This is a feature of Arabic expository style which may be rendered in English simply as: 'This phase was the longest . . . '.

4. In this kind of text, linkers such as ومع ذلك are merely discourse-organizational and, as such, are best left out in English: 'A number of

127

achievements stand to the credit of this period . . . '.

GLOSSARY

General survey of the economy	عرض عام للحالة الاقتصادية
With the year . . .	بحلول العام المالي . . .
phase	مرحلة
have together laid down	ساهمت جميعها بوضع
a strong foundation	الأسس الراسخة
the country's sustained economic growth	للنمو المستقر والمتوازن لاقتصاد البلاد
in the long term	على المدى البعيد
the unification of the country	توحيد البلاد
and lasted until	وانتهت بـ . . .
the successful implementation of	التطبيق الناجح
the stabilization programme	برنامج التوازن والاستقرار
covering a span of more than	واستغرقت فترة زمنية تزيد عن
a quarter of a century	الربع قرن
the discovery of oil	اكتشاف الزيت
provided the resources	توفير الموارد
turned the wheel of economic development	حركت عجلة . . .
the most challenging	أكثرها مشقة وتحدياً
began with extremely limited resources	قد بدأت بموارد محدودة جداً
rich in values and aspirations	غنية بقيمها وتطلعاتها
had virtually no infrastructure	فإنها في الحقيقة كانت تفتقر لتجهيزات البنية الأساسية
the potential for development	امكانيات التنمية
oil revenues were inadequate	إيرادات الزيت لم تكن كافية
the task ahead was difficult	كان س أمام مهمة طويلة وشاقة
a full-fledged government machinery	جهاز حكومي متكامل
socio-economic change	التغيير الاجتماعي والاقتصادي
broke the link with	انقطعت صلة س بـ . . .
with is subsistence past	حالة الكفاف التي سادت في الماضي
the foundations were being laid	بدأت ترسية دعائم
the development of a modern economy	التنمية لإقامة اقتصاد حديث

TEXT 9B (iii)

كلمة معالي نائب رئيس الوزراء وزير الخارجية الأردني
أمام مجلس الجامعة العربية في القاهرة

أود في البداية القول إنني ما كنت لأتأخر أمس عن اجتماعكم لولا أن استبقاني جلالة الملك بمعيته[1] وهو يجري اتصالاته مع اخوانه القادة العرب للعمل على احتواء الوضع الذي بدأنا نواجه فجر أمس.

وكان أن حضرت في معية جلالته للقاء[2] أخيه سيادة الرئيس محمد حسني مبارك وأنني لا أرى حاجة الى شرح طبيعة علاقتنا بأشقائنا في العراق والكويت. < ... >

منذ اللحظات الأولى لسماعنا بالتطورات، بادر جلالة الملك الحسين وعلى الفور إلى الاتصال مع أشقائه للتفكير معهم في كيفية احتواء الأزمة عربياً، لأننا نعرف مدى تأثرنا كأمة في أمننا واستقرارنا بأية مضاعفات. < ... >

لقد عاد جلالة الملك حسين لتوه من بغداد وأود أن أبلغكم نبأ الاتفاق على عقد القمة المرجوة في المملكة العربية السعودية يوم الأحد القادم، بحضور المعنيين باحتواء الأزمة وإيجاد الحل المناسب. أنا أتفق مع ما قاله الأخ أبو اللطف وسواه في جلسة الأمس بإن الموضوع يتطلب المعالجة من قبل القادة، والآن بما أنه تم والحمد لله الاتفاق على موعد لقاءهم، فالمؤمل ألا يجري ما يمكن أن يزيد من صعوبة الوضع وتعقيده ويجعل مهمة القادة أكثر صعوبة، ان لم تكن مستحيلة.

[41]

NOTES

1. The dominant rhetorical function here is 'apologizing', which the literal rendering: 'I wish to say that I would not have missed . . . etc.' simply would not serve. Instead: 'I would first of all like to apologize for not having been able to attend your meeting yesterday. I was with His Majesty . . . '.

2. The relationship between this sentence and the preceding discourse must be made explicit as it is opaque if literally handled: 'I was also at the meeting which His Majesty had with . . . '.

GLOSSARY

Address by X to Y	كلمة س أمام ص
Deputy Premier	نائب رئيس الوزراء
first of all	في البداية
while he contacted	وهو يجري اتصالاته
his fellow Arab leaders	اخوانه القادة العرب
with a view to containing the situation	للعمل على احتواء الوضع
we have been facing since early yesterday morning	الذي بدأنا نواجه فجر أمس
as soon as we heard	منذ اللحظات الأولى لسماعنا
HM immediately initiated contact	بادر س وعلى الفور الاتصال مع
in order to find a way	للتفكير معهم في كيفية
to contain the crisis	لاحتواء الأزمة
within an Arab context	عربياً
we realize the extent to which	نعرف مدى
our security as a nation may be affected	تأثرنا كأمة في أمننا
any further development	بأية مضاعفات
has just returned	عاد لتوه
I wish to inform you of an agreement	وأود أن أبلغكم نبأ الاتفاق
in the presence of those concerned	بحضور المعنيين
find the appropriate solution	وإيجاد الحل المناسب
what X and others said	ما قاله س وسواه
the matter requires the involvement of	يتطلب المعالجة من قبل القادة
it is hoped that nothing will happen	المؤمل أن لا يجري ما يمكن
that may render their task that much more difficult	أن يجعل مهمة القادة أكثر صعوبة

III. Bearing in mind the distinctive features of the various forms of personalized reporting studied so far, translate Texts 9A (i), 9A (ii) and 9A (iii) (reproduced here for easier reference) into Arabic.

TEXT 9A (i)

Report of the Auditors to the Proprietors
Edinburgh, 28th April 1992[1]

We have audited the accounts of the Bank of Scotland presented on pages 50 to 70 in accordance with Auditing Standards. In our opinion the accounts give a true and fair view of the state of affairs of the Bank and of the Group at 29th February 1992 and of the profit and cash flows of the Group for the year then ended and have been properly prepared in accordance with the Companies Act 1985.

NOTES

1. Like its Arabic counterpart, this kind of report is highly formulaic and a cliché-for-cliché translation would be called for.

GLOSSARY

Report of the Auditors	تقرير مدققي الحسابات
to the Proprietors	السادة المساهمون
presented on pages	الواردة على صفحة س
cash flows	السيولة النقدية
have been properly prepared	تم إعدادها وفق الأصول المرعية
Companies Act	قانون الشركات

TEXT 9A (ii)

UN Secretary-General's Annual Report
to the General Assembly

At the beginning of this year, I undertook a special effort to pursue the convening of an international peace conference on the Middle East. With the widespread support of the international community, I held numerous consultations with the parties and the members of the Security Council. These consultations focused on both the principle of a conference and questions of procedure. The views expressed to me differed in nuance and detail, but[1] it was generally hoped that they could be sufficiently narrowed to make possible the convening of a conference at which the more difficult substantive issues could be tackled in a constructive spirit. Unfortunately, it has not yet proved possible to obtain the agreement of all the parties to the principle of an international conference and this[2] has hindered my efforts to make progress on the procedural issues. Bilateral efforts to promote the peace process have also apparently run into difficulties. In spite of these set-backs the search must by all means be sustained for a comprehensive settlement through a negotiating process, under United Nations auspices, in which all parties would participate.

NOTES

1. In keeping with the conventions of reporting in both English and Arabic, this concessive structure, which is here unmotivated, may be subdued as follows: غير أنه كان من المؤمل لدى جميع الأطراف.

2. The connection 'and this' may be pragmatically glossed as: مما أعاق جهودي.

GLOSSARY

undertook a special effort	بذلت جهداً خاصاً
to pursue the convening of	في متابعة مسألة عقد
held numerous consultations	عقدت العديد من المشاورات
consultations focused on	وركزت هذه المشاورات
questions of procedure	المسائل الإجرائية
differed in nuance and detail	تباينت من حيث التركيز والتفاصيل
it was generally hoped	كان من المؤمل
could be sufficiently narrowed to	يكون بالامكان تقريب وجهات النظر
the more difficult substantive issues	المسائل الجوهرية الأكثر تعقيداً
Unfortunately, it has not yet proved possible	ولسوء الحظ لم يكن حتى الآن بالإمكان
hindered my efforts	أعاق جهودي
make progress on	تحقيق التقدم
Bilateral efforts	الجهود الثنائية
have apparently run into difficulties	كما تعثرت أيضاً على ما يبدو (الجهود . . .)
set-backs	العقبات
the search must be sustained	أن يستمر البحث
through a negotiating process	من خلال عملية المفاوضات
under United Nations auspices	برعاية الأمم المتحدة

TEXT 9A (iii)

Norman Schwartzkopf's Memoirs
The Gulf War Ceasefire

I looked at the map. 'OK.[1] Let's go with Safwan airfield' [as a possible site for the ceasefire talks with the Iraqis]. Safwan was the Iraqi military landing strip just north of the Kuwaiti border and only two miles from the road junction I'd ordered the US VII Corps to take the morning before.

Minutes later [General John] Yeosock called back. 'We don't have any forces there.'

I stared hard at the situation map. The entire sector around the airfield was clearly marked as being held by us. I'd also been given confirmation reports to that effect when I'd arrived in the war room that morning. 'If we're not on the airfield itself, we must have units nearby, right? Just move some troops into that area'. Yeosock said he would.

I was becoming uneasy. Safwan was in a sector crucial to our ability to block the escape of Iraqi heavy equipment from Kuwait and root out any remaining Scud storage bunkers. I'd assumed our forces had spent the time since the shooting stopped doing just that.[2] Now I wasn't so sure.

Then Yeosock called back and confirmed my worst fears: we had nobody at Safwan – not at the airfield and not at the nearby mountain where the Scuds were reportedly hidden, let alone at the road junction I had explicitly ordered the army to take. Helicopters had flown combat patrols along the highway and had reported no enemy forces, he said, but troops had never set foot in the sector. I felt as though I'd been punched in the gut.

NOTES

1. This kind of text is normally heavy on pragmatic/attitudinal meaning which has to be made explicit in Arabic. For example, the function of both the quotation marks and 'OK' must be made explicit: وقلت موافقاً على مضض. Also the explicitly marked and implicit قصر must be brought out clearly.

2. An implicit adversative.

GLOSSARY

'OK, Let's go with Safwan . . .'	وقلت موافقاً على مضض «تريدون صفوان، فليكن ...».
just north	لا يبعد سوى مسافة قصيرة عن الشمال
and only two miles from	كما لا يبعد سوى ميلين عن
road junction	ملتقى الطرق
the US VII Corps	الفيلق السابع الأمريكي
ordered X to take	أمرت س باحتلال
the morning before	قبل يوم واحد لا أكثر
called back	اتصل هاتفياً ليقول
I stared hard at	حدقت ملياً
the situation map	خارطة الموقع
The entire sector	القاطع بأكمله
clearly marked	كان قد تم تحديده على أنه
held by us	تحت سيطرتنا
confimation reports to that effect	تقارير تؤكد تلك الحقيقة
war room	غرفة العمليات
we must have X, right . . . ?	أليس من المنطقي أن أتوقع أن تكون لدينا ...؟
Just move some troops into	إذاً ما عليك إلا أن تحرك بعض القوات إلى
said he would	وهو أمر رد عليه س بالإيجاب
I was becoming uneasy	ازداد قلقي
a sector crucial to	قاطعاً حيوياً بالنسبة
block the escape	إعاقة تهريب (تسريب)
root out	استئصال
the remaining Scud storage bunkers	ما تبقى من مستودعات صواريخ سكد تحت الأرض
Now I wasn't so sure	لكني بدأت الآن أفقد الثقة في ذلك
confirmed my worst fears	مؤكداً أسوأ مخاوفي
we had nobody	لم تكن لدينا أي قوات
not at . . . and not at . . .	لا في ... ولا في ...
where X were reportedly hidden	التي يقال إن س خبأ فيها
let alone at	ناهيك عن
I explicitly ordered X to take	كنت قد أصدرت أوامر واضحة للجيش باحتلاله
Helicopters had flown	وكانت الطائرات المروحية قد قامت بالفعل بـ

134

combat patrols	دوريات ميدانية
reported no enemy forces	ولم تفد بوجود أية قوات معادية
but	إلا أنه استدرك قائلاً
X had never set foot in	أن القوات لم تطأ قدماً
as though I'd been punched in the gut	شعرت كمن طُعِنَ في الصميم

UNIT NINE: Additional Texts

I. Bearing in mind the distinctive features of the Report (the Formulaic, the Executive and the Personalized), translate Texts 9C (i), 9C (ii) and 9C (iii) into English.

TEXT 9C (i)

إحياء ذكرى رئيس كينيا الراحل فخامة السيد جوموكينياتا

قام رئيس المؤتمر العالمي لمكافحة العنصرية بالنيابة عن المؤتمر[1] بإرسال البرقية التالية إلى وزير خارجية كينيا: طلب إلي المؤتمر العالمي لمكافحة العنصرية المنعقد في جنيف أن أقدم لكم والى حكومة وشعب كينيا من خلالكم أخلص التعازي في وفاة «مزي» جوموكينياتا. لقد كان الراحل حقاً أباً لهذه الأمة والصانع الأول لتحرير افريقيا من الاستعمار.

إن هدف هذا المؤتمر[2] هو استئصال العنصرية والتمييز العنصري. وقد كان هذا هدف من أهداف السياسة الرئيسية التي صبا إليها الرئيس كينياتا. وسوف تظل ذكراه وما ضربه من مثل مصدر إلهام لنا جميعاً في هذا العمل المتواصل.

[2]

NOTES

1. Adverbial to be fronted cataphorically: 'On behalf of the conference, the president sent . . . '.

2. As we have consistently recommended, this Nominal deviation from expository norm must be responded to through a texture that slightly marks this departure: 'This conference has as its objective . . . ' and not, e.g., simply: 'The objective of this conference is . . . '.

GLOSSARY

tribute to the memory of	احياء ذكرى
the late president of Kenya	رئيس كينيا الراحل
His Excellency	فخامة
the following telegram	البرقية التالية
X has asked me to	طلب الى س أن
offer to you	أقدم لكم
and through you to X and Y	وإلى س و ص من خلالكم
its most sincere condolences	أخلص التعازي
on the occasion of the passing of	في وفاة
he was truly the father of the nation	لقد كان حقاً أباً لهذه الأمة
a prime architect of	الصانع الأول لـ
the emancipation of Africa	تحرير افريقيا
colonialism	الاستعمار
eradication	استئصال
his memory	ذكراه
his example	ما ضربه من مثل
an inspiration to us all	مصدر إلهام لنا جميعاً
in this continuing work	في هذا العمل المتواصل

TEXT 9C (ii)

تقرير مجلس الإدارة عن السنة المنتهية
في ٣١ كانون الأول/ ديسمبر ١٩٧٨

حضرات السادة المساهمين

يسر مجلس إدارة بنك قطر الوطني أن يقدم لكم تقريره السنوي الرابع عشر متضمناً الميزانية العامة وحساب الأرباح والخسائر للعام المالي المنتهي في ١٩٧٨/١٢/١٣م.

إنه لمن دواعي سرورنا القول بإن السنة المالية قيد العرض قد شهدت تقدماً ملموساً ومضطرداً في تحقيق زيادة مرتفعة في موجودات البنك وأرباحه ونمواً كبيراً في توسيع نشاطه العملي.

لقد بلغ مجمل موجودات البنك في نهاية السنة ٣,٣٨٥,٢١٥,٥٢٧ ريالاً قطرياً (باستثناء الحسابات التي لها مقابل «كونترا» والبالغة ١,٦٣٧,٥٨٢,٤٣٨ ريال قطري) في

136

مقابل مبلغ ۲،۰٤۲،۷٦۹،۱۰۲ ريال قطري بنهاية سنة ۱۹۷۷م. أي بزيادة بلغت نسبتها ٦٦٪ عن السنة السابقة.[1]

بلغ صافي الربح ٥۲،۲۹۳،۰٥٤ ريالاً مقابل ٤٥،٤۸٥،٤۸٥ ريالاً تحققت عام ۱۹۷۷ أي بزيادة مقدارها ۱٥٪ وذلك بعد اقتطاع جميع المصاريف والاحتياطات المتعلقة بالطوارئ، وقبل استقطاع الاحتياطي القانوني والاحتياطي الخاص البالغين ٤۳،۹٥۸،۲۱۰ ريال من أصل الأرباح المحققة.

لقد تم اعتماد مبلغ ۸،٤۰۰،۰۰۰ ريال ليوزع حصص أرباح على حملة أسهم البنك بنسبة ۲۰٪ من رأس المال الذي تمت زيادته في ۱۹۷۸/۱/۱م بمبلغ ۱٤ مليون ريال ليصبح ۳۲ مليون ريال، بينما تم توزيع مبلغ ٥،٦۰۰،۰۰۰ ريال ليصبح حصص أرباح لعام ۱۹۸۸م عن رأس المال في تلك السنة والبالغ ۲۸ مليون ريال.

[37]

NOTES

1. This entire chunk may be more neatly expressed in English as follows: 'Total assets of QR. 3,385,615,527 (excluding contra items of liability totalling QR. 1,637,582,438) reflect an increase of 66% on the previous year's figure of QR. 2,042,769,102.'

GLOSSARY

Report of the Board of Directors	تقرير مجلس الإدارة
to the Shareholders	حضرات السادة المساهمين
for the year ended 31st December	عن السنة المنتهية في ۳۱ كانون الأول
X is pleased to present	يسر س أن يقدم لكم
the balance sheet	الميزانية العامة
profit and loss account	حساب الأرباح والخسائر
It is a pleasure to report	إنه لمن دواعي سرورنا القول بإن
the year under review	السنة المالية قيد العرض
has seen yet another period	قد شهدت
spectacular growth	تقدماً ملموساً ومضطرداً في تحقيق زيادة مرتفعة في
with regard to assets	في موجودات البنك
profitability	أرباح
expansion in operational activity	نمواً كبيراً في نشاطه العملي

total assets	مجمل الموجودات
excluding contra items of liability	باستثناء الحسابات التي لها مقابل «كونترا»
net profit	صافي الربح
charging all expenses	بعد اقتطاع جميع المصاريف
making provisions for contingencies	(بعد اقتطاع) الاحتياطات المتعلقة بالطوارئ
transfer to statutory reserve of . . .	استقطاع الاحتياطي القانوني البالغ
special reserve of . . .	الاحتياطي الخاص البالغ
a dividend of . . .	حصص الأرباح
has been approved for payment	تم اعتماد . . . ليوزع (حصص أرباح)

TEXT 9C (iii)

ذل السيجارة

أقلعت عن التدخين ألف مرة، وعدت إليه ألف مرة ومرة.

وكنت أدخن مائة وعشرين سيجارة في اليوم، ولم أكن استعمل عود الكبريت إلا مرة أو مرتين في اليوم. وذات ليلة في شهر ديسمبر كانت الأمطار تسقط بغزارة في القاهرة وأصوات الرعد والبرق تهز فراشي، واستيقظت لأدخن سيجارة وفوجئت[1] أن البيت ليس فيه سيجارة واحدة. وكانت الساعة الرابعة صباحاً فقمت من فراشي وارتديت ملابسي ووضعت حول عنقي كوفية من الصوف وغطيت نفسي بمعطف ثقيل ونزلت إلى الشارع أبحث عن دكان سجائر أشتري منه الدخان أو فاعل خير يمشي في الشارع أشحذ منه سيجارة.[2] ووجدت كل الدكاكين مغلقة ولم أجد أحداً في الشارع يدخن سيجارة وركبت سيارتي ومضيت أبحث عن محل سجائر مفتوح. وبعد نصف ساعة وجدت محلاً في ميدان التحرير اشتريت منه علبة سجائر.

وعدت إلى بيتي وفي فمي سيجارة وكنت أسعد رجل في العالم ولكن عدت ومعي برد شديد أبقاني في الفراش سبعة أيام.

ثم دخلت السجن، وفي السجن كانوا يضايقوني بالتحكم في عدد سجائري. مرة يسمحون لي بعشر سجائر في اليوم، وفي اليوم التالي يجعلونها سيجارة واحدة، ثم خمس سجائر ثم لا سجائر. وشعرت بذلال عجيب لم أعرف مثله طول حياتي.

[42]

138

NOTES

1. To bring out the contrast, an adversative together with the expression of strong feeling must be used: 'But to my dismay . . . '.

2. Once again, an adversative is used to relay the contrast: 'But I found all the shops closed . . . '.

GLOSSARY

the degradation of wanting a cigarette	ذل السيجارة
I've given up smoking	أقلعت عن التدخين
a thousand times	ألف مرة
I've gone back to it	وعدت إليه
I used to smoke	كنت أدخن
I only used to need a match once or twice	لم أكن أستعمل عود الكبريت إلا مرة أو مرتين
one night in December	وذات ليلة في شهر ديسمبر
the rain was bucketing down	كانت الأمطار تسقط بغزارة
the roar of thunder and lightning	أصوات الرعد والبرق
were shaking my bed	تهز فراشي
I found there was not a single cigarette in the house	أن البيت ليس فيه سيجارة واحدة
put on some clothes	ارتديت ملابسي
wrapped a woollen scarf around my neck	وضعت حول عنقي كوفية من الصوف
a tobacconist	دكان سجائر
a charitable passer-by	فاعل خير
from whom I might beg	أشحذ منه
I got into my car	ركبت سيارتي
went off looking for	ومضيت أبحث
and felt like the happiest man in the world	وكنت أسعد رجل في العالم
brought back a terrible cold	عدت ومعي برد شديد
then I went to prison	ثم دخلت السجن
annoy me by controlling	يضايقوني بالتحكم في
at one time . . . , the next time . . . , then . . . , then	مرة . . . وفي اليوم التالي . . . ثم . . .

139

I've never felt so degraded
   in all my life

وشعرت بإذلال عجيب لم أعرف مثله طول حياتي

II. Texts 9D (i), 9D (ii) and 9D (iii) illustrate the three modes of reporting
in English. Translate into Arabic.

TEXT 9D (i)

Message addressed to the President of the Conference
by the President of the Council of State of Guinea-Bissau

On behalf of the people and the Council of State of Guinea-Bissau, and on
my own behalf, I have the honour to send cordial greetings to Your
Excellency, and through you to all the delegations participating in this
important Conference.

   In reaffirming our total support for the objectives of the Conference,
which constitute a common goal for the developing countries, we hope that
irreversible progress will be made towards new forms of cooperation, while
recognizing the importance of the continuation of an effective North-South
dialogue with a view to the acceleration of independent national economic
development of our countries for the benefit of our peoples and humanity as
a whole.

   With best wishes for success.

(Signed) Luis CABRAL

[14]

GLOSSARY

Message addressed to X by Y	رسالة موجهة من س الى ص
the Council of State of	مجلس الدولة
On behalf of . . .	بالنيابة عن
on my own behalf	بالأصالة عن نفسي
to send cordial greetings	أرسل تحياتي الصادقة
to Your Excellency	لسعادتكم
In reaffirming our total support	اننا وإذ نؤكد من جديد دعمنا الكامل
constitute a common goal for	تشكل هدفاً مشتركاً
irreversible progress	تقدماً مضطرداً
the continuation of an effective dialogue	مواصلة حوار بنّاء

with a view to

the acceleration of development

With best wishes for success

من أجل

دفع عجلة التنمية

مع خالص تمنياتي لكم بالنجاح

TEXT 9D (ii)

CHAIRMAN'S STATEMENT

In my last statement, I said[1] that 1991 would be a very challenging year. In the event, the advertising industry suffered from some of the worst trading conditions for over 40 years, with total spending declining by 3% in constant prices. To compound the industry-wide problems, the Group started 1991 in a weak financial position, with an inappropriate management structure and a lack of focus in many of the operating units.

I am pleased to be able to report[2] that we have made considerable progress in addressing these problems despite the lack of evidence in the advertising industry. The outlook for 1992 is for stability,[3] although the US market is expected to remain challenging.

The Recapitalization was successfully completed in April 1991,[4] thus providing a sounder financial base for the future. As a result, we are able to turn our attention to the operating units and carry out a widespread restructuring of management and operations. The new structures have reduced costs, improved efficiencies and clarified reporting lines within the Group. They have been designed to focus management's attention on their areas of expertise and to allow them to concentrate on serving their clients.

(. . .)

Maurice Saatchi
Chairman

[43]

NOTES

1. To convey the personalized element adequately, *last* and *said* may be fused to yield something like: سبق أن قلت في كلمتي الأخيرة.

2. A subtle, implicit adversative can be perceived at this juncture. In Arabic, we would have made this connection more explicit and opted for something like: وبالرغم من هذا. However, in this kind of text, the primary function is less to report than to impress, and the intended subtlety may

141

.إنه ليسعدني أن أفيدكم علماً بأننا. . . :thus be preserved by, for example

3. The discourse seems to flow better when this element is given end-
    position: وعلى الرغم من أن السوق الأمريكية من المتوقع أن تظل غير مشجعة فإن
    هناك ما يشير إلى أن عام ١٩٩٢ سيكون عام استقرار.

4. The 'completion' together with the date may best be rendered as a
    fronted adverbial: . . . وبحلول أبريل ١٩٩١ تم بنجاح إعادة بناء رأس المال.

GLOSSARY

Chairman's Statement	كلمة رئيس مجلس الادارة
a very challenging year	عاماً عسيراً
In the event	وفعلاً
some of the worst trading conditions	ظروف كان بعضها من أسوأ ما شهده السوق
total spending declined by 3%	هبط إجمالي . . . بنسبة
in constant prices	من الأسعار الثابتة
To compound problems	ومما فاقم المشاكل التي عانى منها
industry-wide problems	قطاع الإعلان برمته
weak financial position	وضع مالي ضعيف
inappropriate management structure	بنية إدارية غير ملائمة
a lack of focus in many units	عدم تمكن الوحدات المختلفة من وضع أهداف محددة
operating units	الوحدات الميدانية
to be able to report	يسعدني أن أفيدكم
made considerable progress	تحقيق تقدم ملموس
in addressing these problems	في مواجهة هذه الصعوبات
lack of evidence in	وإن لم تظهر أية مؤشرات واضحة
Recapitalization	إعادة بناء رأس المال
thus providing	مما وفر
sounder . . . for the future	قاعدة مالية أقوى تحسباً للمستقبل
turn our attention	نوجه اهتمامنا
widespread restructuring	إعادة هيكلة . . . على نطاق واسع
clarified reporting lines	جعل قنوات الاتصال أكثر وضوحاً
focus management's attention on	تركيز اهتمام الإدارة
their areas of expertise	مجالات اختصاصاتها
concentrate on serving their clients	تمكينها من التركيز على خدمة عملائها

142

TEXT 9D (iii)

From Lord Carrington's Memoirs

January 1981 found us in Morocco, and from there[1] we flew to Egypt for conversations with President Sadat. Sadat at that time had faith in the ability of the Perez Government in Israel to come to some sort of settlement with the Arabs.[2] He believed that Saudi Arabia and Jordan should be associated with his long, difficult peace negotiations by the end of 1981, perhaps – but not yet.[3] Sadat was an impressive man of great charm and geniality whom I had met before and always liked. I told him I had admired his instant hospitality to the Shah, when the latter appeared after his fall friendless in a once welcoming, even sycophantic world. Sadat shrugged. What else, he asked, could one do?[4]

We had two days in hand after the Egyptian visit and booked cabins on a Nile steamer, through Luxor. It was necessary to keep in touch with London in case of crisis and the embassy in Cairo had detached a young man to keep communication with us by driving along the bank sufficiently near our boat. The Ambassador was with us.

At about eleven o'clock one evening some apparently urgent message came through. The young man motored up and down what might in other conditions be called the tow-path and eventually saw what he supposed was our boat.

[44]

NOTES

1. To sustain evaluative narrative, fronting this adverbial in Arabic is most appropriate: .ومن هناك استقلينا الطائرة إلى مصر

2. This is a coordinated detail which, to be brought/out, must be initiated thus: .كما كان يعتقد أيضاً أن السعودية والأردن ينبغي

3. The pragmatics of this utterance must be glossed with the gloss placed parenthetically to modify the date, thus: ربما بحلول نهاية عام ١٩٨١ ولكن .ليس قبل ذلك

4. To portray this entire scene, extensive glossing may be necessary:

وهنا هز السادات كتفيه وقد أحرجه بعض الشيء وقال «. . . ما عسى المرء .أن يفعل في ظرف كهذا»

GLOSSARY

January 1981 found us in Morocco	دخل علينا يناير ٨١ ونحن في المغرب
for conversations with	للتحدث مع
Sadat at that time had faith in. . .	وكان السادات آنذاك على ثقة من مقدرة حكومة
to come to some sort of settlement with	على التوصل الى نوع من التسوية مع
an impressive man	رجلاً مثيراً للإعجاب
of great charm and geniality	دمث الأخلاق محبوباً
and always liked	وأثار إعجابي دائماً
his instant hospitality to	باستضافته العفوية لـ . . .
appeared after his fall friendless	بعد سقوطه وحيداً منبوذاً
in a once welcoming, even sycophantic world	في عالم متملق زائف كان يوماً ما
	يتظاهر له بكل الحب
We had two days in hand	وجدنا أنفسنا غير مرتبطين بأي التزام ليومين آخرين
booked cabins	حجزنا مقصورات
a Nile steamer, through Luxor	باخرة تمخر عرض النيل عبر الأقصر
to keep in touch with London	لنكون على اتصال بلندن
in case of crisis	تحسباً من حدوث أزمة
the embassy had detached X	انتدبت السفارة س
driving along the bank	كان يقود سيارته على طول الشاطئ
sufficiently near	على مقربة من

PART III: *Translating Argumentation*

OVERVIEW

As we have hopefully been able to demonstrate so far, literal translation is most appropriate for the ultra-detached kind of texts such as those encountered in legal documents. The literal approach has had to be gradually relaxed as different kinds of texts emerged allowing varied degrees of 'evaluativeness', 'emotiveness', etc. Like detachment, a certain degree of evaluativeness is thus inevitable in almost any kind of text. However, a text type whose primary focus is on 'persuasion', and one for which the success of a purely literal approach to translation is not always guaranteed, is argumentation. The context for argumentation specifies that the intention is one of comparing, contrasting and assessing concepts in order to reach a verdict (rightly of wrongly) regarding what is to be favoured. This act of 'managing' may be compared with exposition, whose primary objective is to 'monitor' a situation and portray it as explicitly as one can.

Managing determines its own text-structure formats. Setting a scene and reviewing the various aspects of the scene is a format that cannot be effective in acts of persuasion because it is least involved. Here, what is required is setting a 'tone' and critically evaluating the content of what is being postulated as the point of departure for a given argument.

Thus, on the one hand, we may put forward a thesis in which we, rightly or wrongly, believe passionately. This thesis is normally followed by an extensive defence. For example: 'It is not only conceivable but inevitable

145

that . . . Take X, for example . . .' (see the Through-argument: Units Ten and Eleven).

Alternatively, we may put forward someone else's thesis and one by which we are least convinced, in which case the text would be formated as follows: thesis cited, followed by our opposition and a substantiation of the stance we have adopted. For example: 'Indeed, it is conceivable that . . . However, a more constructive approach would be to . . .' (see the Implicit Counter-argument: Unit Thirteen). The signal for the opposition may sometimes be suppressed (see the Suppressed Counter-argument: Unit Fourteen).

Finally, we may cite someone's unsavoury thesis and, in citing it, express our reservation explicitly. For example: 'While it is conceivable that . . ., a more constructive approach would be to . . .'. Here, our opposition, which would be detailed once the initial thesis is disposed of, does not have to wait as it does in counter-arguments (see the Explicit Counter-argument: Unit Twelve).

To relay these subtle and at times highly opaque sets of intentions, the texture of argumentative texts is bound to be least explicit. Diction will be subtle and vocabulary highly emotive. Syntax will be intricate and word order highly marked. In short, aspects of text construction with which we have had no cause to deal in exposition (e.g. cleft sentences: 'It is X which . . .') will be very prominent, relaying all kinds of complex and important rhetorical meanings.

UNIT TEN:
The Less Involved Through-argument

I. Consider Text 10A (i) as an example of a legal Article and one on the basis of which the other two texts were developed: Text 10A (ii) is an example of an expository Summary; and Text 10A (iii) is an example of a Through-argument and one which continues from Text 10A (ii). Reflect on the subtle differences of texture and structure.

TEXT 10 A (i)

المادة السابعة والعشرون

أ. الشريعة الإسلامية هي المصدر الأساسي الذي تستند اليه محكمة العدل الإسلامية الدولية في أحكامها. (. . .)

[1]

TEXT 10 A (ii)

قضايا كبرى

يثير إنشاء المحكمة الإسلامية عدداً من القضايا المهمة نعرض لاثنين منها تتسمان بالطابع العملي وهما:

أولاً: تقوم المحكمة على أساس الشريعة الإسلامية ويختار قضاتها من فقهاء الشريعة ذوي الخبرة في مجال القانون الدولي ذلك أن أحكام المحكمة وفتاواها سوف تستند إلى الشريعة الإسلامية وإلى مصادر القانون الدولي العام إذا أعوز القضاة النص الشرعي. على أن لا تتناقض قواعد القانون الدولي المطبقة مع أحكام الشريعة. (. . .)

[23]

TEXT 10 A (iii)

قضايا كبرى

(. . .)

والحق أن اختيار الشريعة الإسلامية أساساً لاختيار القضاة، واستنباط الأحكام، يطرح قضية بالغة الأهمية، ذات جانبين، أولهما ضرورة تنشئة عدد من القضاة الذين يجمعون بين التمكن من علوم الشريعة، ومن القانون الدولي العام، وثانيهما ضرورة تقنين القانون الدولي الإسلامي، بحيث تتوافر لدينا قواعد صالحة للتطبيق في العلاقات الدولية، ومستمدة في الوقت نفسه من تراث الفقهاء المسلمين واجتهاداتهم عبر العصور من خلال النصوص الشرعية. وبديهي أن المحكمة، وهي هيئة قضائية دولية، ليست مختصة بتفسير أحكام الشريعة الإسلامية، إلا فيما يتعلق بالنزاع أو الحكم الصادر بشأنه.

[23]

II. Bearing in mind the distinctive features of objective through-arguments in Arabic, translate into Arabic the following text samples which follow on from one another. Text 10B (i) is an example of a legal Article, Text 10B (ii) is an example of an expository Summary based on the legal Article, and Text 10B (iii) is an example of an objective Through-argument.

TEXT 10 B (i)

Article 6
State Immunity

1. A State is[1] immune from the jurisdiction of another State in accordance with the provisions of the present articles.
2. Effect shall be given to State immunity in accordance with the provisions of the present articles.
[45]

NOTES

1. Here, the verbal elements *is* has the legal force which 'shall' enjoys in legal article construction and must thus be rendered using the present simple: . . . تتمتع أية دولة بحصانة من.

GLOSSARY

State Immunity	حصانة الدولة
immune from the jurisdiction	تتمتع س بالحصانة من الولاية القضائية
Effect shall be given	تكون . . . سارية المفعول

TEXT 10 B (ii)

Commentary

The formulation of a general rule of State immunity posed[1] serious problems due to[2] divergent views as to the theoretical foundations or contents of such a rule; various points of departure are available.[3] The rule of the immunity of one State from the jurisdiction of another could be formulated as an exception to the basic norm of territorial sovereignty. It could be seen[4] in terms of the interrelationships between various aspects of sovereignty: territorial sovereignty and national sovereignty or sovereignty equality among States. A formulation along those lines would involve an assumption or presumption of consent on the part of the State of the territory, not to exercise its jurisdiction over another equally sovereign State or its property, even though the latter State's activities may have been conducted in the territory of the former State.

[45]

NOTES

1. The verbal sentence structure is used here to relay the expository tone of the reporting summary: . . . أثارت صياغة.

2. To consolidate the expository tone, this subordinate sentence may be turned into a main verbal one: . . . ويعزى هذا إلى الشعب.

3. The connector here is a substantiator in form though not in function; it is merely a discourse-organizational device: . . . اذ أن هناك منطلقات.

4. To use a mere additive here (i.e. 'و') could be misleading as it presents

the element in question as further explanation of the preceding discourse. Such an erroneous impression may be blocked by the use of كما يمكن which signals that the element in question actually reads: 'It could also be seen'.

GLOSSARY

serious problems	مشاكل خطيرة
contents of	مضامين
an exception to the basic norm	استثناء من القاعدة الأساسية
territorial sovereignty	السيادة الإقليمية
interrelationships	صلات الترابط
the various aspects of	الجوانب المختلفة
sovereignty equality	المساواة في السيادة
assumption or presumption	افتراض أو تسليم
consent on the part of X	بأن س ترضى بـ . . . .
the State of the territory	الدولة صاحبة الإقليم
equally sovereign State	دولة أخرى مساوية لها في السيادة
the latter State	الدولة الأخيرة
the former State	الدولة الأولى

TEXT 10 B (iii)

As the topic is entitled 'Jurisdictional immunities of States and their property',[1] it would appear that the more appropriate approach would be to begin by examining the concept of State immunity itself. In that connection two or more theoretical trends might be perceived as to the contents of a rule of State immunity in contemporary international law. It might be held that there exists a universal and basic principle of State immunity from which might be carved exceptions under certain circumstances. It might also be held, on the other hand, that there is no such general rule, but rather various rules allowing State immunity in some circumstances and not allowing it in others. Yet[2] another position which might be held is that while[3] a general rule on State immunity may well exist, that general rule recognizing State immunity also comprises, at one and the same time, certain restrictions or exceptions to that immunity.

[45]

NOTES

1. The evaluative tone is set in Arabic by: (a) keeping the subordinate clause fronted; and (b) nominalizing the main clause: ولما كان عنوان الموضوع . . . فإن النهج الأنجع فيما يبدو هو . . .

2. This is an 'empty' device whose function is only discourse-organizational and should not be treated as an adversative: وثمة موقف آخر يمكن الأخذ به . . .

3. One way of handling this structure is to treat the 'while' subordinate clause as a main clause, leaving out 'while' and introducing the following clause with an adversative: وهو أنه قد تكون هناك فعلاً قاعدة عامة لحصانة الدولة ومع ذلك فإن تلك القاعدة العامة التي تقر بحصانة الدولة تتضمن . . .

GLOSSARY

examine the concept	بحث مفهوم
In that connection	في هذا السياق
two or more theoretical trends	اتجاهين أو أكثر من الاتجاهات النظرية
perceive	يتصور
contemporary	المعاصر
It might be held that	يمكن القول بإن
that there exists	ثمة (مبدأ عاماً)
a universal and basic principle	مبدأ عاماً وأساسياً
exceptions might be carved	قد ترد (فيه) استثناءات
on the other hand	من ناحية أخرى
but rather	بل بالأحرى
allowing	تجيز
comprises, at one and the same time,	تتضمن وفي نفس الوقت
certain restrictions to X	قيوداً معينة على
exceptions to X	استثنائات من . . .

III. Bearing in mind the distinctive features of through-argumentation in both English and Arabic, translate Texts 10 A (i), 10 A (ii) and 10 A (iii) (reproduced here for easier reference) into English.

TEXT 10A (i)

المادة السابعة والعشرون

أ. الشريعة الإسلامية هي¹ المصدر الأساسي الذي تستند إليه محكمة العدل الإسلامية الدولية في أحكامها. <...>

NOTES

1. Whereas in English, 'is' would carry the verbal binding element of this article, the Arabic would have been more consistent with legal writing had the legal 'is' been rendered as: . . . تعد/تعتبر الشريعة الإسلامية.

GLOSSARY

the Islamic *shari'a*	الشريعة الإسلامية
the main source	المصدر الأساسي
judgements	أحكام

TEXT 10A (ii)

قضايا كبرى

يثير¹ إنشاء المحكمة الإسلامية عدداً من القضايا المهمة نعرض لاثنين منها تتسمان² بالطابع العملي وهما:

أولاً: تقوم المحكمة على أساس الشريعة الإسلامية ويختار قضاتها من فقهاء الشريعة ذوي الخبرة في مجال القانون الدولي ذلك أن أحكام المحكمة وفتاواها سوف تستند إلى الشريعة الإسلامية وإلى مصادر القانون الدولي العام إذا أعوز القضاة النص الشرعي. على أن لا تتناقض قواعد القانون الدولي المطبقة مع أحكام الشريعة. (. . .)

NOTES

1. Observe the Verbal sentence structure as used for detached exposition in Arabic: يثير: 'has given rise'.

2. The relevance of يتسمان بالطابع العملي can only be established by making the cause-effect relationship explicit: 'as they pertain to the operational

aspects of the court's establishment'.

GLOSSARY

critical issues	قضايا كبرى
crucial issues	قضايا مهمة
two of which will occupy us here	نعرض لإثنين منها
Firstly	أولاً
is founded upon	تقوم المحكمة على أساس
expert jurisprudents	فقهاء الشريعة
who have wide experience in	ذوي الخبرة في مجال
this is due to the fact that	ذلك أن
edicts	فتاوى
which complement the Islamic legal text	إذا أعوز القضاة النص الشرعي
this is provided that	على أن
do not conflict with	لا تتناقض
rules of international law	قواعد القانون الدولي
provisions of Islamic law	أحكام الشريعة

TEXT 10 A (iii)

قضايا كبرى

(. . .)

والحق أن¹ اختيار الشريعة الإسلامية أساساً لاختيار القضاة، واستنباط الأحكام، يطرح قضية بالغة الأهمية، ذات جانبين، أولهما ضرورة تنشئة عدد من القضاة الذين يجمعون بين التمكن من علوم الشريعة، ومن القانون الدولي العام، وثانيهما ضرورة تقنين القانون الدولي الإسلامي، بحيث تتوافر لدينا قواعد صالحة للتطبيق في العلاقات الدولية، ومستمدة في الوقت نفسه من تراث الفقهاء المسلمين واجتهاداتهم عبر العصور من خلال النصوص الشرعية. وبديهي أن المحكمة، وهي هيئة قضائية دولية،² ليست مختصة بتفسير أحكام الشريعة الإسلامية، إلا فيما يتعلق بالنزاع أو الحكم الصادر بشأنه.

NOTES

1. Observe the Nominal structure involved in argumentation: والحق أن اتخاذ
الشريعة أساساً . . . يطرح قضية بالغة الأهمية.

2. This is a قصر and has to be used to stress the positive aspects: 'is competent to interpret the provisions of Islamic law but only in so far as these relate to a particular conflict or the judgement issued regarding it . . .'.

GLOSSARY

the choice of judges	اختيار القضاة
the derivation of judgements	استنباط الأحكام
this is twofold	ذات جانبين
the need to prepare	ضرورة تنشئة
who combine competence in X with	الذين يجمعون بين التمكن من ومن
the second aspect of this issue	وثانيهما
the need to codify	ضرورة تقنين
applicable rules for the regulation of	قواعد صالحة للتطبيق في . . .
X will have to be derived from	ومستمدة من
the heritage of jurisprudents	تراث الفقهاء
their scholarly endeavours	واجتهاداتهم
in interpreting legal texts	من خلال النصوص الشرعية
throughout the ages	عبر العصور
here it goes without saying	وبديهي
an international judicial body	هيئة قضائية دولية

UNIT TEN: Additional Texts

I. Texts 10C, which illustrates through-argumentation in Arabic, is taken from an academic article, 'The Sociology of the Arab World'. Translate into English.

TEXT 10C

ان العصبية القبلية هي أهم مركبات الثقافة البدوية . فهي مناط الأمن في الصحراء والرجل الذي لا ينتمي الى قبيلة تحميه قد يكون مصيره الهلاك . ولذا فهو مضطر أن ينضمّ إلى قبيلة قوية عن طريق الولاء أو المكاتبة أو المحالفة، فهو من جانب يقوم بواجباته نحو القبيلة التي والاها، حيث يهب لنجدتها عندما تغزوها قبيلة أخرى ويشارك في أداء المغارم التي تفرض عليها . وهي من[1] جانبها تدافع عنه في حياته وتأخذ بثأره بعد قتله .

154

إن العصبية القبلية هي التي جعلت البدو أكثر من غيرهم اهتماماً بالنسب[2] وصيانة المرأة. فالنسب له أهميته عندهم لأنه يعرفهم بقيمة الفرد من حيث أصله وإلى أية قبيلة ينتمي. وهم كذلك يحرصون على صيانة المرأة لأن المرأة وعاء النسب. ولهذا فهم يسرعون إلى قتل المرأة عند الاشتباه بسلوكها. إن المرأة السيئة السلوك تدخل في دماء القبيلة دماءً غريبة عنها وهي بذلك تفسد الخصال النبيلة التي ورثتها القبيلة عن الآباء والأجداد. ومن هنا جاء تحذيرهم من الزواج بالمرأة الحسناء ذات النسب الوضيع حيث قالوا: «اياكم وخضراء الدمن» فهم بهذا المثل يشبهون الحسناء غير النسيبة بالزهرة التي تنبت في مزبلة.

[46]

NOTES

1. There is a need for a contrastive 'on the other hand . . .', which is a typically argumentative signal.

2. A cleft sentence to relay the force of the nominal: 'It is tribalism which . . .'; or a pseudo-cleft: 'Tribalism is what has made the bedouin more concerned than others about . . .'.

GLOSSARY

tribalism	العصبية القبلية
the most important element in	أحد أهم مركبات
bedouin culture	الثقافة البدوية
the fulcrum (mainstay) of security	مناط الأمن
is sure to perish	قد يكون مصيره الهلاك
he feels it necessary	فهو مضطر
powerful tribe	قبيلة قوية
through loyalty, clientage or alliance	عن طريق الولاء أو المكاتبة أو المحالفة
on his part, he	فهو من جانب
he would be performing	يقوم بـ (واجباته)
to which he has allied himself	التي والاها
he responds to its call for help	يهب لنجدتها
when invading	عندما تغزو
takes part in paying dues imposed	ويشارك في أداء المغارم التي تفرض
on the part of the tribe, on the other hand,	وهي من جانبها
it defends him while he is alive	تدافع عنه في حياته

avenges him when he is killed	وتأخذ بثأره بعد قتله
lineage	النسب
the chastity of woman	صيانة المرأة
lineage is important	فالنسب له أهميته عندهم
it makes them aware of	تعرّفهم
the worth of the individual	قيمة الفرد
in terms of his origin	من حيث أصله
they are careful not to overlook	فهم يحرصون على
the seedbed of lineage	وعاء النسب
they hasten to murder	يسرعون الى قتل
whose conduct is suspect	عند الاشتباه بسلوكها
a badly behaved woman	المرأة السيئة السلوك
only taints the purity	تدخل في . . . دماء غريبة عنها
and thus corrupts the noble traits	تفسد الخصال النبيلة
inherited from its ancestors	التي ورثتها عن الآباء والأجداد
it is in this context that they warned against	ومن هنا جاء تحذيرهم من الزواج
the very attractive but low-born woman	المرأة الحسناء ذات النسب الوضيع
Beware of the flower which grows in dung	إياكم وخضراء الدمن
grows on a rubbish tip	تنبت في مزبلة

II.   Text 10D is an example of a Through-argument in English. The sample
is taken from an academic article on 'Culture and Health'. Translate the
text into Arabic, bearing in mind the distinctive features of through-
argumentation in both English and Arabic.

TEXT 10D

Any health programme,[1] however sound, is liable to fail if those who
introduce it do not work to bridge the cultural gap between the trained
health worker and the people he serves.

Sickness introduces an entirely new dimension into any society. It is[2] an
unwelcome intruder, it threatens people, and it may lead to death. A society's
attitudes and practices in respect of the sick reflect its understanding and
interpretation of the causes of disease. In some societies it has been the
custom to isolate the sick and take no care of them. This practice probably
originated with infections such as smallpox or pulmonary tuberculosis,
which were often transmitted to members of the patient's family or others

living in the same compound. In many places, a basic reluctance to go near the sick can still[3] affect the behaviour of members of the health team, inclining them to neglect their patients.

Even if the patient is not neglected,[4] the form of treatment he receives is usually derived from the ideas of his society about the supposed cause of his illness. If supernatural or magical forces are thought to be the cause, recourse is had to traditional methods; if natural forces are considered responsible, a modern form of care may be chosen.

[47]

NOTES

1. To preserve both the attention-attracting function and the evaluative tone of this utterance, the Nominal is most appropriate: إن أي برنامج
   صحي أياً كان قدره من الصواب يغلب أن يخفق إذا . . .

2. Substantiation begins here and must be signalled appropriately: فهو
   دخيل مقيت.

3. Two elements must be distinguished here:

   (a) *still*, which is best attached to 'we can still see a basic reluctance': لا
   نزال نشهد نفوراً متأصلاً من;

   (b) *can*, which has 'probability' as its modal meaning and is best attached to 'can affect': ربما كان له أثر على سلوك.

4. The agent may be retrieved here as it is commonsensically known to be
   'the people': وحتى لو لم ينصرف الناس عن المريض

GLOSSARY

however sound	أياً كان قدره من الصواب
is liable to fail	يغلب أن يخفق
those who introduce it	أولئك المشرفين عليه
bridge the cultural gap	سد الفجوة الثقافية
introduces an entirely new dimension	يدخل بعداً جديداً كل الجدة
an unwelcome intruder	دخيل مقيت
attitudes and practices in respect of	مواقف س من . . . وتصرفاته إزاء . . .
understanding and interpretation	فهم وتفسير
In some societies, it has been the custom	نهجت بعض المجتمعات على

take no care of them	إهمال رعايته
probably	من المرجح
This practice originated	هذه العادة تكون قد نشأت
smallpox	الجدري
pulmonary tuberculosis	التدرن الرئوي
often transmitted	كانت في الغالب تتنقل
compound	مبنى
a basic reluctance	نفوراً متأصلاً
inclining them to	يدفعهم الى
derived from	مستمداً من
the supposed cause	ما يفترض أنه سبب . . .
supernatural or magical forces	قوى خارقة للطبيعة أو سحرية
recourse is had to	لجئوا إلى
a modern form of care	أسلوب الرعاية الحديث

UNIT ELEVEN:
The More Involved Through-argument

OVERVIEW

This form of argumentation is once again characterized by the statement of a thesis to be endorsed extensively. The only difference between through-arguments to be presented in this unit and those studied so far lies in the nature of the fields tackled (not highly technical, certainly), the tenor (semi-formal) and the mode (even when written, the subjective Through-argument sounds as though it were spoken).

I. Consider Texts 11A (i) and 11A (ii) as examples of through-arguments. The text samples are taken from the genre 'book review'. Note how exposition is allowed to creep into Text 11A (ii).

TEXT 11A (i)

فيما الدول الكبرى، صاحبة القرار، وعلى رأسها الولايات المتحدة، راعية محادثات السلام في عاصمتها واشنطن، تسعى الى حل قضية الشرق الأوسط وقلبها فلسطين، لا يزال بعض المتنورين يرى أن خط الأحداث سائر في الاتجاه المعاكس، لا إلى إعادة فلسطين والقدس، بل إلى تفكيك فلسطين وتدويل القدس.

هذا ما تبنى عرضه الباحث الفلسطيني واصف عبوشي في كتابه «تفكيك فلسطين». ومن كلمة فيه للمؤرخ الأمريكي مونتي بالمر أنه: «أفضل كتاب حتى اليوم عن دور بريطانيا في فلسطين . . .».

الكتاب بحث معمق وموثق عن الظرف الذي أدى ـ غداة الحرب العالمية الأولى ـ إلى إنشاء فلسطين ثم كيف آل الأمر إلى تفكيكها لمصلحة اسرائيل.

واصف عبوشي في كتابه، بعيد عن أية غوغائية أو ديماغوجية يغرق فيها الخطاب السياسي العربي في معالجة الأمور، التزم أن يخبر قراءه الغربيين كيف فلسطين صارت اسرائيل.

[30]

159

TEXT 11A (ii)

هذا الكتاب بين أيدينا هو تاريخ من وجهة نظر تأخذ جانب الحروب الصليبية التي دارت خلال الأعوام ١٠٩٤ و١١٨٤، وفيه تسجيل لتاريخ ملوك بيت المقدس الصليبيين. الكتاب أبرز وأهم المصادر التي وضعت في تلك الحروب فضلاً عن أنه بمثابة أقدم وثيقة غير إسلامية عن الفترة المؤرخ لها.

مؤلف الكتاب هو وليم الصوري المولود في العام ١١٣٠ والذي يعده الباحثون الأوروبيون واحداً من أعظم المؤرخين لتلك الحقبة على الإطلاق، فهو أتقن اللاتينية والفرنسية واليونانية وكان لديه إلمام بالعربية.

ولما كان وليم الصوري مشرفاً على ديوان الرسائل في بلاط مملكة بيت المقدس فإن ذلك قيض له المصادر السرية والعلنية ما لم يقيض لغيره من المؤرخين الذين عاصروه فضلاً عن كونه شغل منصب سفير الملك الصليبي عموري في بلاد أمانويل امبراطور بيزنطية في ذلك الحين ومراكز دينية تدرج فيها إلى أن بلغ القمة في سلك الكهنوت رئيساً لأساقفة صور، ما جعل تاريخه حافلاً بالمعلومات والتفاصيل التي لا نجد لها مثيلاً في التصانيف التاريخية الأخرى التي وضعت في تلك الحروب.

يؤرخ وليم الصوري للحروب العنيفة التي وقعت خصوصاً في مركزي ثقل العالم العربي الشام ومصر وكذلك للحروب التي دارت في بعض أقاليم أعالي العراق وآسيا الصغرى. وفي مقدمة الكتاب، يتقصى المترجم حياة المؤرخ ويبدي حيرته من عدم معرفة الكثيرين لأصوله ويستعرض المؤكد والثابت حول شخصيته . . . .

[30]

II. Now consider and translate into Arabic Texts 11B (i) and 11B (ii) as examples of through-arguments. The two Letters to the Editor (a genre which utilizes a similar kind of evaluative discourse to that of the book review) are in response to GATT, an issue summarized in an expository fashion in Text 11B (iii).

TEXT 11B (i)

Sir: The blame for the disastrous breakdown in the GATT talks lies not so much[1] with the Americans or the Europeans, or even with Jacques Delors, as with the spirit of stubborn intransigence that democratic electors expect their politicians to adopt –[2] my country's interest today, tomorrow and always.

The drawback to this as far as Britain is concerned is that we are the ones who will suffer most from a world trade war, because we are the ones who

have most to lose[3] by a reduction and most to gain from an expansion of world trade. What this shows, therefore, is that if we are on the edge of Europe, or right outside it, we lose out always; we must get ourselves into the heart of Europe, where we can exercise some moderating influence.
[33]

NOTES

1. The *not so much . . . as* structure may be rendered as follows:

    إن مسؤولية الفشل لا تقع على عاتق . . . ولا . . . ولا حتى . . . بقدر ما هي نتيجة
    . . . لـ.

2. This illustrates the need in Arabic to explicate the pragmatic function of punctuation:

    أي أن يرددوا مصلحة بلادي اليوم وغداً ودوماً.

3. To preserve the emphatic focus in this sentence, *we lose out always* may be (a) fronted or (b) relayed through 'restriction' هو أننا سوف لا نجني الا الخسارة: (قصر).

GLOSSARY

The blame	مسؤولية
the disastrous breakdown	الفشل الذريع
GATT talks	الذي مهد لمحادثات الغات
the spirit of stubborn intransigence	روح العناد الشديد الذي يطغى على
democratic electors	الناخب الديموقراطي
drawback	الجانب السلبي
as far as Britain is concerned	بقدر ما يتعلق الأمر ببريطانيا
will suffer most	سنكون أشد معاناة من غيرنا
from a world trade war	في حالة نشوب حرب تجارية عالمية
have most to lose	سنكون أكبر الخاسرين من
a reduction	تقلص
most to gain	أكبر الرابحين
from an expansion	لو حدث العكس
What this shows, therefore,	إن ما يمكن استخلاصه من هذا إذن
we must get ourselves into	هو أن لا نكون إلا في
where we can exercise	حيث يتسنى لنا القيام بـ

a moderating influence   دور توفيقي

TEXT 11B (ii)

Sir: At the centre of the GATT trade war apparently being initiated by the US is[1] American irritation at European Community subsidy for producers of various oilseed crops. It would be a pity[2] if your readers and Britain's shoppers were to be so bedazzled by US self-righteousness in this regard that they overlooked some of the hidden subsidies at work in American food production. I am concerned in particular with the estimated $50m that Washington has provided since 1985 to the Diamond Walnut Company in California in order to promote its product in Europe and elsewhere, in direct competition with European walnuts.

[33]

NOTES

1. To relay the full force of this text-initial tone-setter, some manipulation of word order may be necessary: إن غيظ الأمريكيين من الدعم الذي تقدمه المجموعة الأوروبية لـ . . . هو ما يكمن وراء حرب الغات . . .

2. Contrary to what might at first be concluded, this is a continuation of the tone-setter and not a substantiator. In fact, this text has no proper substantiator, as the three sides of the argument are more or less listed as three aspects enjoying equal status: . . . ما إذا للأسف مدعاة حقاً وسيكون.

GLOSSARY

European Community subsidy for producers of oilseed crops	الدعم الذي تقدمه المجموعة الأوروبية لـ . . . منتجي محاصيل الزيوت النباتية
It would be a pity if	وسيكون حقاً مدعاة للأسف
shoppers	المستهلك
X is bedazzled by Y	انبهر ص بـ س
self-righteousness	الورع الزائف
so bedazzled that	إلى حد يكون معه
overlooked X	يغفل عن التمحيص في
at work	التي تجري على قدم وساق
concerned with	يثير قلقي
the estimated $50m	ما يقدر بـ

162

| in order to promote its product | لترويج منتجاتها |
| in direct competition with | في منافسة مباشرة مع |

TEXT 11B (iii)

General Agreement on Tariffs and Trade (GATT)

GATT, in force since 1 January 1948, is[1] the only multilateral instrument which lays down agreed rules for international trade. It is subscribed to by 94 countries, Contracting Parties, which together account for four fifths of world trade. Another country has acceded provisionally, and a further 30 apply the agreement on a *de facto* basis.

The basic aim of GATT is[2] to liberalize world trade and place it on a secure basis, thereby contributing to economic growth and development and the welfare of the world's peoples.

[29]

NOTES

1. To reflect the expository tone, a Nominal must be resisted and a Verbal sentence structure used, with the meaning of *is* appropriately spelt out:

   تعتبر الاتفاقية العامة للتجارة والتعرفة الجمركية . . .

2. Once again, a Nominal must be resisted and the *aim . . . is* transformed into the Verbal: . . . وتهدف الاتفاقية بشكل أساسي إلى.

GLOSSARY

lays down agreed rules	التي تنص على قواعد متفق عليها
It is subscribed to by X	وقد وقع على هذه الاتفاقية
Contracting Parties	الأطراف المتعاقدة
together account for	تشكل في مجموعها
world trade	التجارة الدولية
acceded provisionally	كما انضم إليها بصفة مبدئية
a further 30 apply the agreement	وتطبقها على أساس . . . ٣٠ دولة أخرى
place it on a secure basis	وإرساء دعائمها على أساس أمتن
thereby contributing to	مساهمة بهذا
growth and development	التنمية والنمو
the welfare of the world's peoples	رفاهية شعوب العالم

III. Bearing in mind the distinctive features of through-argumentation in both English and Arabic, translate Texts 11A (i) and 11A (ii) (reproduced here for easier reference) into English.

TEXT 11A (i)

طرد وتفكيك

فيما الدول الكبرى، صاحبة القرار، وعلى رأسها الولايات المتحدة، راعية محادثات السلام في عاصمتها واشنطن، تسعى إلى حل قضية الشرق الأوسط وقلبها فلسطين، لا يزال بعض المتنورين يرى أن خط الأحداث سائر في الاتجاه المعاكس، لا إلى إعادة فلسطين والقدس، بل إلى تفكيك فلسطين وتدويل القدس.

هذا ما تبنى الباحث الفلسطيني واصف عبوشي عرضه في كتابه «تفكيك فلسطين». ومن كلمة فيه للمؤرخ الأمريكي مونتي بالمر أنه: «أفضل كتاب حتى اليوم عن دور بريطانيا في فلسطين . . .».

الكتاب بحث معمق وموثق عن الظرف الذي أدى ـ غداة الحرب العالمية الأولى ـ إلى إنشاء فلسطين ثم كيف آل الأمر إلى تفكيكها لمصلحة اسرائيل.

واصف عبوشي في كتابه، بعيد عن أية غوغائية أو ديماغوجية يغرق فيها الخطاب[1] السياسي العربي في معالجة الأمور، التزم[2] أن يخبر قراءه الغربيين كيف فلسطين صارت اسرائيل.

NOTES

1. Notice the necessary toning-down of what could have sounded too sweeping a set of generalizations had the Arabic يغرق فيها الخطاب السياسي been literally rendered. Thus, 'with which Arab political discourse is normally imbued'. Similarly, في معالجة الأمور: 'in dealing with matters of this kind'.

2. To support the idea of التزم, a 'restriction' may be necessary here: 'committed only to informing his western reader'.

GLOSSARY

expulsion and dismemberment	طرد وتفكيك
at a time when the decision-making great powers	فيما الدول الكبرى صاحبة القرار
at the forefront of which is	وعلى رأسها الولايات المتحدة
the sponsor of the peace talks	راعية محادثات السلام
in its own capital	في عاصمتها
all seek a settlement	تسعى إلى حل
Middle East question	قضية الشرق الأوسط
and its core	وقلبها
some of the more enlightened observers still	لا يزال بعض المتنورين
the drift of events	خط الأحداث
is going in the opposite direction	سائر في الاتجاه المعاكس
to the return of	إلى إعادة
but to the dismemberment of	بل إلى تفكيك
internationalization of	تدويل
this is the scene which X has taken it upon himself to present	هذا ما تبنى س عرضه
to date	حتى اليوم
a documented in-depth piece of research	بحث معمق وموثق
into the conditions which	عن الظرف الذي أدى
on the eve of the First World War	غداة الحرب العالمية الأولى
led to the creation of	أدى إلى إنشاء
how X was later to be dismembered	كيف آل الأمر إلى تفكيكها
in favour of Israel	لمصلحة اسرائيل
without any sensationalism or demagogy	بعيدة عن أية غوغائية أو ديماغوجية

TEXT 11A (ii)

وليم الصوري
عمل موسوعي

هذا الكتاب بين أيدينا هو تاريخ من وجهة نظر تأخذ جانب الحروب الصليبية التي دارت خلال الأعوام ١٠٩٤ و١١٨٤، وفيه تسجيل لتاريخ ملوك بيت المقدس الصليبيين. الكتاب أبرز وأهم المصادر التي وضعت في تلك الحروب فضلاً عن أنه بمثابة أقدم وثيقة غير إسلامية عن الفترة المؤرخ لها.

مؤلف الكتاب هو وليم الصوري المولود في العام ١١٣٠ والذي يعده الباحثون الأوروبيون واحداً من أعظم المؤرخين لتلك الحقبة على الإطلاق، فهو أتقن اللاتينية والفرنسية واليونانية وكان لديه إلمام بالعربية.

ولما كان وليم الصوري مشرفاً على ديوان الرسائل في بلاط مملكة بيت المقدس فإن ذلك قيض له المصادر السرية والعلنية ما لم يقيض لغيره من المؤرخين الذين عاصروه فضلاً عن كونه شغل منصب سفير الملك الصليبي عموري في بلاد أمانويل امبراطور بيزنطية في ذلك الحين ومراكز دينية تدرج فيها إلى أن بلغ القمة في سلك الكهنوت رئيساً لأساقفة صور، ما جعل تاريخه حافلاً بالمعلومات والتفاصيل التي لا نجد لها مثيلاً في التصانيف التاريخية الأخرى التي وضعت في تلك الحروب.

يؤرخ وليم الصوري للحروب العنيفة التي وقعت خصوصاً في مركزي ثقل العالم العربي الشام ومصر وكذلك للحروب التي دارت في بعض أقاليم أعالي العراق وآسيا الصغرى. وفي مقدمة الكتاب، يتقصى المترجم حياة المؤرخ ويبدي حيرته من عدم معرفة الكثيرين لأصوله ويستعرض المؤكد والثابت حول شخصيته . . . . .

GLOSSARY

William of Tyre	وليم الصوري
encyclopaedic work	عمل موسوعي
the present work is a history book	هذا الكتاب الذي بين أيدينا هو تأريخ
from a perspective well-disposed to	من وجهة نظر تأخذ جانب
the Crusades which took place	الحروب الصليبية التي دارت
the Crusader kings of Jerusalem	ملوك بيت المقدس الصليبيين
the book itself is the most outstanding source	الكتاب أبرز المصادر
not to mention that it is	فضلاً عن أنه بمثابة

on the period in question	عن الفترة المؤرخ عنها
one of the greatest historians ever to write	من أعظم المؤرخين لتلك الحقبة على الاطلاق
had some knowledge of Arabic	وكان لديه إلمام بالعربية
in charge of the chancellery	مشرفاً على ديوان الرسائل
Royal Court of the Kingdom of Jerusalem	بلاط مملكة بيت المقدس
he had privileged access to	قيض له
both confidential and public documents	المصادر السرية والعلنية
which no other contemporary historian had	ما لم يقيض لغيره من المؤرخين الذين عاصروه
the position of ambassador of the crusader King Amalric II	شغل منصب سفير الملك الصليبي عموري
he was also the incumbent of religious offices through which he rose to	ومراكز دينية تدرج فيها إلى أن بلغ
the top of the ecclesiastical hierarchy	القمة في سلك الكهنوت
and became the archbishop of Tyre	رئيساً لأساقفة صور
all this availed him (his book) of information unparalleled	ما جعل تاريخه حافلاً بالمعلومات التي لا نجد مثيلاً لها
other historical chronicles	التصانيف التاريخية الأخرى
which record events of those wars	التي وضعت في تلك الحروب
the two centres of Arab world power	مركزي ثقل العالم العربي
the translator tackles the life of	ويتقصى المترجم حياة
expresses puzzlement	ويبدي حيرته
at how little is known about his origins	من عدم معرفة الكثيرين لأصوله
what is known and established	المؤكد والثابت
about his life	حول شخصيته

UNIT ELEVEN: Additional Texts

I. Text 11C (i) is an example of a Through-argument drawn from a book review in English. Text 11C (ii) is taken from the predominantly expository section of the same review. Bearing in mind the features of both exposition and through-argumentation in English and Arabic, translate the two texts into Arabic.

TEXT 11C (i)

... best schools are those that teach children to be their own masters, ... and capable to work,[1] rather than to be good and obedient only as ... they are under control. Children must be[2] taught to become men who ... eed to be watched in everyday life, and they should be educated in ... ner as to be capable of mastering themselves.'

..., the way to freedom always leads from education to self-education. It is therefore the main task of every educator to emancipate his students, to open up new prospects for them, to teach them how to learn, work and create rather than to fill their heads with ready-made clichés and stereotypes. The only 'must'[3] for a teacher is the capacity to transmit and communicate, the capacity to use metaphors that will[4] present new knowledge to the pupils in as vivid and concrete form as possible. School is[5] not merely a preparation for later life, it is life itself in which students test their abilities and simultaneously become free.

[48]

NOTES

1. To preserve the rhetorical force of 'willing and capable', a structure which parallels that of 'to teach children to be . . .' may be attempted in Arabic, thus: إن أفضل المدارس هي تلك التي تعدّ الأولاد ليكونوا معلمي أنفسهم وتزرع فيهم الإرادة والقدرة على العمل.

2. This is another thesis and a new tone-setter. The Nominal structure is thus appropriate to signal the new side-argument: إن الأولاد ينبغي تعليمهم أن يصبحوا رجالاً لا حاجة إلى مراقبتهم كما ينبغي تربيتهم بشكل يمكنهم من . . .

3. See note 2 above.

4. Here, 'will' has the epistemic modality of 'would': الاستعارات التي من شأنها تسهيل عرض المعارف.

5. See note 2 above.

GLOSSARY

their own masters	ليكونوا معلمي أنفسهم
rather than	بدلاً من
good and obedient	ودعاء مطيعين
only as long as	ما داموا

they are under control	ـ حضرة المربّي
not need to be watched	لا حاجة إلى مراقبتهم
mastering themselves	السيطرة على أنفسهم
leads to self-education	يفضي إلى التربية الذاتية
emancipate	يحرر
open up new prospects	يفتح أمامهم آفاقاً جديدة
create	يبدع
ready-made clichés	أفكار جاهزة
The only 'must'	الفريضة الوحيدة
transmit and communicate	ينقل ويوصل
use metaphors	يستعمل الاستعارات
present knowledge	عرض المعارف
in as vivid form as possible	في شكل يتسم بأقصى ما يمكن من الحيوية
concrete	. . . ومن الملموسية
not merely a preparation for	ليست إعداداً لـ
later life	حياة لاحقة
and simultaneously become free	فيما هم يتحولون إلى أحرار

TEXT 11C (ii)

Trstenjak spent[1] his entire life fighting for the emancipation of his country and of himself. Stressing[2] freedom as the common denominator of all that is human, Trstenjak upheld the highest ideal of education and of human life as a whole. He developed a pluralistic concept of freedom, whereby each individual and each nation achieve emancipation.

For his dedicated service to his people, his homeland has honoured him by instituting an annual award bearing his name, which is given to those educators who carry on his emancipatory educational mission.
[48]

NOTES

1. Just a reminder, the Verbal structure is used here to relay the elements of detachment involved: لقد كرّس «ترستنجاك» حياه بكليتها للنضال من أجل.

2. Given its occurrence in this kind of text and thus its unmarked status, this subordinate clause is best embedded within the main clause: وكان «ترستنجاك» انطلاقاً من اعتبار أن الحرية هي . . . يقيم أسمى الاعتبار للتربية . . .

169

SSARY

ation of his country	تحرير أمته
ation) of himself	وتحرره بالذات
c concept of freedom	كانت لـ . . . نظرة تعددية إلى الحرية
ncipation	تحقيق الحرية
ated service	تخليداً لذكراه وللخدمات التي قدمها لشعبه
his . and has honoured him	شرفته بلاده بـ
instituting an award	إنشاء منحة
carry on his mission	الحاذين حذوه
emancipatory educational mission	حذوه في التربية التحررية

II. Texts 11D (i) and 11D (ii) are examples of the Through-argument in Arabic. The texts belong to the genre 'Letter to the Editor' and to that of the academic article respectively. They both illustrate how the use of certain persuasive strategies in Arabic differs from those seemingly similar modes used in English. Consider the two texts carefully and translate into English.

TEXT 11D (i)

تعقيباً على مقال فهمي هويدي «هكذا خدعونا في مسألة البوسنة» أود أن أضيف بعض النقاط المكملة للموضوع. مما لا شك فيه أن[1] قضية البوسنة والهرسك هي امتداد لسلسلة الصراع الأوروبي بين الإسلام والغرب. بل أكاد أقول أنها صليبية القرن العشرين وصدى لفزع الغرب الرهيب من انتشار وتقدم الإسلام واكتساحه لأوروبا، خصوصاً بعد انهيار الشيوعية، لذلك لا ندهش كثيراً إذا ما رأينا[2] دول الغرب العظمى تتخذ بعض المواقف التي يصفها الكاتب بالتخاذل واللامبالاة تجاه مسلمي البوسنة والهرسك، وتمييع الأمور بالتصريحات والنداءات الجوفاء التي لا تحرك ساكناً ولا تروع ظالماً.

فحقيقة الأمر أن جميع الدول الأوروبية بطريقة أو بأخرى تشارك في صنع هذه المجزرة البشرية موهمة العالم بأنه صراع عرقي أو قومي، ومستغلة في نفس الوقت هذا الصراع لتذويب العناصر المسلمة في تلك البقعة من البلقان. فالآباء والأمهات يقتلون على أيدي الصرب والأبناء ينصّرون في ملاجئ ومعسكرات أوروبا. فالمصلحة مشتركة والعدو واحد وما تلك المساعدات الغذائية إلا مسكنات للضمير العالمي والعربي

والإسلامي لكي لا يجاهر ويندد ويستنكر موقف تلك الدول.

[49]

NOTES

1. We must make sure that this ما لا شك فيه أن is rendered as a signal for a Through-argument and not one which can be opposed (Counter-argument). We suggest: 'Without a shadow of a doubt . . .'.

2. The surprise is directed at the writer, describing certain positions adopted by the great powers of the west towards the Muslims as 'feeble', 'indifferent' and 'sweeping things under the carpet through empty rhetoric'.

GLOSSARY

I read with interest the article '. . .' by X	تعقياً على مقال س « . . .»
cheated on the issue of	خدعونا في مسألة
add one or two points to round off the discussion	أضيف بعض النقاط المكملة للموضوع
is another link in the chain of confrontation between	هي امتداد لسلسلة الصراع
In fact I could almost say that/I could go further than this and say	بل أكاد أقول
the crusades of the 20th century	صليبية القرن العشرين
echoing the west's looking in absolute terror on	صدى لفزع الغرب الرهيب من
the spread and sweep of Islam over	انتشار وتقدم الإسلام واكتساحه
the demise of communism	انهيار الشيوعية
we shouldn't therefore be too surprised to	لذلك لا ندهش كثيراً إذا
which neither helps the victim nor deters the aggressor	التي لا تحرك ساكناً ولا تروع ظالماً
the fact of the matter	وحقيقة الأمر أن
have participated in this human massacre	شاركت في صنع هذه المجزرة البشرية
deluding the world that	موهمة العالم بأنه
it is merely ethnic or nationalistic strife	صراع عرقي أو قومي
exploiting this to annihilate	مستغلة هذا في تذويب

fathers and mothers are being killed	الآباء والأمهات يقتلون على أيدي
at the hands of	
children are being forced into Christianity	والأبناء ينصرون
refugee camps of Europe	في ملاجئ ومعسكرات
there is no conflict of interest	فالمصلحة مشتركة
the food aid is only a palliative	وما تلك المساعدات الغذائية إلا مسكنات
international conscience	الضمير العالمي
so that it does not cry out, condemn and	لكي لا يجاهر ويندد ويستنكر
denounce	

TEXT 11D (ii)

ولا شك¹ أن الشاعر العدواني قد اطلع على شعر شعراء المدينة القدامى والمحدثين
وتبلور² مفهوم المدينة عنده، وازداد وعيه بها، ففاضت قريحته وتغيرت رؤيته لموضوعه،
ولم يقنع من مدينته ببقائه متفرجاً خارجها، مبهوراً بصفاتها المثالية، أو ناقماً غاضباً على
صفاتها القبيحة .

لقد تناول شعره المدينة من داخلها، من خلال المعايشة والمعاناة، تناولها كرمز
للقيد، يكبح انطلاقة الفكرة الطموحة، تناولها كبؤرة عفنة أحياناً من كثرة ما ينبعث
منها من فساد، تناولها كرمز على الاستلاب تضيّق الخناق على كل ما فيها حتى ضاق
بها، فجاءت قصائده تعبر عن هذا الضيق وبينت أسبابه .

ولقصيدة «صفحة من مذكرات بدوي» أهمية خاصة في هذا المجال، فالقصيدة تسير
في التقاليد التي ابتدأتها مقطوعة ميسون بنت بحدل القديمة، حيث التقابل القوي بين
البادية والحاضرة، بين الصحراء والمدينة .

[50]

NOTES

1. As in note 1 to Text 11D (i) above, we preserve the strength of لا شك
    here, but this time through word order: 'X was without doubt . . .'.

2. Here, there are a number of implicit discourse relations which must be
    brought out in the English: وتبلور 'thus crystallized in his mind'; وازداد
    وعيه بها 'which enhanced his awareness of it'.

GLOSSARY

familiar with the work of	قد اطلع على شعر
old and contemporary city poets	شعراء المدينة القدامى والمحدثين
this poetic talent poured forth	ففاضت قريحته
his approach to his subject changed	وتغيرت رؤيته لموضوعه
he was not content that	ولم يقنع
in his city he would remain a spectator	من مدينته ببقائه متفرجاً خارجها
only bedazzled by its idealistic features	مبهوراً بصفاتها المثالية
or only angrily resentful of	أو ناقماً غاضباً على
tackled X from within	تناول س من داخلها
through plodding along and through suffering	من خلال المعايشة والمعاناة
as a symbol of the chain	كرمز للقيد
which curbs the upsurge of every ambitious thought	يكبح انطلاقة الفكرة الطموحة
stagnant swamp	بؤرة عفنة
because of the many corruptions emanating from it	من كثرة ما ينبعث منها من فساد
an act of plunder	الاستلاب
tightens the noose around	تضيق الخناق
until he had enough	حتى ضاق بها
his poems came to express this	فجاءت قصائده تعبر عن
X is particularly significant	لـ س أهمية خاصة
the old piece of	مقطوعة
X and Y are set in striking juxtaposition	حيث التقابل القوي بين س و ص

UNIT TWELVE: The Explicit Counter-argument

OVERVIEW

It is probably safe to conclude that Arabic favours through-argumentation over counter-argumentation. Within the latter form, Arabic tends towards a mode to which we will here refer as explicit counter-argumentation. An adversary's thesis is cited, but the citation is initiated by a signal which specifically indicates that the structure in question is a concessive, that this thesis is somehow flawed, and that a rebuttal is forthcoming. These signals include: 'although', 'despite', 'in spite of', etc.

The structure of an explicit Counter-argument is thus fairly straightforward: a signal of concession, a thesis cited to be opposed, a counter-thesis (all in one sentence), a substantiation and some form of conclusion.

Like all modes of argumentation, the texture of the explicit Counter-argument is essentially evaluative. Comparison and contrast predominate, diction is fairly emotive and structure is often marked. However, within the text type argumentation, explicit counter-argumentation is one of the more detached forms. It is least confrontational and in this it is akin to through-argumentation. Furthermore, while the primary function of the explicit Counter-argument is to persuade, various forms of exposition such as summarizing and reporting are allowed as subsidiary functions.

I.   Texts 12A (i), 12A (ii) and 12A (iii) are examples of the explicit Counter-argument in Arabic. Consider them carefully.

TEXT 12A (i)

لا يستطيع باحث أن يزعم بأن العرب في جاهليتهم كانوا يقبعون خلف ستار حديدي. وكتب التاريخ والسير والأدب تجزم بوجود صلات سلمية وحربية لم تنقطع بين العرب من جهة، والفرس والأحباش والهنود والرومان من جهة أخرى وكانت الحيرة وبصرى وغيرهما مراكز تلتقي فيها الثقافات وتتلاقح.

وبالرغم مما ذكرنا، وتسليماً بحقيقة التأثر والتأثير بين العرب وجيرانهم، فإننا نزعم بأن صلة العربي في الجاهلية بجزيرته العربية المترامية الأطراف وتعايشه مع الحيوانات وخوفه منها، وما كانت أسفاره وحروبه توحيان إليه من تأمل كان له الأثر الفعال في الإكثار من ضرب هذه الأمثال متأثراً بالحيوان والبيئة. ومما لا شك فيه أن الإنسان

تجتمع فيه جملة من أخلاق البهائم، وأن محاولة استقراء دقيقة للحيوانات التي وردت لها أمثال على هذه الصيغة تجعلنا نقف على حقائق سنبيّنها في الجدول التالي:

الذئب. عدد الأمثال ٥٠. الصفات المتصلة بالأمثال: الغدر، البر، الجوع، الخبث، الخفة، الشجاعة . . .

[51]

TEXT 12A (ii)

وبالنسبة للوضع في المملكة الأردنية الهاشمية، فإنه يمكن استنتاج وملاحظة مفارقتين هامتين، وخاصة إذا ما انصرف اهتمامنا إلى ملاحظة حجم السكان وسوق العمل في السنوات الأخيرة.

فمن ناحية أولى، يلاحظ أن عدد السكان الإجمالي قد وصل عام ١٩٧٩ إلى حوالي ٢١٠٢٥٠٠ نسمة. وهو في جميع الأحوال لا يعتبر عدداً كبيراً، ولا يشكل ـ كما يحاول البعض التشويه والتبرير ـ معوقاً تنموياً. بل على العكس من ذلك، فإن التقدير الطبيعي لاحتياجات التنمية الجادة، والمستهدفة إيجاد مجتمع متطور ومتحلل من كل روابط التبعية التي تكبل معظم دول العالم الثالث، يتطلب أضعافاً مضاعفة من السكان العاملين والملتزمين بأهداف التطور.

ورغم ذلك، فقد شهد المجتمع الأردني خلال مرحلة طويلة، وربما منذ نشأة المملكة الأردنية الهاشمية كدولة متحدة مع ما يسمى بـ «الضفة الغربية»، هجرات متواصلة لأهم الطاقات العاملة فيه، وربما أكثرها كفاءة وقوة، سواء كان ذلك إلى الدول العربية المجاورة أم إلى دول العالم الأخرى، الأمر الذي أدى الى تفريغ المجتمع من الطاقات الضرورية لتطويره.

[52]

TEXT 12A (iii)

على الرغم من عراقة وأصالة الحديث عن ثنائية الموروث والمكتسب، أو عن ثنائية الذات والموضوع في كثير من مجالات البحث الإنساني، وعلى الرغم من تأكيد حقيقة أن الوجود الفردي والإنساني يعبران عن مزيج من هذه الثنائيات فإن الفقه الاداري قد تأخر في إدراكه لذلك، وفي إبرازه أثر المتغيرات البيئية على الوجود الاداري وحركته وصيرورته.

ومع ذلك فإن سرعة الإذعان لهذا الأمر بعد أول دعوة طالبت بضرورة ربط الحديث عن النظام الإداري بالحديث عن البيئة العامة من حوله جعلت الفقه الإداري

175

يلحق بغيره في هذا المضمار. حتى ان تكثيف الحديث فيه أدى إلى إبراز المدخل البيئي كواحد من أهم المداخل الرئيسية التي تستهدف تفسير الظاهرة الإدارية أو غيرها من الظواهر تفسيراً بيئياً بهدف تحديد مدى الترابط الوثيق بين عوامل البيئة أو متغيراتها وبين موضوعات الإدارة وتطورها.

[52]

II. Bearing in mind the distinctive features of explicit counter-argumentation in Arabic, study Texts 12B (i), 12B (ii) and 12B (iii) carefully and translate into Arabic.

TEXT 12B (i)

Though western powers supported UN resolution 385, in which the Security Council recognized the illegality of South Africa's occupation of Namibia, they twice vetoed General Assembly measures aimed at enforcing it. Partly to avoid a third such 'triple veto',[1] Andrew Young of the US Carter Administration, together with Dr David Owen, Britain's Labour Foreign Secretary, and their collegues from France, West Germany and Canada, set about an initiative aimed at accomplishing South African withdrawal. These efforts would have failed in their aims[2] had the strength of SWAPO's exiled leadership not been incontrovertibly proven to the Western 'Five', all Security Council members at the time.

[53]

NOTES

1. A case of avoidable cataphora: بالرغم من أن القوى الغربية ساندت قرار الأمم المتحدة . . .

2. A hypothetical conditional with a 'double negative': إلا أن هذه الجهود لم تكن لتذهب إلا هباءً لو لم تكن . . .

GLOSSARY

western powers	القوى الغربية
recognized the illegality of	أقر عدم شرعية
they twice vetoed	استعملت حق النقض مرتين
General Assembly measures	إجراءات تبنتها الجمعية العامة
aimed at enforcing (a resolution)	استهدفت تنفيذ هذا القرار

176

X of the US Carter Administration	س. ممثل حكومة كارتر
set about an initiative	ومن بين ما استهدف . . . في طرحهم مبادرة . . .
accomplishing X's withdrawal	أكمل انسحاب جنوب افريقيا
Western 'Five'	القوى الخمس العظمى
all Security Council members	كانت أعضاء دائمين في مجلس الأمن
at the time	آنذاك

TEXT 12B (ii)

Despite its many faults, I should not like to suggest that I regret[1] the appearance of this book, or to deny that it will have its uses.[2] Contemporary Turkish literature and thought are so little known[3] outside Turkey that any book which opens a window upon this culture for those who do not know the language is to be welcomed. When viewed in this light, the inaccuracies and confusions in the present work are considerably outweighed by the large mass of authentic and interesting information which the author has assembled.

[54]

NOTES

1. A pragmatic 'politeness' strategy which is in keeping with the conventions of the academic 'review' as a genre and must therefore be preserved in Arabic, thus: وبالرغم مما في هذا الكتاب من أخطاء فإني لا أود أن
.يُفهم كلامي على أنه تعبير عن أسفي لصدور هذا الكتاب

2. A pragmatic 'downgrading' strategy whose opaque modality should not be lost sight of in translation: أو أنه إنكار لما فيه من فوائد.

3. A substantiation most effectively conveyed through the use of a Nominal, with 'so little ... that' best handled through a semantic قصر in Arabic: فالفكر والأدب قلّما يعرفه خارج تركيا.

GLOSSARY

opens a window upon	يفتح نافذة على
is to be welcomed	لا يسعنا إلا أن ننوه به
When viewed in this light	ومن هذا المنظور
X is considerably outweighed by Y	فإن أي س يبدو ضئيلاً إذا ما قورن بـ ص

177

inaccuracies and confusions	خطأ أو خلط
the large mass of information	القدر الكبير من المعلومات
authentic and interesting information	المعلومات الهامة والموثقة
X has assembled	التي جمعها المؤلف

TEXT 12B (iii)

Visions apart,[1] West Germany has a vital economic interest in strengthening the EC, which accounts for about half Germany's trade and more than 60% of its massive export surplus. On balance,[2] it stands to gain still more from the single market due to start at the end of 1992.

Even so,[3] this vital economic interest has not made West Germany a model European.[4] While preaching budgetary discipline and free trade, it fought at least as hard (latterly harder) as the French for a wasteful, trade-distorting common farm policy;[5] it accused other member states of subsidizing industry while doing the same itself; and it preserved[6] monopolies in postal services and transport and kept its financial sector wrapped in a cocoon of regulation while extolling the virtues of competition and open markets.

[55]

NOTES

1. An ellipted form of concession which may be rendered as:

   إذا ما تركنا جانباً مسألة التصورات المستقبلية فإن لألمانيا الغربية مصالح اقتصادية حيوية.

2. This anaphoric reference must be made more explicit in Arabic: وفي التحليل النهائي فإن المانيا من المتوقع أن.

3. To lend the argument further persuasive appeal, the wording used in handling the initial concessive (note 1 above) must not be varied in tackling the present concessive: ومع ذلك فإن هذه المصالح الاقتصادية الحيوية.

   Note how, to preserve what borders on irony, this repetition is most effectively counter-balanced by the way *vital economic interest* is expressed when it first occurred above. That is, lexical variation or repetition is never unmotivated.

4. A substantiator which may best be expressed through a Nominal whose subject is *West Germany* = *it* and with the 'while clause' inserted

parenthetically immediately after the subject: فألمانيا الغربية وبينما تنصح
بسياسة مالية صارمة . . فإن هذا لم يمنعها من أن تتبنى . . .

5. This explicates the substantiation and is best introduced as a separate Verbal with 'while': . . . وبينما تهم الدول الأعضاء.

6. The parallelism displayed by this sentence and the previous one may be iconically preserved, thus: . . . وبينما تبقى على التأميم في مجال الخدمات.

GLOSSARY

a vital economic interest	مصالح اقتصادية حيوية
in strengthening X	في تعزيز س
the EC, which accounts for	السوق الأوروبية التي يتجه إليها
about half Germany's trade	نصف تجارة ألمانيا
massive export surplus	فائض صادراتها الهائل
On balance	في التحليل النهائي
due to start at	التي من المقرر أن تفتح أبوابها
preaching budgetary discipline	تنصح بسياسة مالية صارمة
fought hard	هذا لم يمنعها من أن تتبنى بنفس القدر من الحماس
and latterly harder	هذا الحماس الذي تزايد مؤخراً
a wasteful, trade-distorting policy	سياسة لم تجن التجارة منها سوى التبذير والاختلال
common farm policy	سياسة فلاحية مشتركة
kept X wrapped in a cocoon of regulation	تبقى س مسيجاً بالقوانين البيروقراطية
extolling the virtues of	تتغنى بمزايا
competition and open markets	المنافسة وانفتاح الأسواق

III. Now reconsider Texts 12A (i), 12A (ii) and 12A (iii) (reproduced here for easier reference) and translate into English.

TEXT 12A (i)

لا يستطيع باحث أن يزعم بأن العرب في جاهليتهم[1] كانوا يقبعون خلف ستار حديدي. وكتب التاريخ والسير والأدب تجزم بوجود صلات سلمية وحربية لم تنقطع بين العرب من جهة، والفرس والأحباش والهنود والرومان من جهة أخرى وكانت الحيرة وبصرى وغيرهما مراكز تلتقي فيها الثقافات وتتلاقح.

وبالرغم مما ذكرنا، وتسليماً بحقيقة التأثر والتأثير بين العرب وجيرانهم، فإننا نزعم بأن صلة العربي في الجاهلية بجزيرته العربية المترامية الأطراف وتعايشه مع الحيوانات وخوفه منها، وما كانت أسفاره وحروبه توحيان إليه من تأمل كان له الأثر الفعال في الإكثار من ضرب هذه الأمثال متأثراً بالحيوان والبيئة. ومما لا شك فيه أن الإنسان تجتمع فيه جملة من أخلاق البهائم، وأن محاولة استقراء دقيقة للحيوانات التي وردت لها أمثال على هذه الصيغة تجعلنا نقف على حقائق سنبيّنها في الجدول التالي:

الذئب. عدد الأمثال ٥٠. الصفات المتصلة بالأمثال: الغدر، البر، الجوع، الخبث، الخفة، الشجاعة . . .

NOTES

1. This adverbial may best be fronted: 'claim that, in the pre-Islamic era, the Arabs . . .'.

GLOSSARY

no researcher can claim	لا يستطيع باحث أن يزعم
were shielded behind an iron veil (curtain)	يقبعون خلف ستار حديدي
books on biography	كتب السير
assert authoritatively the existence (of)	تجزم بوجود
in times of war and peace (of) unbroken links	صلات سلمية وحربية لم تنقطع
the Ethiopians, the Byzantines	الأحباش والرومان
al-Hira	الحيرة (اسم مدينة)
different cultures met and cross-fertilized	تلتقي فيها الثقافات وتتلاقح
despite this, and in recognition of	بالرغم مما ذكرنا وتسليماً بحقيقة
influenced and were influenced by	التأثر والتأثير
we submit	نزعم
vast peninsula	جزيرته مترامية الأطراف
coexistence with and fear of	لتعايشه مع س وخوفه منها
reflection which X afforded him	وما كان س يوحي له من تأمل
proverbs	الأمثال
not to forget that	ومما لا شك فيه أن
animal traits	أخلاق البهائم
a thorough examination	محاولة استقراء دقيقة
animals cited in	الحيوانات التي وردت لها أمثال

the comparative form	هذه الصيغة «افعل»
we have been able to ascertain	تجعلنا نقف على
will list in the following table	نبينها في الجدول التالي
treachery	الغدر
kindness	البر
hunger	الجوع
slyness	الخبث
nimbleness	الخفة
bravery	الشجاعة

TEXT 12A (ii)

وبالنسبة للوضع في المملكة الأردنية الهاشمية، فإنه يمكن استنتاج وملاحظة مفارقتين هامتين،[1] وخاصة إذا ما انصرف اهتمامنا إلى ملاحظة حجم السكان وسوق العمل في السنوات الأخيرة.

فمن ناحية أولى، يلاحظ أن عدد السكان الإجمالي قد وصل عام ١٩٧٩ إلى حوالي ٢١٠٢٥٠٠ نسمة. وهو في جميع الأحوال لا يعتبر عدداً كبيراً، ولا يشكل ـ كما يحاول البعض التشويه والتبرير ـ[2] معوقاً تنموياً. بل على العكس من ذلك، فإن التقدير الطبيعي لاحتياجات التنمية الجادة، والمستهدفة إيجاد مجتمع متطور ومتحلل من كل روابط التبعية التي تكبل معظم دول العالم الثالث، يتطلب أضعافاً مضاعفة من السكان العاملين والملتزمين بأهداف التطور.

ورغم ذلك، فقد شهد المجتمع الأردني خلال مرحلة طويلة، وربما منذ نشأة المملكة الأردنية الهاشمية كدولة متحدة مع ما يسمى بـ «الضفة الغربية»، هجرات متواصلة لأهم الطاقات العاملة فيه، وربما أكثرها كفاءة وقوة، سواء كان ذلك إلى الدول العربية المجاورة أم إلى دول العالم الأخرى، الأمر الذي أدى الى تفريغ المجتمع من الطاقات الضرورية لتطويره.

NOTES

1. This adverbial element is parallel to the 'as far as X is concerned', and should be dispensed with initially too: 'and particularly if we were to . . . , it is possible to identify two paradoxes worth noting'.

2. The parenthesis may be inserted immediately after 'nor': 'nor, as some distorting and self-justificatory accounts would have us believe, . . . '.

GLOSSARY

as far as the situation in X is concerned	بالنسبة للوضع في . . .
focus on an examination of	انصرف اهتمامنا إلى ملاحظة
the size of the population	حجم السكان
market demands	سوق العمل
on the one hand, it may be noted	فمن ناحية أولى، يلاحظ أن
the total population	عدد السكان الإجمالي
by any standard	في جميع الأحوال
nor does this number constitute	ولا يشكل
a developmental impediment	معوقاً تنموياً
on the contrary	بل على العكس من ذلك
a proper assessment	التقدير الطبيعي
the requirements of serious development	احتياجات التنمية الجادة
designed to create a society	المستهدفة إيجاد مجتمع
advanced and free of the ties of subsidiarity	متطور ومتحلل من كل روابط التبعية
which bind most of	التي تكبل معظم
many times that number of	أضعافاً مضاعفة من
working inhabitants committed to	السكان العاملين والملتزمين بـ
for a long time	خلال رحلة طويلة
since the creation of X as a unified state	منذ نشأة س كدولة متحدة
including what came to be called	مع ما سمي بـ . . . .
a continuous migration of its most important manpower	هجرات متواصلة لأهم الطاقات العاملة
probably of the highest levels of efficiency and productivity	ربما أكثرها كفاءةً وقوةً
whether the destination	سواء كان ذلك إلى
it has deprived society of the potential	أدى إلى تفريغ المجتمع من الطاقات الضرورية

TEXT 12A (iii)

على الرغم من عراقة وأصالة الحديث عن ثنائية الموروث والمكتسب، أو عن ثنائية الذات
والموضوع في كثير من مجالات البحث الإنساني، وعلى الرغم من تأكيد حقيقة أن
الوجود الفردي والإنساني يعبران عن مزيج من هذه الثنائيات فإن الفقه الاداري قد تأخر

في إدراكه لذلك، وفي إبرازه أثر المتغيرات البيئية على الوجود الاداري وحركته وصيرورته .

ومع ذلك فإن سرعة الإذعان لهذا الأمر بعد أول دعوة طالبت بضرورة ربط الحديث عن النظام الإداري بالحديث عن البيئة العامة من حوله جعلت الفقه الإداري يلحق بغيره في هذا المضمار. حتى ان تكثيف الحديث فيه[1] أدى إلى ابراز المدخل البيئي كواحد من أهم المداخل الرئيسية التي تستهدف تفسير الظاهرة الإدارية أو غيرها من الظواهر تفسيراً بيئياً بهدف تحديد مدى الترابط الوثيق بين عوامل البيئة أو متغيراتها وبين موضوعات الإدارة وتطورها .

NOTES

1. There is a comparative element here to convey the intensifier function of 'even': 'In fact, the debate was so intense that the environment issue has become one of . . .'.

GLOSSARY

age-old and deep-rooted nature of the discussion of	عراقة وأصالة الحديث عن
the dichotomy 'inherited' vs. 'acquired'	ثنائية الموروث والمكتسب
'subjectivity' vs. 'objectivity'	الذات والموضوع
in many a field within the humanities	في كثير من مجالات البحث الإنساني
both reflect a combination of	يعبران عن مزيج من
administrative science	الفقه الإداري
has fallen behind in recognizing	قد تأخر في إدراكه لذلك
making prominent	إبرازه
environmental variables	المتغيرات البيئية
administration, its process and development	الوجود الإداري وصيرورته
Yet/Nevertheless	مع ذلك
the receptive response to the first call	سرعة الإذعان بعد أول دعوة
to make the necessary link between	طالبت بضرورة ربط الحديث
catch up with	يلحق
administrative and other phenomena	الظاهرة الإدارية وغيرها
factors and variables are inextricably linked	الترابط الوثيق بين عوامل البيئة أو متغيراتها

183

UNIT TWELVE: Additional Texts

I. Bearing in mind the distinctive features of explicit counter-argumentation in both English and Arabic, translate into English Text 12C (i), which is taken from an editorial and thus tends towards the more subjective end of the spectrum, and Text 12C (ii), which is representative of academic counter-argumentation.

TEXT 12C (i)

ضرب الصرب

القرار المتوقع أن يتخذه مجلس الأمن اليوم بفرض عقوبات شاملة تدريجية على الصرب يجعل المنظمة الدولية والمجموعة الأوروبية على بعد خطوة واحدة أخيرة من التدخل العسكري المباشر في البلد الذي كان يوغوسلافيا. والتدخل العسكري، إذا فشلت العقوبات في تجنبه¹، سيكون خياراً مؤلماً لوضع حد للآلام التي تعانيها الشعوب اليوغوسلافية السابقة نتيجة لاختيارها طريق الاستقلال² الذي فتحه انتهاء الحرب الباردة وكان النتيجة الطبيعية الوحيدة لاستعادة الحقوق التي اغتصبت في كثير من أنحاء العالم على مذبح³ المصالح الدولية وباسم السيادات المقدسة لدول مصطنعة.

وعلى رغم بشاعة الحل العسكري لنزاع كان ينبغي حله بالعقل السليم فإن مسؤوليته الأساسية لا يمكن الا أن تتحملها صربيا التي أصرت على المضي في طريق التعنت والضم بالقوة للدول الجديدة أو لكل بقعة أرض في هذه الدول يقطنها سكان صرب بحجة الحفاظ على ما يسمى بالصرب الكبرى.

[30]

NOTES

1. This has to be approached carefully. The rendering which readily presents itself, 'if sanctions failed to avoid', is ambiguous as to impose sanctions is not enough – sanctions must succeed for military intervention to be avoided. Thus the correct option must be: 'if it proves unavoidable due to the failure of the sanctions . . .'.

2. There is irony here which may be captured by: 'just because these people have opted for the independence road'.

3. Once again, the irony may be preserved by maintaining a semantic

chain: 'that get sacrificed in many parts of the world on the altar of international interests'. Quotation marks will be sufficient to relay the irony in the final segment: 'and in the names of the "inviolable" sovereignty of artificial states'.

GLOSSARY

the strike against the Serbs	ضرب الصرب
impose comprehensive and gradual sanctions against	فرض عقوبات شاملة تدريجية
makes the UN only one last step away from	يجعل الأمم المتحدة على بعد خطوة واحدة أخيرة من
direct military intervention	التدخل العسكري المباشر
in former Yugoslavia	في البلد الذي كان يوغوسلافيا
painful option	خياراً مؤلماً
suffering endured by	الآلام التي تعانيها
the only natural way for	النتيجة الطبيعية الوحيدة
despite the ignominy of	على الرغم من بشاعة
through rational means	بالعقل السليم
the main responsibility	مسؤوليته الأساسية
will sit squarely on the shoulders of Serbia and Serbia alone	لا يمكن إلا أن تتحملها صربيا
Serbia has been wantonly intent on pursuing	صربيا التي أصرت على المضي
the path of intransigence	طريق التعنت
forceful annexation	الضم بالقوة
any stretch of land	كل بقعة أرض
the pretext being to preserve	بحجة الحفاظ على
so-called Greater Serbia	ما يسمى بالصرب الكبرى

TEXT 12C (ii)

وقد تضمنت الخطط الاسرائيلية من وراء إنشاء مثل هذه المدن ثلاثة مستويات من الأهداف: أهداف على المستوى القومي، وأهداف على المستوى الإقليمي، وأهداف على مستوى مدينة بعينها.

وأخذت الأهداف في اعتبارها التناغم والانسجام بين المستويات الجغرافية[1] الثلاثة. ومنذ البداية، فطن مخططو المدن الجديدة في فلسطين المحتلة إلى أن تحقق أحد هذه

الأهداف يبدو سهلاً في جوانبه المادية، لكنه صعباً في جوانبه الاجتماعية التي هي أصعب في القياس .

ورغم أن أهداف إنشاء المدن الجديدة التي بزغت منذ سنة ١٩٤٨ لم تكن واضحة بما فيه الكفاية منذ البداية ـ فيما عدا الرغبة في جعلها هدفاً لاستيعاب المهاجرين ـ إلا أنها بدأت تتضح بعد هذا التاريخ، هي والتعديلات التي أجريت عليها حسبما تستوجب الظروف المحلية من ناحية، والدولية من ناحية أخرى، وذلك٢ من أجل تحقيق أكبر قدر من النفع من إنشائها .

[56]

NOTES

1. To avoid metonymy, this sentence would be introduced by: 'In working out these objectives . . . ', followed by 'consistency and compatibility between the three levels were uppermost in the mind'.

2. To convey what 'وذلك' involves, a recap in necessary first: 'the ultimate aim has always been a utilitarian one – to gain the greatest measure of benefit from the establishment of these towns'.

GLOSSARY

the Israeli planning has involved	تضمنت الخطط الاسرائيلية
three sets of objectives	ثلاثة مستويات من الأهداف
were only too aware that	فطن
may be physically easy to achieve	سهلاً في جوانبه المادية
but not socially	لكنه صعباً في جوانبه الاجتماعية
social aspects being very difficult to measure	التي هي الأصعب في القياس
have sprung into being	بزغت
were not sufficiently clear	لم تكن واضحة بما فيه الكفاية
save for the desire to serve the single aim of	فيما عدا الرغبة
of absorbing new immigrants	في جعلها هدفاً لاستيعاب المهاجرين
these have subsequently become clearer	إلا أنها بدأت تتضح بعد هذا التاريخ
what also become clearer were the modifications	هي والتعديلات
introduced to them	التي أجريت عليها
in accordance with the requirement of	حسبما تستوجب
local conditions	الظروف المحلية

II. Translate into Arabic the following examples of explicit counter-argumentation in English. Text 12D (i) is taken from an editorial and Text 12D (ii) from an academic article.

TEXT 12D (i)

Phew[1]

Though tensions over Europe have hurt the Tories for the past several years, it was[2] the recession that nearly did for them this week. The party that had delivered growth plus low inflation for the elections of 1983 and 1987 had to fight this time on a record of 10% inflation in 1990 followed by a slump in GDP in 1991. The imperative now is to restore the economy. On this, the news is likely to be good – and sooner than most people expect.

The first bearer of good tidings may well be the currency markets. Moneymen would have preferred[3] a decisive result in the election, but remember that for most of the past month the opinion polls were telling them that Neil Kinnock would be in Downing Street. The pound was marked down accordingly. By early this week it was right on the floor of its band in the European monetary system (EMS). Now it will rise,[4] perhaps quickly: a European rope trick, with Mr Major as fakir.

[55]

NOTES

1. A characteristic feature of *The Economist* is its use of cryptic, witty and intertextually* loaded headings. To deal with this kind of reference, which at times carries cultural connotations too complex to dismiss in a word or two, glossing becomes essential. For example, we must first visualize someone saying 'Phew', then portray in words the act involved:
    .وتنفس الصعداء

2. There is added emphasis here which may be captured by a cleft sentence in Arabic: .فإن ما كاد يقضي عليهم بالكامل في هذا الأسبوع هو الركود الاقتصادي

3. A 'text within text' phenomenon, with the possibility of anticipating the 'but' by opting for an explicit counter-argumentative format: وبالرغم من أن رجال المال كانوا يتمنون أن تحقق الانتخابات نتيجة حاسمة فإن علينا أن لا ننسى أن . . . .

4. A sudden shift in argumentative strategy which may be marked as follows: أما الآن فإن الجنيه الاسترليني سترتفع قيمته وربما بسرعة لكن ذلك لن يتحقق إلا إذا استطاع ميجر صنع المعجزات.

   Note how the crucial function of source-text punctuation is decoded and glossed in Arabic.

GLOSSARY

have hurt the Tories	كان لها تأثير سلبي على
delivered growth plus X	استطاع أن يقدم للناخب نمواً ومعدل تضخم منخفض في آن واحد
for the elections of	وذلك في انتخابات
fight on a record of 10% inflation	يخوض الانتخابات ونسبة التضخم قد وصلت وبشكل لم يسبق له مثيل ١٠٪
a slump in GDP	انخفاض حاد في إجمالي الدخل المحلي
The imperative now is to	إن ما يجب القيام به الآن
restore the economy	اصلاح الاقتصاد
On this, the news is likely to be	وفي هذا المجال فإن التوقعات من المرجح أن
and sooner than	وبسرعة تفوق كل الحسابات
bearer of good tidings	أول من يبشرنا بالخير
opinion polls were telling them that	استطلاعات الرأي كانت تفيد
Kinnock would be in Downing Street	كينوك سيصل لا محالة الى رئاسة الحكومة
The pound was marked down accordingly	وهكذا تم تخفيض قيمة الجنيه
By early this week	في بداية هذا الأسبوع
the pound was right on the floor	وصل الجنيه إلى أدنى مستوياته
the floor of its band	ضمن خانته في
the EMS	نظام النقد الأوروبي

TEXT 12D (ii)

While[1] integration of students with learning problems has increased rapidly over the past fifteen years, the movement to place students with mild academic handicaps in regular classes for part or all of their school day has created many problems. Teachers often[2] have ambivalent or negative attitudes toward academically handicapped students, and may feel unprepared to meet their needs. Many questions have been raised about possible negative social effects of integration, as academically handicapped students are frequently rejected by their non-handicapped classmates.

Given the difficulties of integrating students with mild academic handicaps (learning disabilities and mild mental retardation) in regular classes, it is important to know the degree to which this practice is actually beneficial for the academic and social development of these students. It is perhaps even more important to know what kinds of programmes or practices are most effective for meeting the academic and social needs of academically handicapped students in regular classes.

[13]

NOTES

1. To preserve the tenor of academic writing, which is particularly high and which predominates in the style of this article, formal 'concession' may be opted for here: وإذا كان إدماج التلاميذ الذين يواجهون صعوبات تَعَلُم قد انتشر
بسرعة . . . فإن وضع التلاميذ ذوي الاعاقة . . .

2. Substantiation of the counter-expectation begins here: فغالباً ما يقف
المعلمون موقفاً مرتبكاً . . .

GLOSSARY

the movement to place students	إدماج التلاميذ
with mild academic handicaps	ذوي الإعاقة الخفيفة
regular classes	صفوف عادية
for part or all of their school day	لبعض الوقت أو بدوام كامل
has created many problems	يطرح مشاكل عدة
feel unprepared	يشعرون بأنهم غير مهيئين
to meet their needs	للإيفاء باحتياجاتهم
Many questions have been raised about	وتطرح تساؤلات كثيرة حول
possible negative social effects	الآثار الاجتماعية السلبية المحتملة
social effects of integration	الآثار الاجتماعية للادماج
X are frequently rejected by Y	إن ص غالباً ما ينبذون س
non-handicapped classmates	التلاميذ الأسوياء
Given the difficulties of	نظراً الى المشكلات
learning disabilities	يواجهون صعوبات تعليمية
mild mental retardation	يعانون من إعاقة عقلية خفيفة
it is important to know	نرى من المفيد تحديد

189

the degree to which X is beneficial   مدى ملائمة س لـ . . .

this practice   هذه الاستراتيجية

for the academic   لحاجات ص سواء من جهة نموهم على الصعيد المدرسي
    development of X

for the social development of X   أو من جهة اندماجهم الاجتماعي أو «جمعتهم»

It is perhaps more important   ولعل من الأهم

programmes or practices   المناهج والممارسات

most effective for   الأنجح في

meeting the needs   الإيفاء بحاجات . . .

UNIT THIRTEEN:
The Implicit Counter-argument

OVERVIEW

You will recall that the Through-argument commits the text producer to the statement of a thesis in which he or she believes, and then to an extensive substantiation of this thesis. Although the Counter-argument essentially involves responding to more or less the same context as that of a Through-argument (that of passionately advocating a particular point of view), counter-arguments achieve their goals through slightly different structural routes. The Counter-argument commits the text producer to the restatement of an adversary's thesis, which will then be rebutted. This rebuttal is normally followed by a substantiation. In the previous unit, we saw how this is done in an explicit fashion, more or less giving the game away by announcing at the outset that someone's thesis is essentially flawed (e.g. 'Although . . ., . . .').

Like all forms of argumentation, the texture of implicit counter-arguments is highly evaluative, comparing and contrasting concepts, weighing up alternatives and dealing with the pros and cons of a given issue. The ultimate goal of this kind of reasoning is to reach some form of conclusion which is intended (rightly or wrongly) to steer the text receiver in a direction favourable to the text producer's aims. Vocabulary will be highly emotive and structure heavily manipulated. Of course, this is not as much in evidence in objective counter-arguments as it is in the subjective variety. Nevertheless, a general opaqueness of intentions is the rule rather than the exception whatever the form of argumentation.

One particular problem commonly encountered in translating the implicit Counter-argument from and into English or Arabic is that some typically counter-argumentative signals in English are through-argumentative signals in Arabic. For example, the Arabic through-argumentative text-initial signal لا شك, when translated as a sentence-initial, text-initial 'No doubt', would only signal the start of a Counter-argument in English. The English reader would expect a rebuttal ('However . . .', etc.) and, as through-arguments do not have rebuttals as such, communication would inevitably break down.

I.   Consider the following texts, which illustrate the use of typically English counter-argumentative signals that can be signals of through-argumentation in Arabic.

TEXT 13A (i)

(. . .)

Of course, the world now needs international coordination and planning as never before. The new stages of European integration were means to furnish more adequate methods to regulate and direct the economies united by the single market. Yet the procedures devised at Maastricht have undoubtedly aggravated the recession, through concerted measures of deflation. The Maastricht Treaty not only prescribes austerity measures but also seeks to impose a secretive and unaccountable intergovernmental structure and European Central Bank, in the place of the democratic institutions of a federal Europe that are now needed to plan for recovery and for a new model of economic advance.

[57]

TEXT 13A (ii)

Of course, there are plays that justify a three-hour running time, just as there are thousand-page novels from which one wouldn't wish to cut a word. But not many. Peter Ackroyd's 1,200-page biography of Dickens would have been a far better book if someone at his publisher's had been brave enough to edit out all the flatulence, thus reducing the length by at least a quarter. The same can be said of the volume I am trudging through at the moment, *The View from No. 11,* by Nigel Lawson, which runs to a wrist-spraining 1,120 pages.

[58]

TEXT 13A (iii)

Clearly, the Bush years haven't been the best of times. The incomes of many – though by no means all – families have been lagging behind inflation. Someone in one of every four households has lost a job since 1990. Bush can't escape responsibility. He was, after all, vice-president to Ronald Reagan, who oversaw the biggest budget deficits since World War II; the government's chronic need to borrow has kept long-term interest rates high and given Bush little room to offer even token plans to stimulate the economy. Bush compounded the mistake by promising 'no new taxes' during the 1988 campaign and then changing his mind at precisely the wrong moment, the summer of 1990, when a tax hike helped knock a weak economy into recession.

But the malaise has more fundamental causes that are beyond the control of this – or any – president. It is Bush's misfortune to preside over an economy undergoing gut-wrenching structural change. The much-vaunted globalization of economic life is finally hitting home. Worldwide competition for sales is intense in almost every industry. (. . .)

[34]

II. Bearing in mind the characteristic features of argumentative strategy studied so far, consider carefully and translate Texts 13B (i) and 13B (ii) into English. The signals typical of counter-argumentative style in English can be and often are through-argumentative signals in Arabic. However, particularly among western-educated Arabs, the equivalent of some of the English counter-argumentative signals are also in evidence in Arabic, albeit not very commonly. When they are used to signal counter-argumentation, these devices pose no problem for the translator.

TEXT 13 B (i)

<. . .>

لا مشاحة في أن كل هذا حتى لو تم تنفيذه كما يجب[1] ـ الأمر الذي لم يحصل في الواقع ـ لم يكن كافياً على الإطلاق لتحقيق الفصل المطلوب بين قضية لبنان وقضية المنطقة، ولكن هذا كان من المحتمل أن يساعد لبنان على معايشة مشكلة الشرق الأوسط في حدود قدرته على احتمال أوزارها وذلك ريثما يتحقق الحل النهائي لها، فإذا لم يكن في المتناول فك الترابط بصورة قاطعة بين القضيتين، فقد كان الهدف، بتعبير واقعي، التوصل إلى صيغة تعايش بين لبنان ومشكلة المنطقة. لقد كان التعايش مع قضية المنطقة، في وجه من الوجوه، هو واقع الحال في لبنان منذ أن نبتت مشكلة الشرق الأوسط وحتى منتصف عقد السبعينات تقريباً.

[60]

NOTES

1. It may be helpful to dispense with these parenthetical elements
    cataphorically: 'Even if it had been possible to carry out as it should
    have been, there is no gainsaying that all of this would not have been
    sufficient . . .'. Notice that the second parenthesis, الأمر الذي لم يحصل في
    الواقع, is redundant, as the idea is expressed by 'had been/would have
    been . . .'.

GLOSSARY

achieve the desired separation	لتحقيق الفصل المطلوب
the Lebanese issue and that of the region	قضية لبنان وقضية المنطقة
it was likely	كان من المحتمل
to coexist with the Middle East question	لبنان على معايشة مشكلة . . .
shoulder its burdens	احتمال أوزارها
until such a time as	ريثما
a final solution was achieved	يتحقق الحل النهائي لها
if it hadn't been feasible to	فإذا لم يكن في المتناول
to achieve an absolute separation	فك الارتباط بصورة قاطعة
the aim would have been, to put it realistically, to	فقد كان الهدف بتعبير واقعي
some form of coexistence	صيغة تعايش بين
in some sense	في وجه من الوجوه
a fact of life	واقع الحال
appeared on the scene	نبتت

TEXT 13B (ii)

<. . .>

تلك هي الصورة العامة للشاعر حين يرى نفسه مقسماً بين عالمين ففي العالم الأول كان
مطلق الصراح يقول ما يشاء ويغني كما يحب، أما[1] في العالم الثاني فهو إذا غنّى
بحساب، وإذا قال شيئاً فإن هذا الشيء يراعى فيه أن يكون محكوماً بنظام جديد جاءت
به نظرية جديدة.

صحيح أنه في الحالة الأولى سيكون مستمتعاً بالحرية، ضارباً في شعابها، وأنه لا
يحس قيداً من القيود مما يوفر له طلاقة في رقم الصورة وطلاقة في التعامل مع

194

الموسيقى، بالإضافة الى طلاقة في التناول، فليس هناك رقيب على فكره ـ ولكن متى كانت الحياة كالغابة التي لا يحكمها قانون؟² ومتى كان الفن بلا حدود؟ ومتى كانت حرية الشاعر مطلقة حتى ولو تصادمت هذه الحرية المطلقة مع حرية الآخرين؟³ لقد كان لا بد من تهذيب الإنسان، ولا بد من إدخاله عالم الحضارة .

[49]

NOTES

1. This is a functional contrastive لما: 'However, . . . '.

2. Rhetorical questions imbued with irony: 'But when was life ever like a jungle unruled by any law? And when was art ever unbounded? When was the freedom of the poet ever absolute?'

3. This is tricky. It is not: 'even if in conflict with . . . '; it is actually: 'particularly (when) (if it happened to be) in conflict with the freedom of others'.

GLOSSARY

torn between	مقسماً بين
would be totally free	كان مطلق الصراح
saying what he likes and singing what takes his fancy	يقول ما يشاء ويغني كما يحب
he would not be unconstrained	غنى بحساب
this would take cognizance of the rules of a new system	فإن هذا يراعى فيه أن يكون محكوماً بنظام جديد
emanating from a new theory	جاءت به نظرية جديدة
roaming about unfettered	ضارباً في شعابها
not feeling the shackles of any	لا يحس قيداً من القيود
provide him with total fluency	مما يوفر له طلاقة
in articulating the image	في رقم الصورة
facility in interacting with	طلاقة في التعامل مع
ease in tackling	طلاقة في التناول
no one is to censure his thought	ليس هنالك رقيب على فكرة
has had to be acculturated	كان لا بد من تهذيب

195

III. Bearing in mind the characteristic features of modes of counter-argumentation in English and Arabic and how the two modes can be similar, though they are more often different, translate Texts 13A (i), 13A (ii) and 13A (iii) (reproduced here for easier reference) into Arabic.

TEXT 13A (i)

Of course, the world now needs[1] international coordination and planning as never before. The new stages of European integration were means[2] to furnish more adequate methods to regulate and direct the economies united by the single market. Yet the procedures devised at Maastricht have undoubtedly aggravated the recession, through concerted measures of deflation.[3] The Maastricht Treaty not only[4] prescribes austerity measures but also seeks to impose a secretive and unaccountable intergovernmental structure and European Central Bank, in the place of the democratic institutions of a federal Europe that are now needed to plan for recovery and for a new model of economic advance.[5]

NOTES

1. As always with this kind of text, the initial sentence sets the tone with a thesis cited to be opposed later. The Nominal in Arabic, together with 'strawman gambit signals'* such as 'of course', 'clearly', etc., ensure that the desired focus is properly relayed: صحيح أن العالم يحتاج اليوم أكثر من أي وقت مضى الى تنسيق . . .

2. The citing of an opponent's thesis to be subsequently rebutted may take more than one sentence to implement, as in this text. Sentence 2 may thus be combined with صحيح أن ellipted as: وأن المراحل الجديدة التي قطعها الاندماج الأوروبي كانت سبيلاً . . .

3. As *concerted measures of deflation* can give the impression of a 'positive course of action', an ironic touch may perhaps not be out of place here to bring out the intended meaning: 'through the mess they got us into': وذلك بفضل الإجراءات المعقدة التي استهدفت الحد من التضخم . . .

4. Following the 'opposition' (*Yet . . .*). 'substantiation' is produced as evidence, signalled thus: . . . فمعاهدة ماستريخت لا تقف عند فرض.

5. The modality involved in conditionally making the point that 'a federal Europe has not yet happened, and were it to happen, something else

would happen', must be made explicit, thus: هذا كله عوضاً عن المؤسسات الديموقراطية التي كان يمكن لأوروبا فدرالية أن تحققها والتي نحن بأمس الحاجة إليها الآن. . . .

GLOSSARY

European integration	الاندماج الأوروبي
were means	كانت سبيلاً من سبل
furnish more adequate methods	طرح طرق أكثر فاعلية
regulate and direct	تنظيم وتوجيه
the procedures devised at	التدابير التي تم ابتكارها
have undoubtedly aggravated	لا شك أنها كانت وراء تفاقم
the recession	حالة الركود
not only prescribes	لا تقف عند فرض . . . فحسب
austerity measures	اجراءات تقشفية
but also seeks to impose	بل تسعى إلى فرض
intergovernmental structure	بنية حكومية دولية
secretive and unaccountable	تكتنفها السرية وليس عليها رقيب
a European Central Bank	بنك مركزي أوروبي
in the place of	هذا كله عوضاً عن
are now needed to	والتي نحن بأمس الحاجة إليها الآن
plan for recovery	لتخطط للانتعاش
a new model of economic advance	ولنموذج جديد للتطور الاقتصادي

TEXT 13A (ii)

Of course, there are plays that justify[1] a three-hour running time, just as there are thousand-page novels from which one wouldn't[2] wish to cut a word. But not many.[3] Peter Ackroyd's 1,200-page biography of Dickens would have been a far better book if someone at his publisher's had been brave enough to edit out all the flatulence, thus reducing the length by at least a quarter. The same can be said of[4] the volume I am trudging through at the moment, *The View from No. 11,* by Nigel Lawson, which runs to a wrist-spraining 1,120 pages.

NOTES

1. The initial elements of this kind of text necessitate a 'dynamic equivalence' approach to translation. It does matter what *Of course,*

there are plays that justify . . . etc. literally means in Arabic; but **what is crucial is the effect they are intended to produce on the target reader.** Thus, sentence 1 may be rather liberally rendered as: لا شك أن هناك من المسرحيات ما يبرر عرضها ساعات وساعات.

2. To relay the subtle point of 'intimacy', the modality of this utterance may be rendered by something like: دون أن يشعر المرء بالحاجة إلى أن يحذف منها ولو كلمة واحدة.

3. This heavily ellipted utterance must be explicated in Arabic, thus:
إلا أن مثل هذه الأعمال قلّما وُجدت.

4. A new Nominal sentence to signal the start of a new side argument:
. . . والشيء نفسه ينطبق على الجهد الذي اخوض الآن غماره والذي.

GLOSSARY

a three-hour running time	عرضها ساعات وساعات
just as there are	تماماً كما أن هناك من . . .
X's biography of Dickens	. . . سيرة «ديكنز» التي ألفها
1,200-page biography	في كتاب من ١٢٠٠ صفحة
would have been	كان يمكن لها أن تكون
a far better book	أفضل بكثير
someone at his publisher's	لو أن أحداً من دار النشر التي أخرجت الكتاب
had been brave enough to	كان على قدر من الشجاعة يمكنه من
edit out all the flatulence	التخلص من الحشو
thus reducing the length	مما يقلص حجم الكتاب
by at least a quarter	بالربع على الأقل
I am trudging through at the moment	الذي أخوض الآن غماره
The View from No. 11	إطلالة من نافذة منزل وزير المالية
by X	بقلم س
runs to a wrist-spraining 1,120 pages	ويقع في ١١٢٠ صفحة تقصم الظهر

TEXT 13A (iii)

Clearly, the Bush years haven't been the best of times.[1] The incomes of many – though by no means all – families have been lagging behind inflation. Someone in one of every four households has lost a job since 1990.[2] Bush can't escape responsibility. He was, after all, vice-president to Ronald

Reagan, who oversaw the biggest budget deficits since World War II; the government's chronic need to borrow has kept long-term interest rates high and given Bush little room to offer even token plans to stimulate the economy. Bush compounded the mistake by promising[3] 'no new taxes'[4] during the 1988 campaign and then changing his mind at precisely the wrong moment, the summer of 1990, when a tax hike helped knock a weak economy into recession.

But the malaise has more fundamental causes that are beyond the control of this – or any – president. It is Bush's misfortune to preside over an economy undergoing gut-wrenching structural change. The much-vaunted globalization of economic life is finally hitting home. Worldwide competition for sales is intense in almost every industry. (. . .)

NOTES

1. To relay the 'strawman gambit' of this 'thesis cited to be opposed', a form of words such as the following may be used: صحيح أن سنوات بوش في البيت الأبيض لم تكن لتخلو من الصعوبات.

2. To highlight the 'disastrous effect', the time adverbial may be fronted: ومنذ سنة ١٩٩٠ أصبح واحد من بين كل أربعة معيلي عائلة عاطلاً عن العمل.

3. There is an interesting intertextual allusion that must be preserved here. Bush became notorious for one of his presidential campaign speeches in which he announced: 'Read my lips. No new taxes!' Of course, once elected, he went back on this promise. The gloss for the sentence in question may thus be something like: وفاقم بوش هذا الوضع بإطلاق وعود خاوية أثناء حملته الانتخابية عام ١٩٨٨.

4. A cryptic reference which must be explicated in Arabic: بإطلاق وعود خاوية أثناء . . . ومن ثم نكث هذه الوعود في وقت لم يكن مناسباً على الاطلاق.

GLOSSARY

many – though by no means all – families	فدخل العديد من العائلات وإن لم تكن كلها
lagging behind inflation	دون مستوى التضخم
X cannot escape responsibility	ولا يستطيع س. أن يتملص من تحمل مسؤولية ذلك
after all	إذ لا ينبغي أن ننسى أنه
oversaw the biggest deficits	الذي شهد عهده أكبر عجز مالي منذ . . .
chronic need to borrow	اضطرار الحكومة المزمن إلى

199

keep X high	أبقى س مرتفعة
long-term interest rates	معدلات الفائدة على المدى الطويل
give X little room to offer	لم يمنح س فرصة طرح
even token plans	خطط ولو رمزية
stimulate the economy	لإنعاش الاقتصاد
compounded the mistake	وفاقم س هذا الوضع
a tax hike	القرار برفع الضرائب
knock X into recession	اقتصاداً كان يتداعى الى حالة الركود السائدة
the malaise	حالة اليأس
has more fundamental causes	جاءت نتيجة لعوامل أساسية
are beyond the control of this	تفوق قدرة
It is X's misfortune	لم تكن سوى سوء حظ س
preside over	إدارة دفة
undergoing structural change	يعيش تحولات هيكلية
gut-wrenching	(تحولت هيكلية) صعبة
the much-vaunted	الذي بالغ س في تمجيده
globalization of economic life	تصدير نمط الحياة الاقتصادية
X is intense	يحتد التنافس
Worldwide competition for sales	التنافس على المبيعات في كل أنحاء العالم
in almost every industry	وفي كل قطاع من قطاعات الصناعة تقريباً

UNIT THIRTEEN: Additional Texts

1. Text 13C is an example of a complex Counter-argument: we have an adversary's thesis cited, then an opposition. But before we issue a proper substantiation, we embark on a rebuttal of the entire argument developed so far including our own (half-hearted) reservation. A substantiation may finally be issued, acting as a conclusion. This is what we shall term the 'double-tier' Counter-argument. To become better acquainted with the form, consider and translate the following text into Arabic.

TEXT 13C

Undoubtedly, one of the reasons why the New Order government dominated by Suharto and his generals has been able to stay in power for so long, despite the criticisms that have been levelled at it by both civilian intellectuals and politicians and critics within the armed forces, has been the economic stability of the country and the tangible benefits of development to the country over the last twenty years. Criticism of the government's complicity in corruption, dissatisfaction at the financial manipulations of the enormously wealthy Jakarate elite and unhappiness with the government's human rights record may stir intellectuals to protest, but[1] the majority of these issues are not of critical importance, provided that their own economic opportunities continue to expand. It is clear, however, that those opportunities are going to be dramatically curtailed in the near future. The fall in the[2] price of oil has already had an impact, and the recent 45 per cent devaluation is going to hit salaried middle-class officials very hard. It is not hard to foresee that a deterioration of the economic status will affect the way in which the country will react both to future criticisms of the government and the government's attempts at self-justification.

On the other hand, it would be foolish to predict anyone's downfall.[3] As *The Road To Power* has shown, the New Order government has remarkable[4] powers of resilience, and the armed forces are still sufficiently united to take concerted action against any serious opposition.

[61]

NOTES

1. As a 'text within text', the subsequent *but* may be anticipated by opting for an explicit counter-argumentative format: 'Although . . . '. Note that with 'Although . . .', the adversative signal (e.g. 'but') becomes redundant: وبالرغم من الانتقاد الموجه إلى الحكومة بشأن تورطها . . . فإن هذه كلها أمور ليس من شأنها أن تحتل الصدارة عند . . .

2. Following the 'opposition' proper, this is the 'substantiation' proper, which must be clearly signalled in Arabic: . . . فانهيار أسعار النفط كان له تأثيره.

3. At this point, a rebuttal of the entire two-tier argument developed so far is produced. It must be introduced by something like:

    . . . إلا أنه ومن ناحية أخرى سيكون من الحماقة.

4. Another substantiation is issued to support the opposition just cited: . . . فكما جاء في كتاب «الطريق الى النفوذ».

GLOSSARY

New Order government	حكومة النظام الجديد
dominated by	التي يهيمن عليها

his generals	جنرالاته
stay in power	قادرة على البقاء في السلطة
for so long	طوال هذه المدة
criticisms levelled at it	الانتقاد الموجه إلى
civilian intellectuals	المثقفين المدنيين
critics within the armed forces	النقاد داخل القوات المسلحة
economic stability	الاستقرار الاقتصادي
tangible benefits of	الفوائد الملموسة
development benefits to the country	من إنماء البلاد
complicity in corruption	تورط س في الفساد
dissatisfaction at	الاستياء من
financial manipulation	التلاعبات المالية
enormously wealthy elite	النخبة الجاكارتية ذات الثراء الفاحش
unhappiness with	الشقاء الذي سببه
human rights record	سجل ممارسات الحكومة بخصوص حقوق الإنسان
stir intellectuals to protest	من شأنها أن تدفع المثقفين إلى الاحتجاج
of critical importance	يولي اهتماماً بالغاً بـ
provided that	ما دامت . . .
their own economic opportunities	فرصهم الاقتصادية
continue to expand	تزداد وفرة
dramatically curtailed	سوف تتقلص بشكل مثير
has already had an impact	كان له بالفعل تأثيراً ملحوظاً
foresee that	التنبؤ
deterioration of the economic status	تدهوراً في الوضع الاقتصادي
attempts at self-justification	محاولات تبرير موقفها
remarkable powers of resilience	تمتلك قدرات لافتة للنظر على المرونة والتكيف
sufficiently united to	ما تزال متحدة وبشكل كاف
take concerted action against	التحرك بانسجام لمواجهة
any serious opposition	أية معارضة خطيرة

II. Now study and translate the following double-tier Counter-argument into English.

TEXT 13D (i)

وفي نفس الخطاب أمام الشعب عمدت إلى مهاجمة أمريكا وروجرز بأعنف ما يمكن . . .
وهكذا بدأ فصل جديد من العلاقات السيئة بيني وبين أمريكا . . . مواجهة عاتية
كاملة . . . .

طبعاً أصيب الأمريكان بذهول يوم ١٦ يوليو سنة ١٩٧٢ عندما اتخذت قرار
الاستغناء عن الخبراء السوفييت. ولكنهم حاولوا جهد طاقتهم أن لا يأخذ القرار مكانة
في إعلامهم . . . فالوفاق كان قد بدأ وكان نيكسون قد زار موسكو في مايو ١٩٧٢
أي قبل شهرين فقط من قراري بالاستغناء عن الخبراء السوفييت[1] . . . فكأنما كانت
مؤامرة صمت . . . .

ولكن[2] يخطئ من يقول إني اتخذت قرار طرد الخبراء السوفييت لإرضاء أمريكا أو أية
جهة أخرى . . . لقد كان قراراً وطنياً سعد به شعب مصر كل السعادة فهو قراري
وقرار شعبي وحده.

[62]

NOTES

1. This adverbial may best be fronted: 'Détente had just begun and, only two months before my decision, that is in May 1972, Nixon had been on a visit . . .'.

2. Opposition is best relayed through adversatives such as: 'yet . . .', 'nevertheless . . .'.

GLOSSARY

which I gave to the nation	أمام الشعب
I went out of my way to attack	عمدت إلى مهاجمة . . .
in the most violent language possible	بأعنف ما يمكن
thus, a new chapter of terrible relations	فصل جديد من العلاقات السيئة
an all-out fierce confrontation	مواجهة عاتية كاملة
were stunned by my decision on . . .	أصيب الأمريكان بذهول يوم . . . عندما اتخذت قرار
to dispense with Soviet advisers	الاستغناء عن الخبراء السوفييت
they did their utmost	حاولوا جهد طاقتهم
to prevent reports from acquiring	أن لا يأخذ القرار مكانة في إعلامهم

prominence in their press	
US-Soviet détente	الوفاق
a conspiracy of silence	مؤامرة صمت
it would be erroneous to allege	يخطئ من يقول
in order to appease America	لإرضاء أمريكا
or any other party	أو أية جهة أخرى
a decision taken in the national interest	قراراً وطنياً
and one with which X were extremely happy	سعد به س كل السعادة
it was my decision and that of my people alone	قراري وقرار شعبي وحده

III. Text 13D (ii) is actually a Through-argument in Arabic. Translate into English, making sure you do not set up expectations which would make the English reader anticipate a rebuttal.

TEXT 13D (ii)

من الجاحظ الى ابن خلدون

لا شك[1] إننا مدينون لجيل الموسوعيين العرب العظام من أمثال الجاحظ وابن قتيبة . . . ونظرائهم كثير في جميع المادة الفولكلورية العربية على امتدادها الطويل والعريض في الزمان والمكان العربيين، بل ندين أيضاً لهؤلاء العلماء الموسوعيين بأقدم أساليب الجمع الميداني وبأقدم مناهج التصنيف في بعض المجالات الفولكلورية كالأمثال والأغاني والقصص والحكايات مثلاً.

بل[2] إننا مدينون أيضاً لعالم موسوعي عظيم هو ابن خلدون في مقدمته التي بوأته مركز الصدارة في فلسفة التاريخ ونشأة العلوم الاجتماعية، مدينون له[3] بتأسيس علم الفولكلور العربي نفسه وكان ذلك نفحة من نفحات العبقرية الخلدونية الخالدة فعلى يديه أخذت المادة الفولكلورية الضخمة التي جمعها جيل الموسوعيين شكلها المنهجي وإطارها العلمي ولأول مرة في الفكر العربي والعالمي. فهو أول عالم يقوم بدراسة العلوم الشعبية أو الفولكلورية من حيث هي أدب شعبي وعادات وتقاليد ومعتقدات ومعارف شعبية وحرف وصناعات وفنون جمعها[4] في إطارها العلمي الصحيح ضمن دراسته عن علم العمران والاجتماع البشري.

[63]

NOTES

1. An unopposable لا شك would be something like: 'Without doubt . . . '.

2. As we have already had an 'indeed', this بل may be read pragmatically to mean: 'specifically, we are indebted to . . . '.

3. This highly marked word order may be reflected in a similar word order marking in English: 'Indebted as we are to . . . '.

4. Perhaps it would be useful to have a new 'recap' sentence here: 'He placed all this in a proper . . . '.

GLOSSARY

we are all indebted to	إننا مدينون لـ
that generation of great Arab encyclopaedists	لجيل الموسوعيين العرب العظام
such as . . . , to name but a few	من أمثال . . . ونظرائهم كثير
for the compilation of folkloric materials	جمع المادة الفولكلورية
covered a vast expanse of time and place	على امتدادها الطويل والعريض
throughout the Arab lands	في الزمان والمكان العربيين
indeed, we are indebted	بل ندين أيضاً
encyclopaedist scholars	العلماء الموسوعيين
the oldest compilation methods relying on fieldwork	أقدم أساليب الجمع الميداني
classification methodologies	مناهج التصنيف
stories and tales	القصص والحكايات
in his *Muqaddima*, the book which enabled him to occupy a position of prominence,	في مقدمته التي بوأته مركز الصدارة
the emergence of the social sciences	نشأة العلوم الاجتماعية
a stroke of eternal Khaldunian genius	نفحة من نفحات العبقرية الخلدونية
at his hands, X took its methodological form	فعلى يديه أخذت س شكلها المنهجي
adopted a scientific framework	(أخذت) اطارها العلمي
in Arab and world thought	في الفكر العربي والعالمي
as the literature of the people	من حيث هي أدب شعبي
popular wisdom	معارف شعبية
crafts and trades	حرف وصناعات
in a proper scientific perspective	في إطارها العلمي الصحيح

culture, civilization and social anthropology علم العمران والاجتماع البشري

IV. Texts 13D (iii) and 13D (iv) are examples of English Implicit counter-argumentation. The sample included here, however, introduces a new problem. This is to do with the existence, within the 'macro'-counter-argument, of a 'micro'-counter-argument (text within text). When translating micro-counter-arguments into Arabic, a useful strategy is to opt for an explicit form of counter-argumentation بالرغم من and to leave out the adversative signal. It should be emphasized that this is not an invariable rule but merely a suggested strategy. Both implicit and explicit counter-argumentation are perfectly aceptable here, though the latter form strikes one as being more idiomatic in Arabic 'micro-texts'. Try this strategy on the following text.

TEXT 13D (iii)

Playing Party Games

In December 1984, in the debate on the Joint Declaration, Mr Richard Luce, who was then a Foreign Office minister, assured parliament that 'we[1] all fully accept that we should build up a firmly based, democratic administration in the years between now and 1997'. (. . .)

But what would guarantee those freedoms after 1997? One reason for Hongkong's[2] political apathy is that British colonialism has served them well. The governor is a[3] dictator, but a benevolent one. The police are everywhere – one policeman for every 200 people is surely excessive – but they rarely come at dawn even for dishonest folk, and they do not lock people away without trial. There are virtually no[4] institutions of democracy in Hongkong, but it is perfectly possible to insult the governor in public or demonstrate in the streets. Compare this with Singapore, a[5] country with all democracy's institutions but few of Hongkong's freedoms.
[55]

NOTES

1. The switch from the reporting mode (*assured parliament*) to speaking in the first person (*we all fully accept*), which is not normally permitted in Arabic genres such as the news report, is rhetorically motivated here ('undertaking as part of an assurance') and must thus be preserved: صرّح

.مؤكداً للبرلمان بأننا جميعاً نقبل قبولاً تاماً ضرورة . . .

2. Following the opposition just issued, one would expect a 'substantiation'. Instead, however, a new side-argument begins and must be
marked as such with a separate Nominal: إن أحد أسباب الركود السياسي
.الذي تعاني منه هونغ كونغ هو . . .

3. To relay the force of these substantiators and preserve the repetitive
succession of the list, the structure: فبالرغم من ديكتاتورية الحاكم فهو رجل
خيَر . . . may be used throughout.

4. A new side-argument begins here and must thus be marked with a
separate imperative: . . . قارن هذا مع الوضع في بلاد سنغافورة.

5. We may here revert back to the strategy: بالرغم من أنها بلاد تتمتع فبالرغم من
.بجميع المؤسسات الديموقراطية فهي لا تملك الا القليل من حريات هونغ كونغ . . .

GLOSSARY

the debate on	النقاش حول
Joint Declaration	الاعلان المشترك
was then a Foreign Office minister	والذي كان آنذاك وزيراً في الخارجية البريطانية
assured parliament	صرح مؤكداً للبرلمان
build up a democratic administration	انشاء ادارة ديموقراطية
firmly based	ثابتة الدعائم
what would guarantee	من الذي سيضمن
political apathy	عدم الاكتراث السياسي
colonialism has served them well	الاستعمار الذي أسدى لها خدمات جمة
a benevolent dictator	حاكم خيَر رغم استبداده
is surely excessive	وهي سمة مبالغ فيها دون شك
they rarely come at dawn	نادراً ما تداهم عند الفجر
even for dishonest folk	حتى المشتبه بهم
lock people away	تسجن أحد
without trial	دون محاكمة
insult X in public	اهانة س علناً
demonstrate in the streets	التظاهر في الشوارع
Compare this with	قارن هذا مع

TEXT 13D (iv)

(. . .)

The Eurocrats pledge that they will follow scrupulously the principle of 'subsidiarity', the notion that the Commission will act only in cases where it can do a better job than individual governments. [But] who will set the standards for subsidiarity remains an open question. European leaders meeting in Birmingham this week will wrestle with it,[1] but they will not solve it. A recent Commission describes[2] the huge free-trade area as a 'house under construction' in which 'the shell of the building[3] has been completed, but it is still difficult to move around the house, since the finishing work still has to be undertaken'. This omits[4] the awkward fact that the house's 360 million tenants must move in by 1 Jan. The 'finishing work' will have to be done with the occupants in residence.

[34]

NOTES

1. Here is another example of a 'text within text': in the middle of the macro-counter-argument, this micro-text may be handled more explicitly thus: فبالرغم من أن القادة الأوروبيين المجتمعين في برمنكهام هذا الأسبوع سينكبون على دراسته فإنهم سوف لن يفلحوا في الإجابة عليه بشكل نهائي.

2. Although a substantiator in function, this sentence may be treated as a side-narrative, with an initial Verbal structure to mark the scene-setter: ويصف تقرير صدر مؤخراً عن . . .

3. Metaphors occur in a chain-like fashion and this intertextual element must be thematically preserved; *construction, shell, building, house,* etc. must all be made to link up with one another by the lexical choices made in their renderings: دار في طور البناء، هيكل البناية، من الصعب التحرك داخل الدار، لمسات الديكور الأخيرة، مستأجري الدار، ينتقلوا إلى الدار.

4. A subtle counter-argument which must be made explicit in Arabic: إلا أن هذا لا يأخذ في الحسبان الحقيقة المحرجة.

GLOSSARY

the Eurocrats pledge	بيروقراطيو بروكسيل يقطعوا على أنفسهم العهد بأن
follow scrupulously	سيطبقوا مبدأ . . . بحذافيره
the principle of 'subsidiarity'	مبدأ أولوية الدولة
act only in cases	سوف لن تتدخل إلا في حالات
it can do a better job	تستطيع فيها إنجاز مهمة ما بشكل أكثر فاعلية
individual governments	من الحكومات المختلفة منفردةً
who will set the standards	من سيضع معايير
remains an open question	يطرح نفسه سؤالاً لا يجد من يجيب عليه

V. The reverse of the pattern 'English implicit counter-argumentation becoming Arabic explicit counter-argumentation' is also possible is some contexts. You have to judge appropriateness for yourself, but if it is possible to render a given, say, '*Although* structure' in Arabic as a 'thesis cited + adversative signal' structure in English, then the latter is the more idiomatic rendering of the source text's explicit Counter-argument. Try this on the following text.

TEXT 13D (v)

ويتضح من هذا العرض[1] بالنسبة للمشكلات القبلية ومحاولات معالجتها وبعض التحولات في العراق، سواء قبل عصر مدحت باشا أو أثناء هذا العصر، الاختلاف البيّن بين عوامل المشكلة القبائلية العراقية وعوامل مثل هذه المشكلة في قلب الجزيرة العربية، وإن تشابهت[2] في كثير من مظاهر الحياة البدوية، وعلى الرغم من[3] اتصال البادية العراقية بالبادية النجدية كما أشرنا من قبل، لا يفصلهما أي حاجز طبيعي من جبال أو أنهار أو أودية، حيث[4] كانت قبائل الباديتين تتجول فيها حيث تشاء في غاية السهولة والحرية ومن غير قيد ولا شرط، بسبب[5] امتداد العصور العثمانية قروناً متتابعة بالإضافة إلى هذه الطبيعة الجغرافية[6].

لذلك بدا لنا على الرغم من أنها مشكلة قبائلية أو بدوية، كأنهما مشكلتان منفصلتان، من حيث[7] النمو ومن حيث وسائل التصدي والعلاج والتنفيذ، ومن ثم بدا أيضاً أنه[8] لا شيء يمكن أن يستعار أو يتشبه به في مجال توطين القبائل وتثبيتها في قلب الجزيرة العربية.

[64]

NOTES

1. A drastic restructuring of this text is necessary. The initial elements: يتضح من هذا العرض . . . الاختلاف البين . . . وقلب الجزيرة العربية be must deferred to be used later as part of the 'opposition'. What we need first is a 'thesis cited to be opposed'. This is provided by: الطبيعة . . . وان تشابهت .الجغرافية

2. In order to implement the new structure, the reference for وان تشابهت must be retrieved from the initial elements which are deferred: 'The Iraqi tribal problem and that confronted in the Arabian peninsula have a number of aspects of bedouin life in common.'

3. As we continue with using these elements as a thesis cited to be opposed, على الرغم من is left out: 'and the Iraqi desert merges into the Najdi desert . . .'.

4. حيث here becomes: 'furthermore . . .'.

5. This بسبب provides us with: 'Finally, the Ottoman era extended uninterruptedly . . .'.

6. Here we introduce the opposition which is presented first in the Arabic text: 'This review, however, has made clear that, as far as tribal problems are concerned, as well as attempts at solving them and certain transformations in Iraq, whether before or during the era of Midhat Pasha, factors relating to the Iraqi tribal problem and those confronted in the heart of the Arabian peninsula are substantially different.'

7. To signal that من حيث is a substantiator here, the addition of: 'this is justified in terms of . . .', may be necessary.

8. It is more effective to get in here: في مجال توطين القبائل, 'that, when it comes to discussing settlement and stabilization of the tribes in the heart of the Arabian peninsula, there is nothing which could have been borrowed from or can be compared with the Iraqi experience'.

GLOSSARY

unseparated by any natural barrier	لا يفصلهما أي حاجز طبيعي
such as mountains, rivers	من جبال أو أنهار

used to roam as they pleased	تتجول حيث تشاء
with utmost ease and freedom	في غاية السهولة والحرية
without constraints or conditions	ومن غير قيد ولا شرط
which, added to the nature of the geography	بالاضافة الى هذه الطبيعة الجغرافية
we have therefore felt that	لذلك بدا لنا
in spite of the problem being seen as	على الرغم من أنها مشكلة قبائلية أو بدوية
it should be seen as two separate	(بدا لنا) كأنهما مشكلتان منفصلتان
the way it developed	من حيث النمو
the means proposed to combat and	ومن حيث وسائل التصدي والعلاج والتنفيذ
actually resolve it	

UNIT FOURTEEN:
The Suppressed Counter-argument

OVERVIEW

In the previous unit, we discussed the problem of counter-argumentative signals and how these may not be text-typologically equivalent in English and Arabic. For example, 'No doubt', when occurring text- and sentence-initially, is very likely to usher in a Counter-argument in English (i.e. it will be followed by an adversative such as 'however' and a substantiation). As we have discovered, this is not always the case in Arabic as من المؤكد can and often does signal a Through-argument (i.e. a thesis followed by an extensive substantiation).

This unit also deals with counter-argumentative signals. Here, however, we will be concerned with whether these signals are suppressed or not. In both English and Arabic, counter-argumentative signals may occur in either form. When not suppressed, these pose no particular problems. However, when suppressed, the issue becomes more complicated and translators will have to negotiate text structure properly in order to be able to retrieve the missing link.

This is a particular problem when translating into Arabic. Though by no means in each and every case, Arabic tends towards the unsuppressed expression of discourse relations. There are substantiating particles (e.g. إذ، فَـ، حـيـث) which have no equivalents in English. Adversatives are no exception and, except in rare contexts, they are normally used in an unsuppressed fashion. The translator must therefore first retrieve the signal, if missing from the English text, and then restore it in the Arabic text.

I.   Consider Texts 14A (i) and 14A (ii) carefully. They both illustrate missing argumentative signals. In general terms, whether these signals are explicitly or implicitly expressed is not an ad hoc matter, but one that is determined by the ultimate function of the text (whether it is purely argumentative or an argument with a subsidiary expository function), the degree of objectivity (whether the argument is factual or impressionistic) and the kind of publication (whether the argument is scholarly in a book, sophisticated in the quality press or pedestrian in a tabloid). For example, Text 14A (i) is of the scholarly type, using academic discourse within the genre 'book introduction'. Text 14A (ii) is from a serious review article.

TEXT 14A (i)

(. . .)

Existing studies of development in the Gulf region have mostly restricted their concern to one aspect of development. A substantial number of surveys of mineral resources, studies on the feasibility of individual projects or the effectiveness of existing undertakings (especially in the oil industry), and studies of the functioning and development of individual economies have been undertaken. There have also been studies dealing with individual social or political aspects of the development process. What is lacking is an overall perspective of development, integrating the political, social and economic aspects, providing some conception of the nature of the economies, societies and policies which are emerging in the Gulf, and assessing the options and alternatives which lie ahead. This study attempts, in an introductory manner, to supply such a perspective.

[65]

TEXT 14A (ii)

Even today many theories of education hold that the main task of schools and educators consists in transmitting the acquired historical experience of mankind to the younger generation. Trstenjak was among the first to see that this notion was self-contradictory, because insistence on traditional experience stifles the primal freedom-instinct among the young. Pupils treated as mechanical sponges, taking in all that they are told, will not be able to create anything new. Aware of this, in opposition to the authoritarian tradition in teaching, Trstenjak insisted on the importance of 'learning how to learn', of conditioning the young to be creative and to act independently, instead of passively accumulating information to be mechanically reproduced in examinations.

[13]

II. This form of suppressed counter-argumentation is rare in Arabic. But a few examples do exist. Consider Texts 14B (i), 14B (ii) and 14B (iii), which illustrate the ellipted opposition signal, and translate into English. You may try an explicit or a suppressed form in English and check for idiomaticity.

TEXT 14B (i)

وبما لا شك فيه[1] أن تحديد بداية مرحلة الشيخوخة بسنة معينة قد يختلف من مجتمع الى آخر، كما أن الإحالة إلى المعاش يتفاوت من فئة مهنية الى أخرى، وقد تصل الحاجة إلى إبقاء[2] الفرد على رأس عمله ما دام قادراً على أدائه دونما اعتبار لعمره الزمني كما حصل في فرنسا بالنسبة لأساتذة الجامعات. أضف إلى ذلك أن المكتشفات العالمية الحديثة والعناية الصحية التي يلاقيها الفرد في كثير من المجتمعات المتقدمة قد ساهمت في إطالة متوسط العمر للفرد وجعلته أكثر قدرة على استمراريته في الإنتاج[3]. في نفس الوقت، نجد المجتمعات المتخلفة الأكثر فقراً تعاني من سوء التغذية والعناية الطبية، مما عمل على هبوط متوسط العمر للفرد، وتضاؤل قدرة الفرد على الإنتاج في سن مبكرة نسبياً. وعليه فليس من السهل وضع بداية واحدة لكل المجتمعات لمرحلة الشيخوخة.

[66]

NOTES

1. A weaker form of concessive, i.e. one inviting 'opposition', would be appropriate here: 'No doubt', 'Without doubt . . .'.

2. There is an 'instructional' touch here. It is like saying: 'A person may be kept in their work' = ويجوز إبقاء.

3. This is a structure worth noting. Arabic opts for noun + noun, while English prefers this to be modifier + noun: استمراريته في الإنتاج = 'continued productivity', تضاؤل قدرة الفرد في الإنتاج = 'diminished individual productivity'.

GLOSSARY

determining the year at which old age begins	تحديد بداية مرحلة الشيخوخة بسنة معينة
is a matter which may vary	قد يختلف من
from society to society	من مجتمع الى آخر
Similarly	كما أن
the age of retirement will vary . . .	الإحالة الى المعاش تتفاوت من والى
from one professional category to another	من فئة مهنية إلى أخرى
as long as he or she is able to do the job	ما دام قادراً على أدائه
regardless of age	دونما اعتبار لعمره الزمني
as has happened in . . . with	كما حصل في فرنسا بالنسبة لأساتذة الجامعات

added to this is the fact that	أضف إلى ذلك أن
modern scientific discoveries	المكتشفات العلمية الحديثة
the health care	العناية الصحية
a person receives	يلاقيها الفرد
advanced societies	المجتمعات المتقدمة
prolonging the average working life of	قد ساهمت في إطالة متوسط عمر الفرد
the more underdeveloped and poorer societies	المجتمعات المتخلفة الأكثر فقراً
malnutrition and inadequate medical care	سوء التغذية والعناية الطبية
lowering	هبوط
a relatively early age	سن مبكرة نسبياً
thus	وعليه
decide on a particular point . . . and make this applicable to all societies	وضع بداية واحدة لكل المجتمعات

TEXT 14B (ii)

ولم يكن سياق التطور ثلاثي المراحل مقتصراً على تاريخ البشرية الديني بعامة ، بل كان لينطبق على تاريخ الأديان التوحيدية كما جاء في رسالة التوحيد فارتفعت هذه من دين قائم على أوامر وزواجر وطلب للطاعة المطلقة، في إشارة من عبده الى اليهودية،[1] الى دين وجداني مخاطب للعاطفة[2] في المسيحية أو مخاطب للعقل في الإسلام الذي يشرك العاطفة والعقل في الإرشاد إلى سعادة الدين والدنيا .

ولم يكن عبده وحيداً[3] في اتباع النظرة التطورية إلى الدين التي وضعت الإسلام في سياق تطور تاريخي موضوعي مساوق لترقي البشرية وللرقي والصواب فقد رأى السيد جمال الدين أن أوهام الإنسان ترقت برقيه في المعقولات فعبد الإنسان البدائي خسائس الموجودات كالحجر، ثم ترقى فعبد النار فالسحاب والأفلاك، حتى توصل إلى عبادة الأمور المنزهة عن الكم والكيف .

[67]

NOTES

1. This parenthesis has to be made more explicit: 'the latter being a reference by Abduh to Judaism. . . '.

2. An either-or construction: 'Which either addresses emotions as in. . . or reason as in. . .'.

3. Here is the suppressed adversative which may be retrieved in the English text: 'But Abduh was not the only one to adopt the theory of evolution and adapt it to religion.'

GLOSSARY

the context . . . was not restricted	لم يكن سياقاً . . . مقتصراً على
three phase development	التطور ثلاثي المراحل
monotheistic religions	الأديان التوحيدية
Treatise on the Unity of God	رسالة التوحيد
were thus elevated	ارتفعت
a set of commandments, prohibitions	أوامر وزواجر
demands for absolute obedience	طلب للطاعة المطلقة
in the single notion of guidance towards	في الإرشاد إلى
in this world and in the Hereafter	الدين والدنيا
objective, historical, evolutionary context	في سياق تطور تاريخي موضوعي
compatible with	مساوق
progress, development and righteousness	ترقى، رقي، صواب
delusions of man	أوهام الإنسان
as his own cognitive faculties developed	ترقت برقيه في المعقولات
primitive man	الإنسان البدائي
worshipped the most base of entities	عبد خسائس الموجودات
stars	الأفلاك
things transcending quantity and quality	الأمور المنزهة عن الكم والكيف

TEXT 14B (iii)

السفير السعودي في الكويت للمجلة

المجلة: ألم يحن الوقت بعد مرور هذه السنوات من انشاء مجلس التعاون الخليجي لإلغاء الجوازات والتنقل بين دول المجلس من خلال البطاقة الشخصية؟[1]

السفير: التنقل أسهل شيء موجود بين دول مجلس التعاون. والمواطن الخليجي لا يحتاج إلى تأشيرة. ثم[2] أن الجواز يعتبر إثبات هوية، ولا توجد أي صعوبة على الحدود بل «تختم جوازك وتمشي».

[35]

NOTES

1. The pragmatic force of this utterance is one of 'reprimand', which can be reflected in English by something like: 'Isn't it time that . . .', an utterance which comes after the introduction: 'Now that . . .'.

2. This is where the major difficulty in tackling this text lies: ثم أن is a less abrasive way of more straightforwardly issuing an 'adversative', thus: 'However, . . .'.

GLOSSARY

the establishment of the GCC	انشاء مجلس التعاون الخليجي
the abolition of passports	الغاء الجوازات
allowing freer movement	التنقل بين دول المجلس
identity card	البطاقة الشخصية
you stamp your passport	تختم جوازك
and you are on your way	وتمشي

III. Bearing in mind that suppressed argumentation in Arabic is the exception rather than the rule, and that Arabic tends to favour the explicit expression of connectors, translate Texts 14A (i) and 14A (ii) (reproduced here for easier reference) into Arabic.

TEXT 14A (i)

Existing studies of development in the Gulf region have mostly restricted their concern[1] to one aspect of development. A substantial number of surveys of mineral resources, studies on the feasibility of individual projects or the effectiveness of existing undertakings (especially in the oil industry), and studies of the functioning and development of individual economies have been undertaken. There have also been studies dealing with individual social or political aspects of the development process. What is lacking[2] is an overall

217

perspective of development, integrating the political, social and economic aspects, providing some conception of the nature of the economies, societies and policies which are emerging in the Gulf, and assessing the options and alternatives which lie ahead. This study attempts,[3] in an introductory manner, to supply such a perspective.

NOTES

1. To relay the criticism implied and prepare for both the 'dismissive' list of studies and the suppressed opposition which will follow, a peculiar use of the Verbal sentence structure may be opted for: بشكل عام، انحصرت
    اهتمامات دراسات التنمية في منطقة الخليج في جانب واحد من جوانب التنمية.

2. The cleft structure relays a contrastive element which may be signalled by using an adversative in Arabic: إلا أن ما نفتقر إليه هو إطار عام.

3. At this point, exposition starts and a form not unlike that of the Abstract emerges. The Verbal structure is thus most appropriate for the necessarily detached tone adopted in this segment: وتحاول هذه الدراسة
    ... تقديم تمهيدي بشكل.

GLOSSARY

A substantial number of surveys	عدد كبير من دراسات مسح
mineral resources	الموارد المعدنية
the feasibility of individual projects	ودراسات جدوى مشاريع معينة
the effectiveness of existing undertakings	فاعلية مشاريع قائمة
the functioning of individual economies	عمل أنظمة اقتصادية معينة
dealing with individual social aspects	تعالج جوانب اجتماعية معينة
social aspects of the development process	عملية التنمية من جوانب اجتماعية
integrating X and Y aspects	... تتداخل فيه الجوانب الـ
providing some conception of	يعطي فكرة واضحة عن
the nature of the economies	طبيعة الأنظمة الاقتصادية
the nature of societies and policies	طبيعة الأنظمة الاجتماعية والسياسات
assessing the options	تقويم الخيارات
the options and alternatives	الخيارات والبدائل
which lie ahead	التي سنواجهها في المستقبل

TEXT 14A (ii)

Even today many theories of education hold that[1] the main task of schools
and educators consists in transmitting the acquired historical experience of
mankind to the younger generation. Trstenjak was among the first to see that
this notion was self-contradictory,[2] because insistence on traditional
experience stifles the primal freedom-instinct among the young. Pupils
treated as mechanical sponges,[3] taking in all that they are told, will not be
able to create anything new. Aware of this, in opposition to the authoritarian
tradition in teaching, Trstenjak insisted on the importance of 'learning how
to learn', of conditioning the young to be creative and to act independently,
instead of passively accumulating information to be mechanically reproduced in examinations.

NOTES

1. Here, we must try to preserve two kinds of focus: (a) that of the tone-
    setting argumentative function: and (b) that of *even*: واليوم، ما زال هناك
    كثير من منظّري التربية يعتبرون أن . . .

2. The contrast introduced here signals the drift of the text into counter-
    argumentation and this must be appropriately marked in Arabic: إلا أن
    «ترستنجاك» كان بين أوائل الذين أدركوا أن هذه الفكرة تناقض نفسها . . .

3. A substantiation with an interesting use of the negative agentless
    passive: ومتى عومل التلاميذ كالإسفنجة التي تمتص كل ما يقال، باتوا عاجزين عن
    ابتداع أي شيء جديد . . .

GLOSSARY

consists in	تقوم على
transmitting	نقل
the acquired historical experience of mankind	الخبرة التي اكتسبتها الإنسانية على مر تاريخها
the younger generation	الجيل الجديد
insistence on	التشديد على
traditional experience	الخبرة التقليدية
stifles	يخنق
the primal freedom-instinct	غريزة الحرية الفطرية
among the young	عند الناشئة
Aware of this	وانطلاقاً من وعي هذا الأمر

in opposition to	وعلى نقيض
the authoritarian tradition	التقليد السلطوي
conditioning the young	تهيئة الصغار
passively accumulating	يخزنون بصورة سلبية
mechanically reproduced	(معلومات) يعيدونها تلقائياً
in examinations	يوم الامتحان

UNIT FOURTEEN: Additional Texts

I. Bearing in mind the characteristic features of counter-argumentation (both the non-suppressed and the suppressed varieties), study and translate Texts 14C (i) and 14C (ii) into Arabic.

TEXT 14C (i)

Mismanaged Algeria

The country's troubles are so glaring that it is easy to forget Algeria's strengths.[1] At three o'clock in the afternoon in the poor, over-crowded Casbah of Algiers, children leave school not to beg but to do their homework. Investment of some two-fifths of GDP a year during much of the 1960s and 1970s gave Algeria the strongest industrial base in Africa north of the Limpopo. The northern coastal bit of the country, where 96% of its 23m people live, is rich and fertile. It used to[2] feed the Romans. It could feed Algerians if it were better farmed.

These strengths are being wasted.[3] Some 180,000 well-schooled Algerians enter the job market every year. Yet a hobbled economy adds only 100,000 new jobs a year, and some 45% of these involve working for the government. Algeria lacks the foreign currency it needs to import raw materials and spare parts to keep its factories running. The collective farms have routinely fallen short of their targets, leaving Algeria ever more reliant on imported food.
[55]

NOTES

1. To relay the high degree of evaluativeness, and to anticipate the opposition contained in the second paragraph, the Nominal structure is most appropriate here: إن المشاكل التي تعاني منها الجزائر قد تفاقمت إلى حد يجعل
من السهل أن ننسى ما للبلاد من إيجابيات فالأطفال . . .

2. To underline the point of these two utterances, *used to* may be understood as 'could', with motivated parallelism through repetition emerging as a result: ارض خصبة كانت قادرة في عهود مضت على إطعام الرومان. ويمكن أن تكون قادرة على إطعام الجزائر إذا ما تم استغلالها زراعياً بشكل أفضل.

3. Here is the fulcrum of the text: the contrastive nature of this element is a precondition for argumentative opposition. Note the intertextuality involved in the use of the word *strengths*, both here and in the first sentence of the first paragraph: إلا أن هذه الإيجابيات تذهب هباء فبالرغم من . . .

GLOSSARY

the poor, over-crowded Casbah	قصبة الجزائر الفقيرة والمكتظة بالسكان
not to beg	لا ليستجدوا
Investment of some two-fifths of X	استثمار ما يزيد على ثلثي . . .
GDP	إجمالي الناتج المحلي
during much of the 1960s	خلال معظم سنوات الستينات
gave X the strongest industrial base in	جعل من الجزائر أقوى قاعدة صناعية
north of the Limpopo	شمال نهر الليمبوبو
The northern coastal bit	الجزء الساحلي شمال البلاد
96% of its 23m people live	٩٦٪ من سكان البلاد البالغ عددهم ٢٣ مليون
It used to feed	كانت قادرة في عهود مضت على إطعام
well-schooled Algerians	من نخبة المتعلمين
enter the job market	يبحث عن عمل
a hobbled economy	اقتصاداً مترهلاً
lacks the foreign currency it needs	ينقصها ما تحتاجه من عملة صعبة
raw materials	المواد الخام
spare parts to keep factories	قطع الغيار للحيلولة دون توقف مصانعها عن العمل
collective farms	المزارع الجماعية
have routinely fallen short of their targets	عودتنا على إظهار عجزها عن تحقيق أهدافها الانتاجية
leaving X ever more reliant on	مما يجعل س يعتمد وبشكل متزايد

TEXT 14C (ii)

(. . .)

To be sure,[1] Indonesia and Malaysia are far from perfectly open. Mahathir's government in Kuala Lumpur[2] banned not only[3] Salman Rushdie's book *The Satanic Verses*, controversial enough, but even Steven Spielberg's Holocaust film, *Schindler's List*. Many subjects[4] are off limits in Malaysian public life, and the political opposition is routinely denied access to state-run radio and television. Still[5] the country's carefully monitored multiculturalism has allowed Malays, Chinese and Indians to rub shoulders and get to know one another without much rancour. When Louis Farrakhan stopped in Malaysia this year after his visits to such countries as Libya, Iraq and Iran, all government leaders shunned him. Of America's most notoriously anti-Jewish black Muslim, an aide to Anwar says, 'No self-respecting Islamic organization would have anything to do with him.'

[6]Anwar's own experiences abroad of late could not have been more different . . .

[68]

NOTES

1. This is a strawman gambit signal, introducing a claim to be countered subsequently and it is therefore equivalent to 'of course', 'no doubt', etc. In Arabic it is best rendered by something like . . . صحيح أن

2. A substantiator such as ف . . . would be needed here to introduce the following sentence: . . . .فحكومة كوالالمبور

3. A restriction قصر is essential here to relay the force of 'only': لم تمنع كتاب سلمان رشدي «آيات شيطانية» فحسب بل منعت حتى فيلم . . .

4. A Nominal/Equational sentence structure is needed here to relay the evaluativeness: . . . .والعديد من المواضيع محضور الحديث فيها

5. Most baffling for translators of texts like this is the retrieval of the suppressed adversative. The problem is further compounded by the choice of *still* which is here used as equivalent to 'but', 'however', etc. This may be relayed by something like إلا أن . . . or .بالرغم من كل هذا فإن

6. A truly suppressed counter-argument with the adversative completely submerged is found here. The second paragraph must be introduced in

Arabic by an explicit signal such as لكن or إلا أن (avoiding the one that has just been used in the previous paragraph): إلا أن ما شهده أنور مؤخراً من

حفاوة في الخارج . . .

GLOSSARY

far from perfectly open	أبعد ما يكون عن كونهما بلدين منفتحين
controversial enough	وهو كتاب أثار من الجدل ما فيه الكفاية
Holocaust film	فيلم عن الابادة الجماعية لليهود
is routinely denied access	لا يمكنه الوصول قطعاً الى
carefully monitored multiculturalism	التعددية الحضارية التي يتم التحكم فيها بشكل دقيق
to rub shoulders	أن يحتكوا ببعضهم
without much rancour	دون هاجس أو حساسية
shunned him	ابتعد عنه
most notoriously anti-Jewish	الذي ذاع صيته لمناهضته اليهود

II. Texts 14D (i) and 14D (ii) not only illustrate the suppressed form of
    counter-argumentation in Arabic, but also demonstrate how opaque
    this form can be, although it is very rare indeed. Translators into
    English have to renegotiate the entire argumentative strategy and
    remould the text if it is to read acceptably. Consider carefully and
    translate the texts into English.

TEXT 14D (i)

أتابع باهتمام بالغ ما ينشر الآن بجريدتنا «الشرق الأوسط» عن التعليم في وطننا العربي
الكبير وأود أن أشارك في هذا الموضوع المهم والشيق، فالتعليم لا شك[1] هو أساس
تطور أي أمة وقواعد حضارتها. والمتتبع لقضايا التعليم في الوطن العربي يجد أشياء
غريبة ومتناقضة[2] بالرغم من وجود كيان كبير كالجامعة العربية التي من المفترض أن تقوم
بدور أكثر إيجابية عبر أجهزتها المختصة في توحيد نظام التعليم في الوطن العربي والذي
هو أساس الوحدة الحقيقية لأمة تنطق لغة واحدة وتدين لدين واحد بنسبة 99 في المئة .

والتناقض³ تجده في المناهج الموضوعة بمدارس الوطن العربي⁴ بل أحياناً تعديل نظام التعليم من وقت لآخر، كما سيحدث في السودان مثلاً حيث سيتم تعديل المرحلة الابتدائية من ٦ إلى ٨ سنوات.

[59]

NOTES

1. This is an opposable شك لا. The opposition is implicit and the contrastive element starts with والمتتبع لقضايا which should be signalled as follows: 'However, anyone who follows issues relating to education . . . '.

2. Perhaps a new sentence with a recap here: 'This is despite the existence of a large organization . . . '.

3. 'As for the contradiction' moves the spotlight on to this issue here.

4. A necessary repetition of 'contradiction' to relay the force of بل here: 'Indeed, contradiction is often to be found in . . . '.

GLOSSARY

follow with great interest	أتابع باهتمام
education	التعليم
contribute to	أشارك في
important and stimulating	مهم وشيق
the foundation of its civilization	قواعد حضارتها
finds the whole thing shrouded in mystery	يجد أشياء غريبة
which ought to play	التي من المفترض أن تقوم
a more positive role	بدور أكثر إيجابية
specialized agencies	أجهزتها المختصة
the very basis of the genuine unity	أساس الوحدة الحقيقية
a nation 99% of which speak one language and . . .	أمة تنطق لغة واحدة . . . بنسبة ٩٩٪
the curricula in use	المناهج الموضوعة
the constant amendments to . . .	تعديل . . . من وقت إلى آخر
such as the change which Sudan will see shortly	كما سيحدث في السودان مثلاً
the elementary cycle	المرحلة الابتدائية

TEXT 14D (ii)

تفاوتت مواقف الإصلاحيين العرب من الدستورية عملياً¹ حسب مواقفهم السياسية
المتحولة . ولئن² كان الكواكبي ـ وهو يقتبس «الفيري» المفكر الايطالي في عصر الثورة
الفرنسية، على طول طبائع الاستبداد ـ يوافق الناظرين في التاريخ الطبيعي للأديان على
أن الاستبداد السياسي متولد عن الاستبداد الديني، ويؤكد على اشتراك الحاكم والمعبود
في الكثير من الصفات عند الخلفاء الفاطميين و«السلاطين الأعاجم» وغيرهم في تاريخ
الإسلام³، فهو⁴ يستثني من اعتبار التاريخ ذلك الجزء من تاريخ الإسلام الذي اعتبره
هو ومضارعوه نموذجاً مرجعياً ملزماً .

[67]

NOTES

1. The adverbial عملياً is under focus and must therefore be fronted: 'In practice, . . .'.

2. لئن is a concessive here. It could be rendered as 'although'. But, perhaps more idiomatically, it could be left out and the opposition introduced with a 'however' later.

3. This عند adverbial may best be fronted to leave room for a more focused 'that-clause': 'He also stresses that, under the Fatimid caliphs, the Persian sultans and others in the history of Islam . . .'.

4. Here, the opposition begins: 'However, al-Kawakibi excludes . . .'.

GLOSSARY

the stance of the Arab reformists	مواقف الإصلاحيين العرب
constitutionalism	الدستورية
varied as X varied	تفاوتت . . . حسب
changing political positions	مواقفهم السياسية المتحولة
quoting X	وهو يقتبس س
on the ever-pervasive might of	على طول
autocratic instincts	طبائع الاستبداد
theorists in the natural history of	الناظرين في التاريخ الطبيعي
political autocracy is born out of	الاستبداد السياسي متولد عن
the object of worship	المعبود
had a number of features in common	اشتراك س وص في كثير من الصفات

the purview of history	اعتبار التاريخ
his contemporaries	مضارعوه
a binding, model frame of reference	نموذجاً مرجعياً ملزماً

Glossary of Text Linguistics and Translation Terms

Abstract: *see* Exposition.

Agentive Passive: a form of Passive (as opposed to Active) characterized by the mention of the agent introduced by 'by'. In Arabic, this is normally rendered as active with the agent becoming the subject of the sentence (e.g. 'These resolutions were adopted by the Diplomatic Conference' = تبنى المؤتمر الدبلوماسي هذه القرارات). The passive form may also be **Agentless**, in which case the Arabic rendering would be either:

    (a) تم + Verbal Noun (مصدر), (e.g. 'if the impasse is not corrected' = وإذا لم يتم تصحيح هذا الوضع المتأزم);

    or:

    (b) using a passive verb (e.g. 'The Italian translator was stabbed' = طُعِنَ المترجم الإيطالي).

I put forward the hypothesis that option (a) is resorted to when the action involved is positive, while option (b) is reserved for negative processes.

Agentless Passive: *see* Agentive Passive.

Anaphora: this is when a linguistic item (say, a pronoun) is used to refer backward to antecedent elements in the text (e.g. 'The king spoke. In his speech, he said . . . '). **Cataphora**, on the other hand, is when a linguistic item is used to refer forward to subsequent elements in the text (e.g. 'In his speech, the king said . . . ').

Argumentation: a text type in which concepts and/or beliefs are evaluated. Two basic forms of argumentation may be distinguished: **Counter-argumentation** in which a thesis is cited, then opposed; and **Through-argumentation** in which a thesis is cited, then extensively defended. Counter-arguments could be:

(a) **Explicit** (the concession is explicitly signalled by the use of concessives such as 'although', 'while', etc.).

(b) **Implicit** (the opposition is introduced by the use of adversatives such as 'but', 'however', etc.). (This is also known as the **Strawman Gambit**.)

(c) **Suppressed** (the implicit opposition is introduced without the use of an explicit adversative).

Through-arguments are basic argumentative formats which could either be **Less Involved** (objective) or **More Involved** (subjective).

Article: *see* Instruction.

Aspect of the Scene: *see* Text Structure.

Cataphora: *see* Anaphora.

Cliché: a conventional, formulaic form of expression, the use of which is insisted on in certain *registers* such as journalese (e.g. وجدير بالذكر) or legalese (e.g. مع عدم المساس بـ . . . .).

Collocation: like *clichés*, collocations are conventionalized forms of expression. The use of collocations, however, enjoys a wider scope than that dictated by *registers*, for example, to include almost any form of expression. For example, 'wide' and not, say, 'big' collocates with 'scope'.

Concluding Article: *see* Instruction.

Connectors: particles which connect sentences within a sequence of elements that make up the text. Connectors can be additive ('and', etc.), adversative ('but', etc.), causal ('so', etc.).

Connotation: additional meanings that a lexical item acquires beyond its primary, referential meaning, e.g. 'notorious' means 'famous' but with negative connotations. **Denotations**, on the other hand, cover the dictionary, contextless meaning of a given lexical item.

Context: the extra-textual environment which exerts a determining influence on the language used. Three domains of context may be distinguished:

(a) **Communicative**: including aspects of the message such as *register*;

(b) **Pragmatic**: covering *intentionality*;

(c) **Semiotic**: accounting for *intertextuality*.

Counter-argument: *see* Argumentation.

Denotation: *see* Connotation.

Diction: *see* Texture.

Discourse: modes of speaking and writing which involve participants in adopting a particular attitude towards areas of socio-cultural activity (e.g. racist discourse, bureaucratese, etc.).

Discourse-organizational devices: *see* Functional.

Ellipsis: the omission (for reasons of rhetorically motivated economy) of linguistic items whose sense is recoverable from the context.

Entity-oriented Report: *see* Exposition.

Evaluativeness: the comparison or assessment of concepts, belief systems, etc. It is the determining factor in distinguishing *Argumentation* from *Exposition*.

Event-oriented Report: *see* Exposition.

Executive Report: *see* Exposition.

Explicit Counter-argument: *see* Argumentation.

Exposition: a text type in which concepts, objects or events are presented in a **Non-evaluative manner**. Three basic forms of exposition may be distinguished:

(a) **Description**: focusing on objects spatially viewed;

(b) **Narration**: focusing on events temporally viewed;

(c) **Conceptual Exposition**: focusing on the detached analysis of concepts and yielding a number of text tokens. Starting with the most detached and moving on to the least detached, these conceptual expository text forms include: the **Synopsis**, the **Abstract**, the **Summary**, the **Entity-oriented Report**, the **Person-oriented Report**, the **Personalized Report**, the **Event-oriented Report**. The Report can also be **Formulaic** (e.g. the auditors' report), **Executive** (e.g. the company chairman's annual statement) or **Reminiscent** (e.g. memoirs).

Format: *see* Text Structure.

Formulaic: *see* Text Structure, Exposition, Cliché.

Formulaic Report: *see* Exposition.

Free Translation: *see* Literal Translation.

Functional: having a role to perform in the process of the realization of *context by text*. Functional signals are in contrast with Discourse-organizational devices whose role is, as the term suggests, merely organizational (i.e. formal and cosmetic rather than functional and **rhetorically motivated**).

Genre: conventional forms of text associated with particular types of social occasion (e.g. the News Report, the Editorial, the Recipe).

***Idafa* Construction**: a two-element structure in Arabic (Noun + definite article + Noun) (e.g. كرامة الإنسان). The translation problem confronted in dealing with *idafa* involves the use of a series of *idafas* which share a common second element (e.g. كرامة الإنسان + حقوق الإنسان), in which case two ways of dealing with this structure may be distinguished: (a) كرامة وحقوق الانسان; (b) كرامة الإنسان وحقوقه. The latter is said to be finer Arabic, and even more grammatical.

Idiom: *see* Texture.

Implicit Counter-argument: *see* Argumentation.

Initial Article: *see* Instruction.

Instruction: a text type in which the focus is on the formation of future behaviour, either 'with option' as in Advertising or 'without option' as in **Legal Instruction** (e.g. Treaties, Resolutions, Contracts, etc.). Within Legal Instruction, all legal documents may be viewed in terms of an initial part (**Preamble**) and a set of **Articles**. In the construction of Articles, special verbs are used to relay specific instructional forces e.g. 'shall' = legally binding, 'may' = optionality, 'must' = obligatoriness, 'should' = logical necessity, etc.). Articles could be of the open-ended type (i.e. covering almost any content) or more formulaic as in typical **Initial** and **Concluding Articles**.

Intentionality: a feature of human language which determines the appropriateness of a linguistic form to the achievement of a *pragmatic* purpose.

Intertextuality: a precondition for the intelligibility of texts, involving the dependence of one text as a semiotic entity upon another.

Legal Article: *see* Instruction.

Legal Instruction: *see* Instruction.

Less Involved Through-argument: *see* Argumentation.

Literal Translation: a rendering which preserves surface aspects of the message, both semantically and syntactically, adhering closely to source-text mode of expression. **Free Translation**, on the other hand, modifies surface expression and keeps intact only deeper levels of meaning. The choice of method is determined by text properties related to text type, purpose of translation, etc.

Managing: *see* Monitoring.

Marked: *see* Unmarked.

Modality: expressing a distinction of mood, such as that between 'possibility' and 'actuality'.

Monitoring: expounding in a *non-evaluative* manner. This is in contrast to **managing**, which involves steering the discourse towards the speaker's goals.

More Involved Through-argument: *see* Argumentation.

Motivatedness: the set of factors which regulate the text user's choices, whether conscious or unconscious.

Nominal Sentence: in Arabic, the Subject + Verb + Complement structure is normally associated with *evaluative contexts* (e.g. *Argumentation*). The **Verbal Sentence**, on the other hand, has a Verb + Subject + Complement structure and is normally associated with *non-evaluative contexts* (e.g. *Exposition*).

Non-evaluativeness: *see* Evaluativeness.

Opposition: *see* Text Structure.

Person-oriented Report: *see* Exposition.

Personalized Report: *see* Exposition.

Pragmatics: the domain of *Intentionality* or the purposes for which utterances are used in real contexts.

Preamble: *see* Instruction.

Register: the set of features which distinguishes one stretch of language from another in terms of variation in *context* concerning the language user (geographic dialect, idiolect, etc.) and/or with language use (field or subject matter, tenor or level of formality and mode or speaking vs. writing).

Reminiscent Report: *see* Exposition.

Report: *see* Exposition.

Scene-setter: *see* Text Structure.

Strawman gambit: *see* Argumentation.

Stucture: *see* Text Structure.

Substantiation: *see* Text Structure.

Summary: *see* Exposition.

Suppressed Counter-argument: *see* Argumentation.

Synopsis: *see* Exposition.

Text: a set of mutually relevant communicative functions, *structured* and *textured* in such a way as to achieve an overall rhetorical purpose.

Text Structure: the compositional plan of a text. Different *text types* exhibit different structure formats. Some of these are *formulaic* as in the structure of the *Preamble*: 'X and Y, Having met. . ., Considering, Re-emphasizing, . . ., Have agreed . . .'. Other formats are less formulaic, though fairly predictable. For example, a *'managing'* *Counter-argument* has the following structure: Thesis Cited, Opposition, Substantiation, Conclusion. A *'managing' Through-argument* simply has: Thesis Cited, Thesis Extensively Defended. Whether to be rebutted or defended, the thesis cited always **sets a tone**. On the other hand, *'monitoring' Exposition* displays the most open-ended of formats: Scene Set, Aspects of the Scene Tackled.

Text Type: the way the *structure* and *texture* of *texts* are made to respond to their *context*. Three basic text types may be distinguished: *Exposition, Argumentation* and *Instruction*.

Texture: aspects of *text* organization which contribute to the overall effect of texts hanging together and reflect the coherence of *text structure* and the way texts respond to their *context*. Texture includes aspects of message construction such as cohesion, theme-rheme organization, as well as text idiom and diction.

Thesis Cited to be Opposed: *see* Text Structure.

Through-argument: *see* Argumentation.

Tone-setter: *see* Text Structure.

Truncated Relative Clause: a relative clause with the relative pronoun and the copula element ellipted (e.g. 'The report, [*which is*] described in detail in the next chapter, involves . . .').

Unmarked: the state of certain lexical or grammatical items or structures which are considered to be more basic or common than other structures, marked for particular effects. The cleft sentence: 'It was John who did it' is a **marked** form of: 'John did it.'

Verbal Sentence: *see* Nominal Sentence.

Sources of Text Samples

1. *Al-Siyasa*, 15/9/1987, Kuwait.
2. *Report of the World Conference to Combat Racism and Racial Discrimination*, 1978, United Nations.
3. *Draft Convention of the Law of the Sea*, 1981, United Nations.
4. *Al-Jarida al-Rasmiyya*, 28/4/1977, Manama.
5. *Vienna Convention on Diplomatic Relations*, 1961, United Nations.
6. *Al-Kuwait al-Yawm*, 23/2/1988, Kuwait.
7. *Law No. 8 of 1980 on Regulating Labour Relations*, Development Advertising and General Services, UAE.
8. *Human Rights: A Compilation of International Instruments*, 1988, United Nations.
9. A miscellany of Arabic legal documents.
10. A miscellany of English legal documents.
11. *Al-Kuwait al-Yawm*, 23/2/1988, Kuwait.
12. *Al-Siyasa*, 5/9/1978, Kuwait.
13. *Prospects*, Vol. XVI, No. 2, 1986, UNESCO.
14. *Report of the United Nations Conference on the Least Developed Countries*, 1981, United Nations.
15. *Al-Kuwait al-Yawm*, 23/2/1988, Kuwait.
16. *Prospects*, Vol. XVI, No. 2, 1986, UNESCO.
17. *Al-Sharq al-Awsat*, 18/6/1992, London.
18. An Arabic abstract.
19. Abdul Fattah al-Qarashi, '*Ittijahat al-aba' wa al-ummahat al-kuwaitiyin fi tanshi'at al-abna' wa ᶜalaqatiha bi baᶜd al-mutaghayyirat*', *Hawliyaat Kuliyyat al-Adab*, 1986, University of Kuwait.
20. *Specific Matters Arising from the Resolutions, Recommendations and other Decisions Adopted by the UN Conference on Trade and Development*, 1982, United Nations.
21. Muhammad Ibrahim Marsi, '*Adwa' ᶜala malikat saba*', *Hawliyaat Kuliyyat al-Adab*, 1988, University of Kuwait.
22. *Documents of the Diplomatic Conference on Humanitarian Law*, 1978, United Nations.
23. *Al-ᶜArabi*, Kuwait.
24. Report of the UN Secretary-General, 1987.
25. *Dirasat al-Khalij wa al-Jazira al-ᶜArabiyya*.
26. *Dictionary of Diplomacy and International Affairs*, 1974, Librairie du Liban.
27. *Report of the UN Conference on Technical Co-operation Among Developing Countries*, 1978, United Nations.
28. *Bulletin of the Arab-British Chamber of Commerce*, London.
29. *Basic Facts About the United Nations*, 1987.

30. *Al-Hayat*, London.
31. *Al-Thawra*, Baghdad.
32. *The Guardian*, London.
33. *The Independent*, London.
34. *Newsweek*, London.
35. *Al-Majalla*, London.
36. Bank of Scotland Annual Report, 1992.
37. National Bank of Qatar Annual Report, 1978.
38. Norman Schwartzkopf, *It Doesn't Take a Hero*, 1992.
39. National Bank of Qatar Annual Report, 1976.
40. Saudi Arabian Monetary Fund Annual Report, 1982.
41. The White Paper, 1991, Ministry of Information, Jordan.
42. Ali Amin, *200 Fikra*, al-'Asr al-Hadith, 1987.
43. Saatchi & Saatchi Annual Report, 1991.
44. *Reflect On Things Past: The Memoirs Of Lord Carrington*.
45. *Report of the International Law Commission*, 1980, United Nations.
46. Ali al-Wardi, *'Awjuh al-tashabuh wa al-ikhtilaf bayna al-aqtar al-ᶜarabiyya min al-nahiya al-ijtimaᶜiyya'*, *al-Bahith al-ᶜArabi*, 8, 1986.
47. E. Parry, 'The Influence of Culture', *World Health Forum*, 1984.
48. *Prospects*, Vol. XVI, No. 4, 1986, UNESCO.
49. *Al-Sharq al-Awsat*, London.
50. Nuriyya al-Rumi, 'al-ᶜAlam al-shiᶜri li Ahmad al-ᶜUdwani', *ᶜAlam al-Fikr*, 1991.
51. ᶜAfif ᶜAbd al-Rahman, 'al-Amthal al-ᶜarabiyya ᶜala sighat afᶜala', *al-Majalla al-ᶜArabiyya li al-ᶜUlum al-Insaniyya*, 1986.
52. ᶜAbd al-Muᶜti ᶜAssaf, 'al-Biʾa al-ijtimaᶜiyya wa ᶜalaqatiha bi al-nizam al-idari fi al-mamlaka al-urdiniyya al-hashimiyya', *al-Majalla al-ᶜArabiyya li al-ᶜUlum al-Insaniyya*, 1986.
53. Randolph Vigne, 'SWAPO of Namibia', *Third World Quarterly*, Vol. 9, No. 1, 1987.
54. Celia Kerslake, *British Society for Middle Eastern Studies Bulletin*, 1990.
55. *The Economist*, London.
56. *Al-Mudun al-israʾiliyya, Hawliyaat Kuliyyat al-Adab*, University of Kuwait.
57. *New Left Review*, 1992, London.
58. *Independent Magazine*, London.
59. *Al-Sharq al-Awsat*, London.
60. S. al-Huss, *Lubnan ᶜala Muftaraq al-Turuq*, 1984.
61. 'The Politics of Exile', *Third World Quarterly*, 1987.
62. Anwar Al-Sadat, *al-Bahth ᶜan al-dhat*, 1978, al-Maktab al-Masri.
63. *ᶜAlam al-Fikr*, Kuwait, 1991.
64. Modi B. Mansour, *al-Malak ᶜAbd al-ᶜAziz wa muʾtamar al-Kuwait, 1923-1924*, 1992, Beirut/London, Dar al-Saqi.
65. T. Niblock, *Arab Research Papers*, 1978.
66. *Al-Majalla al-ᶜArabiyya li al-ᶜUlum al-Insaniyya*, 21, 1986.
67. From a pre-publication manuscript on 'Secularism in the Muslim World', by Aziz el-Azmeh.
68. *Time*, 30/9/1996.

Select Bibliography

Beaugrande, R. de (1978) *Factors in a Theory of Poetic Translating*. Assen: van Gorcum.
————— and W. Dressler (1980) *Introduction to Text Linguistics*. London: Longman.
Bell, R. (1992) *Translation and Translating*. London: Longman.
Catford, J. C. (1965) *A Linguistic Theory of Translation*. Oxford: Oxford University Press.
Crystal, D. and D. Davy (1969) *Investigating English Style*. London: Longman.
Fowler, R. (1986) *Linguistic Criticism*. Oxford: Oxford University Press.
Gregory, M. and S. Carroll (1978) *Language and Situation: Language Varieties and their Social Contexts*. London: Routledge & Kegan Paul.
Halliday, M. A. K. (1978) *Language as Social Semiotic: The Social Interpretation of Language and Meaning*. London: Edward Arnold.
Hartmann, R. R. K. (1980) *Contrastive Textology*. Heidelberg: Julius Groos Verlag.
Hatim, B. and I. Mason (1990) *Discourse and the Translator*. London: Longman.
————— (1997) *The Translator as Communicator*. London: Routledge.
House, J. (1976) *A Model for Translation Quality Assessment*. Tübingen: Gunter Narr Verlag.
Kelly, L. (1979) *The True Interpreter*. Oxford: Oxford University Press.
Levinson, S. (1983) *Pragmatics*. Cambridge: Cambridge University Press.
Nash, W. (1980) *Designs in Prose*. London: Longman.
Neubert, A. (1985) *Text and Translation*. Ubersetzungswissenschafltiche Beitrage 8. Leipzig: VEB Verlag Enzyklopädie.
Newmark, P. (1981) *Approaches to Translation*. Oxford: Pergamon.
Nida, E. A. and C. R. Taber (1969) *The Theory and Practice of Translation*. Leiden: E. J. Brill.
O'Donnel, W. R. and L. Todd (1980) *Variety in Contemporary English*. London: Allen & Unwin.
Werlich, E. (1976) *A Text Grammar of English*. Heidelberg: Quelle & Meyer.